Mining, Politics, and Development
in the South Pacific

Mining, Politics, and Development in the South Pacific

Michael C. Howard

Westview Press

BOULDER • SAN FRANCISCO • OXFORD

This Westview softcover edition is printed on acid-free paper and bound in library-quality, coated covers that carry the highest rating of the National Association of State Textbook Administrators, in consultation with the Association of American Publishers and the Book Manufacturers' Institute.

Published in 1991 in the United States of America by Westview Press, Inc., 5500 Central Avenue, Boulder, Colorado 80301, and in the United Kingdom by Westview Press, 36 Lonsdale Road, Summertown, Oxford OX2 7EW

Library of Congress Cataloging-in-Publication Data
Howard, Michael C.
  Mining, politics, and development in the South Pacific / by Michael C. Howard.
    p. cm.
  Includes bibliographical references and index.
  ISBN 0-8133-8170-3
  1. Mineral industries—Oceania. 2. Oceania—Economic conditions.
3. Oceania—Politics and government. I. Title.
HD9506.O32H68 1991
338.2'099—dc20   90-19448
                                                                      CIP

Printed and bound in the United States of America

    The paper used in this publication meets the requirements
(∞) of the American National Standard for Permanence of Paper
    for Printed Library Materials Z39.48-1984.

10   9   8   7   6   5   4   3   2   1

Contents

Tables

Preface

The genesis of the present work is to be found in several research projects in which mining emerged as an important consideration. The first of these was my Ph.D. research in the mid-1970s on Australian Aboriginal politics in Southwestern Australia. From it, I developed a general concern with the political debate surrounding mining on land claimed by Aboriginal people. One of the projects to spin off from my initial interest in Aboriginal issues was a study of the global activities of the American-based mining company AMAX and its relations with native peoples. My attention was drawn to AMAX while I was engaged in research in Western Australia in 1980. In August 1980 AMAX became involved in a confrontation over oil exploration with the Yungngona people at Noonkanbah. In 1981, while examining AMAX's activities elsewhere in the world, I came into contact with Ted Wheelwright of the Transnational Corporations Research Project at the University of Sydney, who encouraged me to present a paper on AMAX at the 1982 ANZAAS Conference to be held in Sydney.

Questions of indigenous rights and the activities of transnational corporations were prominent among my interests when I moved to Fiji to work at the University of the South Pacific in 1982. Once in Fiji I continued my research on transnational corporations, while also undertaking studies on labor relations and economic development in the South Pacific. Once again, mining was not the central focus of my research, but gradually it assumed greater prominence. In particular, a good deal of my work came to focus on primary resource development in fishing, forestry, and mining. In regard specifically to mining, I served for a period as an adviser to the Rabi Council of Leaders, the council representing those who had moved to Fiji from the phosphate island of Banaba (or Ocean Island) after the Second World War. I made several brief visits to Nauru, where I was able to become better acquainted with its phosphate industry at first hand. During visits to the Solomon Islands primarily to study industrial relations and later the fishing industry, I also conducted interviews relating to mining on Guadalcanal. Having been interested in the Fijian goldmining industry previously, between 1985 and 1987, prior to the 1987 national election, I became involved in the debate in Fiji concerning the activities of Emperor Gold Mine. Finally, while in Fiji, I became acquainted with the history of the mining industry in the South Pacific, especially in the course of writing *The Political Economy of the South Pacific to 1945* (Townsville: Centre for Southeast Asian Studies, James Cook University, 1987) with Simione Durutalo.

Having produced a number of publications on the South Pacific for the Transnational Corporations Research Project, in 1985 Ted Wheelwright suggested that I prepare a comparative study of the impact of the mining industry on native peoples. Developments in Fiji delayed completion of the work until the latter part of 1987, while I was living in Australia. Published in 1988 as *The Impact of the International Mining Industry on Native Peoples*, the monograph included chapters on AMAX, Brazil, the Philippines and the South Pacific. Preliminary research on native peoples and primary resource development in the Philippines had been carried out in 1986 (further research was carried out in 1989).

The idea for the present book grew out of a desire to explore some of the issues concerning the South Pacific discussed in my comparative study more thoroughly and to bring the material up to date. Since my study for the Transnational Corporations Research Project a great deal has happened in relation to mining in the South Pacific. The most dramatic event undoubtedly is the uprising on Bougainville, but elsewhere in the region there have also been equally important developments. Thematically, I especially wished to look more carefully at the political dimension of mining and at the relationship of mining to national development.

Over the years a number of people have helped me to better understand the many issues surrounding the mining industry. In regard to the present work, I would like especially to thank 'Atu Bain, Simione Durutalo, Donna Winslow, Peter Larmour, Ted Wheelwright, Terence Wesley-Smith, Herb Thompson, and Hans Dagmar for their insights and assistance.

Michael C. Howard

1

Introduction

If asked about the primary resources of the South Pacific, most people would think of coconuts or fish, few would mention timber, much less minerals. Yet such resources are of vital importance to the economies of several of the small Pacific island states, and they are often the subject of very heated political controversy. Before the arrival of Europeans, mining and metallurgy were unknown to Pacific islanders. The discovery of gold in the South Pacific was left to European explorers during the sixteenth and early seventeenth centuries who found traces of alluvial gold on some of the islands for which they gave them names like the Islands of Solomon and the Island of Gold (New Guinea).

The South Pacific did not become another Mexico or Peru, and it was not until the last decades of the nineteenth century, when European colonial expansion in the region provided a new impetus to mineral exploration, that mining began on several of the islands. Gold was found in New Guinea and New Caledonia in the 1870s, and by the 1880s, nickel and chromite mining were important industries on New Caledonia. Guano was removed from many of the region's smaller and more isolated islands during the latter half of the nineteenth century, and around the turn-of-the-century the discovery of rich phosphate deposits led to the development of large-scale mining operations on Nauru, Banaba, Angaur, and Makatea.

The rising price of gold during the interwar years of the twentieth century promoted further exploration throughout the Melanesian area and resulted in the development of large gold mining operations in Papua New Guinea and Fiji. By the time the Second World War began, the mining industry was a major source of export earnings and government revenue for many colonies around the South Pacific.

It was also an industry dominated by a handful of companies, companies that tended to be at least as powerful as the colonial governments: Société le Nickel, Emperor Gold Mining Company, Bulolo G.D. Ltd., New Guinea Goldfields, and the British Phosphate Commissioners.

In recent decades, as most of the countries in the South Pacific have become independent, mining has continued to be of considerable importance, but the issues and problems have changed considerably. Perhaps more than anything else, the relation between the mining industry and the state and the local population has become more open to question. The colonial situation of an all-powerful enclave owned by private foreign interests is no longer so easily accepted. In the case of Nauru, the matter was settled by complete assumption of control over the industry by the newly independent state. In Papua New Guinea the tendency has been to favor some form of equity participation by the state. New Caledonia remains a French colony, but the French state has assumed a dominant interest in the mining industry. Only in Fiji does the colonial pattern prevail, although it has not gone unchallenged.

Increased state intervention, however, has not resolved many of the political and social questions facing the mining sector. There remains, for example, the question of in whose interest the state functions in regard to the mining industry, and in the newly independent states of the South Pacific this is often a hotly contested issue. In most states in the region, indigenous elites groomed by colonial authorities simply assumed power upon independence. All to often, such elites appear to have formed an alliance with mining interests primarily for their own benefit rather than that of the broader population. In the case of Fiji, where continuity from colonial to independent state was greatest and a single party identified with a chiefly oligarchy ruled from 1970 to 1987, the relationship of political leaders to the foreign-owned mining interest remained a close one, differing little from that under colonial rule. Independent Nauru has been ruled for most of its history by a government as authoritarian as Fiji's. Government control of the mining industry has meant that rather than allying itself with foreign interests it has cloaked pursuit of its own interests in the mining sector with a populist mantle. The more chaotic political situation in independent Papua New Guinea has been reflected in a complex relationship between national political leaders and the mining industry characterized by a mixture of pragmatism, corruption, and nationalism.

TABLE 1.1 Mineral Production in the South Pacific, 1986

Country	Mineral and Quantity
Fiji	Gold, 94,902 troy ounces
Nauru	Phosphate, 1,494,000 metric tons
New Caledonia	Nickel, 61,800 metric tons
Papua New Guinea	Gold, 1,127,686 troy ounces
	Copper, 178,211 metric tons
Solomon Islands	Gold, 4,000 troy ounces*

*Estimate.
Source: *Minerals Yearbook, Vol 3: International* (United States Department of the Interior, 1987).

In recent years, mining has been caught up in challenges to the power of these political elites. Mining wealth has played an significant role in financing the patronage systems used to keep governments such as those of Kamasese Mara of Fiji and Hammer de Roburt of Nauru in power. Such a use of wealth has ensured that the mining industry has come under attack by those critical of these governments. In the case of Nauru, this has involved landowners and members of the landless middle class questioning the way in which the Hammer de Roburt government has handled the country's mining wealth. In Fiji, the Mara government's relationship with the Emperor Gold Mining became an important part of a political challenge to the government that culminated in the 1987 electoral defeat of the Mara government. In Papua New Guinea, regional dissatisfaction over the government's handling of wealth derived from the copper and gold mine on Bougainville created problems of national unity at the time of independence. Opposition to government mining policies erupted again on Bougainville in the late 1980s in the form of a guerrilla war that closed the mine and necessitated military intervention.

The situations in Fiji and Papua New Guinea also point to another general issue of even more concern to postcolonial politicians than it was to colonial authorities—land rights. While sympathetic in certain respects to indigenous tenure, British and Australian colonial authorities were often as adamant as the French when it came to the priority of mining claims over other considerations. This did not eliminate local opposition to mining or do away with claims for greater compensation, but these actions received little sympathy from authorities. Postcolonial governments have had to pay more attention to local sentiment in terms of land rights claims and the settlement of compensation, but claimants have not necessarily done any better at the hands of their own national leaders. This is especially true where regional factors come into play as with western versus eastern Fiji and the micronationalism of Papua New Guinea. Broadly, the debate has focused not simply of the level of compensation from mining but, moreover, on the distribution of the revenue between local and national or elite interests.

Mining has also played an important role in labor relations in the South Pacific. During the colonial period, mine workers generally were recruited from outside of the immediate vicinity of the mine, often because of a lack of interest in mining by the local population. In the case of the phosphate mines, many workers were brought from Asia. The colonial authorities sought to regulate such recruitment to ensure that it was not too destabilizing for the colony as a whole and to ensure labor peace at the mine site in the interest of maximizing profits for the mining companies and the government itself. Maintaining a peaceful labor force was not always an easy matter as the mines became one of the early centers of growing proletarian consciousness and of worker militancy. Such tendencies were opposed by the authorities primarily through appeals to communalism by conservative indigenous or ethnic leaders as well as through other tactics of divide and rule. Where such subtle means did not work, force or the threat of force was also an option.

Labor relations in the postcolonial world of the South Pacific are far more complex. Gone are the days when colonial authorities blithely moved people around the world to suit the needs of colonial economies. Recruitment across national boundaries still occurs on Nauru, but even here it must contend with nationalist sentiments of those worried that these foreigners might remain. Elsewhere, the necessity of catering to the employment needs of local populations first has made it impossible to continue overseas recruitment, except in cases where certain skills are not available locally. Concerning matters of wages and labor conditions for mine workers, the growth of unionism in the Pacific has meant that worker demands must be taken more seriously. The attitudes of national political leaders to such demands, however, in many ways differ little from those of earlier colonial authorities. In fact, such national leaders sometimes are even less sympathetic to workers' demands, arguing that these demands are a threat to national well-being.

Environmental questions only recently have begun to be raised about mining. This reflects in part a growing awareness in general among the population of environmental pollution and related health and safety issues. Specifically, questions about pollution caused by mining often has taken place in the context of opposition to mining by local people whose agricultural base is threatened. Government and mining officials, as elsewhere, usually have sought to deny that there is a problem and have been reticent to respond to complaints.

The countries of the South Pacific also have had to confront the problems associated with the reduction of recoverable deposits to the point of mines closing. Nauru is the last of the phosphate islands where mining is still being carried out and its deposits will be exhausted shortly. The primary question facing the resettled Banabans on Rabi and the government of Kiribati for some time, and shortly Nauru as well, has been how best to manage investment funds derived from previous mining. In Papua New Guinea there are older large mines nearing their end, raising a host of questions for the national government, for the mining companies, for landowners, and for the mine workers.

The reverse of the problem of aging mines is the gold rush of the 1980s, covering an area stretching from Papua New Guinea to Fiji, that was brought on by the higher price of gold and technological innovations. Discoveries in Fiji and the Solomon Islands so far have been relatively small, but those in Papua New Guinea have been of such a scale to mean that before long the country will be one of the world's top gold producers. Questions relating to benefits in terms of profits, revenue, and employment from the gold rush have served to heighten controversies over state versus local rights, environmental pollution, and foreign investment. Other technological innovations relating to seabed mining have led to the prospect of yet another mining rush—one that has the potential of encompassing an even greater part of the region and involving a different set of legal questions centering on the Law of the Sea. Thus, rather than fading into the background, mining looks as if it will remain a major concern in the South Pacific for many years to come.

Mining and Social Science in the South Pacific

There are only a few parts of the Third World, such as southern Africa, where one finds a significant social science literature on mining that goes beyond narrow economic factors to look at the broader social, political, and economic context. For most of this century, scholarly writing on the South Pacific has focused on village life and colonial administration. A naive romanticism ensured that studies of the islanders paid little attention to those laboring in mines or on plantations since this did not fit within the ideal of happy, tradition-bound natives living in thatched huts. Gold mining in New Guinea in the 1920s and 1930s and the phosphate diggings on Nauru and Banaba were inspiration for a few popular works, but failed to receive much attention from scholars at the time.[1]

The decolonization process, starting in the 1960s, finally attracted some scholars to mining, and, more specifically, to the political economy of mining. Nancy Viviani produced a history of Nauru which focused on the Nauruan political struggle that eventually would lead to their independence and their take over of the industry itself.[2] The political controversy surrounding development of the Panguna copper mine on Bougainville in the late 1960s and early 1970s, aroused scholarly interest largely in terms of questions of decentralization and possible secession.[3] Despite these two exceptions, the vast majority of works looking at the independence process during the 1960s and early 1970s focused narrowly on political events, and when touching on economic questions, largely ignored the mining sector. Even with New Caledonia, although nickel mining was not ignored, it was relegated to a relatively minor position.

Since the late 1970s, there has been a relative increase in academic writing on various aspects of mining in the South Pacific. In recent years, there have been several historical studies of commercial enterprises in the South Pacific. The mining sector remains underrepresented within the genre, but a recent work by Maslyn Williams and Barrie Macdonald on the British Phosphate Commissioners is a good start.[4] One important growth area in Pacific Island scholarship is labor history and here the mining industry has received a better accounting. This is to be seen in the work of Colin Newbury and Richard Curtain on New Guinea and 'Atu Bain on Fiji, all of which deal with the colonial period.[5] In Papua New Guinea, development of the large Ok Tedi mine near the Indonesian border resulted in a few studies associated with the Ok Tedi Monitoring Project of the Institute of Applied Social and Economic Research, and the Bougainville mine has continued to receive some interest, especially since the outbreak of violence in 1988.[6]

In terms of Pacific Island scholarship as a whole, however, the literature on mining remains undeveloped. The extent to which this is the case can be seen by looking at Coppell and Stratigos's, *Bibliography of Pacific Island Theses and Dissertations*, published in 1983. The work lists only three theses of relevance, all on Papua New Guinea: a 1975 Ph.D. thesis from the University of Papua New Guinea on the history of gold mining in Papua New Guinea, a 1976 B.Ec.(Hons) thesis from the University of Papua New Guinea on the impact of the Panguna mine on local business, and a 1978 LL.M. from

Monash University on taxation.[7] More recent dissertations are Bain's 1985 Ph.D. on gold mining in colonial Fiji and Terence Wesley-Smith's 1988 Ph.D. on underdevelopment in Papua New Guinea, which contains several chapters on the mining sector.[8]

Currently, the political situation in Fiji makes further research on mining in that country difficult. The accumulated information on the mining industry in New Caledonia has grown considerably as a result of general research on the independence movement, but research on mining remains overshadowed by political events. The tradition of secrecy by the Nauru government has placed substantial obstacles on research on Nauru's mining industry, although recent court cases have provided some opportunities for gaining greater insight into the island economy. Mining research has developed the most in Papua New Guinea, primarily because of the crises surrounding the country's two largest mines, but even here much of the work on mining has taken the form of topical papers written by Papua New Guinea specialists whose substantial work has been on other topics. Clearly then, on a descriptive level, a great deal remains to be done. The present work is intended to help alleviate this situation, but it is far from definitive, and in some cases it can do no more than to point to deficiencies in the scholarly literature on mining in the region.

There is also a theoretical side to academic research on mining in the South Pacific. Scholarly writing on mining in the South Pacific over the past ten to fifteen years, to a large extent, has been closely linked to theoretical currents falling broadly within a political economy perspective, associated initially with questions of dependency and, more recently, with analyses of class and with the articulation of modes of production.[9] Until the 1970s, virtually all scholarship on the South Pacific adhered to one or another variant of the functionalist perspective, with the literature of economics and development falling within the modernization and dualism schools of thought.[10] The latter focused on the need to modernize the backwards sectors of the island economies with reference primarily to agriculture and coincided with the efforts of colonial governments to prepare the states under their control for independence in the decades following the Second World War. Mining received almost no attention in this literature, with the exception of Viviani's study of Nauru and a few works on Bougainville in Papua New Guinea.

Writing from a dependency perspective expanded slowly in the South Pacific during the 1970s. The emergence of this literature coincided with the transition to independence of many island states and with concern about neocolonial relations for the newly independent states.[11] These studies focused on external factors such as aid and foreign investment and, especially, the role of transnational corporations. While not ignoring the relationship of dependency to internal factors (such as corrupt, self-serving elites), the emphasis in this writing clearly was on the ways in which outside interests exerted influence on the newly independent island nations. Mining was of little relevance to those studies concerned with dependency in most of the smaller island states, but it was of considerably more importance for those works dealing with the larger states of Fiji and Papua New Guinea. In these instances questions were raised about local control and benefits to be derived from the mining sector.

While the interest in dependency remains among Pacific scholars, especially for those concerned with the smaller, highly dependent states, during the 1980s the attention of critical scholarship turned increasingly to the internal dynamics of South Pacific island states. Among the specific topics addressed were class relations (especially the activities of local elites and labor relations) and the role of the colonial and postcolonial state.[12] These studies coincided with important political changes in the region as the initial postcolonial political consensus began to break down and rival groups emerged to contest the power held by those left in office by the departing colonial authorities. Perhaps the clearest indication of this was the rise of the Fiji Labour Party, which was founded in 1985, and the subsequent resort to military force to regain power by the Fijian oligarchy. Mining received greater attention in this literature, specifically in terms of labor relations within the mining sector and relationships between mining interests and local political elites.

Increasingly during the 1980s, the combined interest by scholars in questions of dependency and in the role of the state and class relations within the overall context of a concern for understanding the evolution of Pacific island societies and questions of underdevelopment and development served to draw attention to the relevance of analysis of modes of production and their articulation within the Pacific. In the early 1980s, Fitzpatrick employed the concept to an analysis of relations between traditional societies and the modern state in Papua New Guinea; Howard, Plange, Durutalo, and Witton employed the term "Pacific mode of production" in their discussion of precolonial Pacific island societies, and examined subsequent social formations in terms of a capitalist mode of production; and Watters used the idea of a "village mode of production" when discussing contemporary island societies dependent on external sources of funds.[13] A short time later, Howard and Durutalo refer to precapitalist societies in the South Pacific as adhering to a "lineage mode of production," and divide the South Pacific roughly into two general variants, one in the west and the other in the east, and then discuss the process of capitalist penetration and formation of the colonial state.[14] Two primary issues arising from these analyses are the nature of traditional modes of production and their subsequent articulation with a capitalist mode of production.

While these initial studies did not refer directly to the mining sector in their analyses of modes of production and relationships between modes of production, they did provide a potential avenue for examining the impact of mining on Pacific island societies. This potential was developed by Wesley-Smith in his Ph.D. dissertation.[15] In his discussion of the precolonial situation in Papua New Guinea, Wesley-Smith refers to "Melanesian modes of production," of which he sees Papua New Guinea as having three (hunting and gathering, horticultural, and husbandry), each distinguished by particular social relations of production. In his analysis of colonial and contemporary Papua New Guinea, he notes:

> Papua New Guinea's transition to capitalism is incompletely realized. The capitalist intrusion has changed irreparably the structure and relations that governed Melanesian life prior to the arrival of Europeans. However, only a tiny minority of Papua New Guineans have become wholly involved in capitalist forms of production. Indeed, most contemporary productive relationships are neither capitalist nor pre-capitalist in nature, but display elements of both.[16]

In regard specifically to the impact of mining on the transition process, Wesley-Smith argues that its impact has been relatively small and that it may even serve to inhibit the process:

> In part, this is because this sort of capital places relatively few direct demands on indigenous modes of production, and because of the localized nature of the demands that are made. But it is also because it provides those who dominate the post-colonial state with ample material support, and obviates the necessity for the technocracy to extract more surplus from the agricultural sector.[17]

The issues raised by Wesley-Smith and the articulation of modes of production approach in general warrant further investigation in light of recent developments in Papua New Guinea as well as in comparative terms in relation to the other states in the region where mining plays an important role.

The present work builds on these dependency and mode of production perspectives. The chapters that follow focus first on the former British and Australian colonies of Fiji, Papua New Guinea, and the Solomon Islands, where mining has centered on gold and, more recently in the case of Papua New Guinea, on copper as well. Next comes the French colony of New Caledonia, whose economy has been dominated by nickel and chromite mining for almost a century. Finally, we will look at the Phosphate islands of Nauru, Banaba, Makatea, and Angaur.[18] In each case attention is paid to the interplay between political and economic factors at the international, national, and local levels over time and to the impact of mining on the island societies. Within this context, the mining sector is examined as it relates to issues surrounding local elites, foreign capital, labor relations, and the state.

Notes

1. The development of the Morobe goldfields is recorded in such popular works as Edmond Demaitre, *New Guinea Gold: Cannibals & Gold Seekers in New Guinea* (London: Geoffrey Bles, 1936); and Ion Idriess, *Gold Dust and Ashes: the Romantic Story of the New Guinea Goldfields* (Sydney: Angus, 1933). Labor recruitment for the goldfields is touched upon in such studies written during this period as, S.W. Reed, *The Making of Modern New Guinea, with Special Reference to Culture Contact in the Mandated Territory* (Philadelphia: American Philosophical Library, 1943); and L.G. Viall, "Some Statistical Aspects of Population in the Marobe District, New Guinea," *Oceania*, Vol. 8 No. 4, 1938, pp. 383-397. Arthur Grimble served as an administrative officer between the world wars and produced two popular accounts after the Second World War which touch on the early days of phosphate mining: *A Pattern of Islands* (London: John Murray, 1952); and *Return to the Islands* (London: John Murray, 1957).

2. Nancy Viviani, *Nauru: Phosphate and Political Progress* (Canberra: Australian National University Press, 1970).

3. Among the important studies of the impact of mining on Bougainville are: Raymond F. Mikesell, *Foreign Investment in Copper Mining: Case Studies of Mines in Peru and Papua New Guinea* (Baltimore: Johns Hopkins University Press, 1975); M.L. Treadgold, "Bougainville Copper and the Economic Development of Papua New Guinea," in *Economic Record*, Vol. 47, No. 118, 1971; M.L. Treadgold, *The Regional Economy of Bougainville: Growth and Structural Change* (Canberra: Development Studies Centre, Australian National University, 1978); Alexander Mamak and Richard Bedford, *Bougainville Nationalism: Aspects of Unity and Discord* (Christchurch: Department of Geography, University of Canterbury, 1974); Richard Bedford

and Alexander Mamak, *Compensation for Development: The Bougainville Case* (Christchurch: Department of Geography, University of Canterbury, 1977); Ralph Premdas, "Secessionist Politics in Papua New Guinea," in *Pacific Affairs*, Vol. 50, 1977, pp. 64-85; Ralph Premdas, "Copper and Secession on Bougainville," *Canadian Review of Studies in Nationalism*, Vol. 4, No. 2, 1977, pp. 247-265; and Douglas Oliver, *Bougainville: A Personal History* (Honolulu: University Press of Hawaii, 1973).

4. Maslyn Williams and Barrie Macdonald, *The Phosphateers: A History of the British Phosphate Commissioners and the Christmas Island Phosphate Commission* (Melbourne: Melbourne University Press, 1985). An earlier company history which also should be mentioned is: "La Societe 'Le Nickel' de la Fondation a la fin de la Deuxiene Guerre Mondial," in *Journal de la Société des Oceanistes*, Vol. 11, 1955, pp. 97-124.

5. Colin D. Newbury, "Colour Bar and Labour Conflict on the New Guinea Goldfields 1935-1941," *Australian Journal of Politics and History*, Vol. 21 No. 3, 1975, pp. 25-38; Richard Curtain, "The Migrant Labour System and Class Formation in Papua New Guinea," *South Pacific Forum*, Vol. 1, No. 2, 1984, pp. 117-41; 'Atu Bain, Vatukoula—Rock of Gold: Labour in the Gold Mining Industry of Fiji, 1930-1970 (Ph.D. Thesis, Australian National University, 1985); and 'Atu Bain, "Labour Protest and Control in the Gold Mining Industry of Fiji, 1930-1970," in *South Pacific Forum*, Vol. 3, No. 1, 1986, pp. 37-59.

6. On Ok Tedi see: Richard Jackson and T.S. Ilave, *The Ok Tedi Monitoring Project* (Boroko: Institute of Applied Social and Economic Research, 1983); Craig Emerson, "Mining Enclaves and Taxation," in *Development*, Vol. 10, No. 7, 1982, pp. 561-71; Richard Jackson, "Mineral Resources and Mining in Papua New Guinea: Digging in for a Difficult Decade," in *Yagl-Ambu*, Vol. 7, No. 2, 1980, pp. 1-8; Richard Jackson, *Ok Tedi: The Pot of Gold* (Boroko: University of Papua New Guinea, 1982); and William S. Pintz, *Ok Tedi: Evolution of a Third World Mining Project* (London: Mining Journal Books, 1984). More generally, see: C. O'Faircheallaigh, "Review of Papua New Guinea's Mineral Policy 1964-82: Some Preliminary Findings," in D. Gupta and S. Polume, eds., *Economic Policy Issues and Options in Papua New Guinea* (Canberra: Development Studies Centre, Australian National University, 1984).

7. W.G. Coppell and S. Stratigos, *A Bibliography of Pacific Island Theses and Dissertations* (Canberra: Research School of Pacific Studies, Australian National University, 1983). The theses in question are: Hyland N. Nelson, Black, White and Gold: Gold mining in Papua New Guinea, 1878-1930 (Ph.D. Thesis, University of Papua New Guinea, 1975); Brian Brunton, Prices, Mining and Taxation in Papua New Guinea (LL.M. Thesis, Monash University, 1978); and Ephraim Umeng, The Impact of Bougainville Copper Limited Operations on Local Business on Bougainville: A Study of Underdevelopment (B.Ec., Hons., Thesis, University of Papua New Guinea, 1976).

8. Bain, Vatukoula; and Terence A. Wesley-Smith, Melanesians and Modes of Production: Underdevelopment in Papua New Guinea with

Particular Reference to the Role of Mining Capital (Ph.D. Thesis, University of Hawaii, 1988).

9. For a general overview of theoretical developments in social science literature in the South Pacific, see Michael C. Howard, "Social Scientists in Paradise," in *Journal of Pacific Studies*, Vol. 9, 1983, pp. 1-8; the essay is an introduction to a special issue of the *Journal of Pacific Studies* which includes survey of the various social science disciplines.

10. The work of E.K. Fisk provides a good example of this perspective. See, for example, E.K. Fisk, *The Political Economy of Fiji* (Canberra: Australian National University Press, 1967).

11. Among the more important studies concerned with dependency, in chronological order, are: Amelia Rokotuivuna, et al., *Fiji: A Developing Australian Colony* (Melbourne: International Development Action, 1973); Paul Shankman, *Migration and Underdevelopment: The Case of Western Samoa* (Boulder, CO: Westview Press, 1976); Ernst Utrect, *Papua New Guinea: An Australian Neo-colony* (Sydney: Transnational Corporations Research Project, University of Sydney, 1977); Azeem Amarshi, Kenneth Good, and Rex Mortimer, *Development and Dependency: The Political Economy of Papua New Guinea* (Melbourne: Oxford University Press, 1979); John Connell, *Remittances and Rural Development: Migration, Dependency and Inequality in the South Pacific* (Canberra: Development Studies Centre, Australian National University, 1980); George Kent, *Transnational Corporations in Pacific Fishing* (Sydney: Transnational Corporations Research Project, University of Sydney, 1980); Stephen Britton, *Tourism, Dependency and Development: A Mode of Analysis* (Canberra: Development Studies Centre, Australian National University, 1981); Stephen Britton, *Tourism and Underdevelopment in Fiji* (Canberra: Development Studies Centre, Australian National University, 1983); Michael C. Howard, Nii-K. Plange, Simione Durutalo, and Ron Witton, *The Political Economy of the South Pacific: An Introduction* (Townsville: South East Asian Studies Committee, James Cook University, 1983); Michael C. Howard, "Transnational Corporations: The Influence of the Capitalist World Economy," in A. Ali and R. Crocombe, eds., *Foreign Forces in Pacific Politics* (Suva: Institute of Pacific Studies, University of the South Pacific, 1983), pp. 264-189; Ernst Utrect, ed., *Fiji: Client State of Australasia?* (Sydney: Transnational Corporations Research Project, University of Sydney, 1984); Michael C. Howard, "Export Processing Zone Advocacy and the Evolution of Development Strategies and Investment Policies in the South Pacific," in Ernst Utrect, ed., *Transnational Corporations in South East Asia and the Pacific* (Sydney: Transnational Corporations Research Project, University of Sydney, 1984); G. Bertram and R.F. Watters, "The MIRAB Economy in South Pacific Microstates," in *Pacific Viewpoint*, Vol. 26 No. 3, 1985, pp. 497-519; Michael C. Howard, "Transnational Corporations and the Island Nations of the South Pacific," in M.K. Saini, ed., *Global Giants: The Other Side* (New Delhi: Indian Institute of Research on Transnational Corporations, 1986), pp. 117-60; Bruce Knapman, "Aid and the Dependent Development of Pacific Island States," in *Journal of Pacific History*, Vol. 21, No. 3, 1986, pp. 139-52; and Paul

Shankman, "Phases of Dependency in Western Samoa," *Practicing Anthropology,* Vol. 12, No. 1, 1990, pp. 12-13, and 20.

12. Critical analyses of the roles of political elites are to be found in Michael C. Howard, "Vanuatu: The Myth of Melanesian Socialism," *Labour, Capital and Society,* Vol. 16, No. 2, 1983, pp. 176-203; and Simione Durutalo, *The Paramountcy of Fijian Interest and the Politicization of Ethnicity* (Suva: University of the South Pacific Sociological Society, 1986). On labor relations, see Michael C. Howard, ed., *Labour History in the South Pacific,* a special issue of *South Pacific Forum,* Vol. 3, No. 1, 1986. On the colonial state, see William Sutherland, The State and Capitalist Development in Fiji (Ph.D. Thesis, University of Canterbury, Christchurch, New Zealand, 1984); and Michael C. Howard and Simione Durutalo, *The Political Economy of the South Pacific to 1945* (Townsville: Centre for Southeast Asian Studies, James Cook University, 1987); also of relevance is the pioneering work of Peter France, *The Charter of the Land: Custom and Colonization in Fiji* (Melbourne: Oxford University Press, 1969). Another work of importance within this overall genre is Simione Durutalo, Internal Colonialism and Unequal Development: The Case of Western Fiji (M.A. Thesis, University of the South Pacific, 1985).

13. P. Fitzpatrick, *Law and State in Papua New Guinea* (London: Academic Press, 1980); Howard, et al., *Political Economy,* pp. 5-7; and R.F. Watters, "The Village Mode of Production in MIRAB Societies," *Pacific Viewpoint,* Vol. 25, 1984, pp. 218-23.

14. Howard and Durutalo, *Political Economy,* pp. 6-7

15. Wesley-Smith, *Melanesians and Modes of Production,* pp. 53-59.

16. Ibid., p. 298.

17. Ibid., p. 303.

18. The condominium of the New Hebrides (now independent Vanuatu) was the scene of some alluvial gold prospecting in the 1930s as part of the general search for gold in the Melanesian region, but little gold was found. During the 1950s, foreign mining companies engaged in a search for phosphate and manganese. The only mine to be developed as a result of this effort was the relatively small Forari phosphate mine in eastern Efate, which began operation in 1962 and closed in 1978. Intensive mineral exploration began again in 1981, following independence and with the advent of the new Melanesian gold rush. To date, exploration has turned up little of commercial value (primarily, a small manganese deposit on Erromango), and almost nothing in terms of possible gold deposits. See J.S.G. Wilson, *Economic Survey of the New Hebrides* (London: Ministry of Overseas Development, 1966); and Republic of Vanuatu, *First National Development Plan, 1982-1986* (Port Vila: National Planning Office, 1982), pp. 165-69.

2

Fiji

The country of Fiji is comprised of an archipelago of over three hundred islands with a population by the late 1980s of around 700,000. There are two main islands, Viti Levu and Vanua Levu, with the majority of people and bulk of economic activity being found on Viti Levu, where the nation's capital, Suva, is located. The population includes two main ethnic communities, indigenous native Fijians and Indo-Fijian descendants of migrants from India. Each of these communities in turn is quite heterogeneous. In addition, there are several smaller communities, including Chinese, Europeans, part-Europeans, and other Pacific islanders.[1]

Fiji's eastern chiefs ceded the islands to Britain in 1874 and Fiji remained under British rule until 1970. To promote development of large-scale commercial enterprises, the colonial authorities standardized Fiji's land tenure system and created a centralized system for administering the land within a structure of chiefly-based indirect rule. Sugar assumed a central place in the colonial economy and since independence the country has remained highly dependent on sugar exports. Copra and gold ranked a distant second and third in importance to the colonial economy. Both of these industries were also controlled by foreign interests. Fiji's economy has diversified since the 1960s as the development of tourism (which became the nation's second most important industry), timber, tuna fishing, and light industry made Fiji's the most diversified and developed economy among the island nations of the South Pacific with a per capita gross domestic product of over U.S.$1,400 by the mid-1980s.

Taking the year 1982 as an example, sugar and molasses accounted for F$130 million out of Fiji's roughly F$168 million worth of exports. Of the remaining F$38 million, gold accounted for over F$15 million, fish and fish products around F$9 million, and coconut products F$5 million. Fiji's economic dependence on sugar exports becomes even greater if we examine the other sectors of its economy more closely. Tourism, Fiji's second industry, is not only largely foreign-owned, but puts relatively little money directly into the Fiji economy. The so-called leakage factor was estimated in the early 1980s to be in excess of seventy-five cents out of every dollar spent by tourists. In addition, tourism has produced relatively little employment over the years. Likewise, the gold industry, which will be examined in greater detail below, produces very little income for Fiji and employs a relatively small number of people.

Newer areas of the economy to be developed include timber and garments. The Fiji Pine Commission was established in 1977. The industry, however, got off to a slow start. Although the government proclaimed that within a few years exports of "green gold" would soar to F$50 million and perhaps even surpass sugar as Fiji's main export, after peaking at F$4 million in 1980, timber exports dropped to under F$2 million the following year. Timber exports remained low into the mid-1980s, when hopes were again revived as a new large joint venture scheme between the Fiji Pine Commission and British Petroleum got underway. The garment industry emerged during the 1980s in response Australian and New Zealand duty concessions and an ability to pay workers exceptionally low wages. Since the 1987 military coups the garment industry has received considerable support by the Mara-Rabuka regime, which views garment exports as an important area of economic growth and profits for its supporters.

An understanding of Fiji's economy cannot be divorced from four important political features: (1) the existence of a powerful oligarchy dominated by a handful of native Fijian chiefs from the eastern part of the country, (2) widespread uncertainty among Fijians in the face of rapid socioeconomic change, (3) the extent to which communalism has been a part of Fijian political life, and (4) regional disparities related to the influence of the eastern chiefs. The latter feature has resulted in a situation where, although productive economic activity is centered in the western part of Viti Levu, political power and the dispersal of government funds has been concentrated in the eastern portion of the country.

Since independence, Fiji's chiefly oligarchy has been headed by Ratu Sir Kamasese Mara, whose Alliance Party held power from 1970 until it lost office to a coalition led by the newly formed Fiji Labour Party in April 1987. A month later, on 14 May 1987, the coalition government of Dr. Timoci Bavadra was overthrown in a military coup, staged by Colonel Sitiveni Rabuka, aimed at putting the chiefly oligarchy back in power. During the remainder of 1987, Fiji experienced a period of political and economic chaos, including a second coup in September. Since 1988, a chiefly-military alliance has held power under Mara's leadership.

Mining in Colonial Fiji

Gold prospecting in Fiji dates back to the 1880s, but production was insignificant until the 1930s, when gold mining quickly became established as one of the colony's leading industries.[2] Ownership of all minerals was vested in the Crown under 1908 legislation. Prospecting was made difficult by the mountainous terrain and thick vegetation of the main islands and was confined mainly to coastal areas. Small alluvial deposits were discovered at several sites as early as the mid-1880s, but no significant mining took place until after the First World War. E. Cresswell, a local prospector, discovered alluvial gold in Vanua Levu and opened a small mine in 1922. Two crushings of 190 tons of ore produced only a small amount of gold and the mine was shut down the following year. The first important mine to be developed was at Yanawai, on Vanua Levu. Prospectors had known of alluvial gold at the site since 1885, but no serious search had been made for its source until the 1920s, when payable deposits were discovered by the Vatukaisia Mining Company Ltd. Mount Kasi Mines Ltd. acquired Vatukaisia's interests and commenced production at Yanawai in 1932.

The world depression of the 1930s adversely effected Fiji's agriculturally-based economy, causing a loss of export earnings and unemployment. As the price of gold rose from U.S.$20 to around U.S.$30 an ounce in the early 1930s, the colonial government saw gold mining as a possible way out of the colony's economic problems. It was a view shared by the administrations of Papua, New Guinea and the Solomon Islands. The colonial government in Fiji passed a new mining ordinance and set out mining regulations in 1934 to encourage local and foreign interests in the industry. A number of small local firms registered and began looking for gold. At the same time, the Mount Kasi Mine company installed a more efficient plant at its mine on Vanua Levu that led to increased production.

The center of mining activity soon shifted to Tavua, in western Viti Levu. The Tavua goldfield attracted important foreign interests associated with Frank Packer and Edward Theodore of Australia (who were also active in gold mining in Papua New Guinea). They formed Emperor Gold Mining Company Ltd. (which merged with

Korowere Gold NL in 1938) to exploit the largest deposit, with proven reserves of over one million tons of ore. Two other smaller mines also began operation, the Loloma mine owned by Loloma (Fiji) Gold Mines NL, and the Dolphin mine owned by Fiji Mines Development Ltd. Although these two mines had much smaller reserves, the Loloma mine 48,000 tons and the Dolphin mine 35,000 tons, the grade of the ore in the mines was much higher than Emperor's Vatukoula mine (Loloma's being 20.0 dwt gold per ton, Dolphin's 20.0, and Emperor's 7.9).

After the initial impetus caused by the sudden rise in the price of gold, the situation soon became more problematic, when the international price of gold was fixed at U.S.$32 an ounce in 1934. The fixed price meant that those in the gold mining industry did not have to worry about the price fluctuations present in many other commodity markets, but sustaining profits meant that costs had to be watched very carefully. Emperor Gold Mining responded by lobbying the government for assistance to keep the mines profitable— starting a pattern that eventually would lead to pleas for outright subsidies. In 1938 the authorities agreed to reduce customs duties on all equipment used in mining of non-British origin to fifteen per cent and that of British origin was allowed to enter duty free.

The value of gold exports rose from virtually nothing in the early 1930s to thirty-five per cent of the colony's exports by 1939 (sugar representing fifty-four per cent). Emperor Gold Mining alone produced 607,385 fine ounces of gold during its first decade of operation, worth £5.6 million. Benefitting from the low taxes and duties of Fiji's colonial economy, Australian mining interests were able to recoup their initial investment in a short time. The concessions to the industry, however, also served to reduce the government's direct financial benefits from mining despite the rise in the overall value of gold exports.

The other area of cost where the government sought to help the mine owners was labor. Paid employment in Fiji during the 1930s was very limited, and the mines soon became one of the most important sources of regular paid work. By 1938, the mining industry employed 1,675 people (Fiji's total population was about 200,000). The Emperor's Vatukoula mine employed 727 people in 1938: 68 Europeans, 77 of mixed origin, 555 native Fijians, 25 Indo-Fijians, and 2 classified as other. The Loloma mine in the same year employed 437: 38 Europeans, 33 of mixed descent, 355 native Fijians, and 1 Indo-Fijian. Thus, although mining was of little importance for Indo-Fijians (who comprised about half of the population and most of whom were employed in the sugar industry), the mines were very important for the other communities. The European population at the time was around 4,000 and the mixed, or part-European, population around 4,500. For these communities, mining accounted for between five and ten per cent of the work force.

Around 1,000 of the country's roughly 100,000 native Fijians were employed in the mining industry. Being closely tied to their villages through the Native Regulations, mining represented one of the few avenues of permanent wage employment open to them. Work in the mines was especially valued in the 1930s because of low prices for their agricultural products. Such employment for native Fijian commoners was viewed ambiguously by the chiefs and religious authorities, however, who appreciated the income it generated as the money found its way back to the villages, but who also feared the loss of control over those living away from the village.

Native Fijians occupied most of the unskilled jobs in the industry, while part-Europeans held most of the jobs requiring more skills, and Europeans occupied the most skilled and managerial posts. Wages in the mining industry for native Fijians and part-Europeans were about average by the standards of the day, but lost ground in relative terms after the mid-1930s, when wage rates became stagnant. Wages in the mining industry ranged from fourteen shillings a week for unskilled workers to twenty-five shillings a week for skilled workers (in addition to quarters and rations). By comparison, unskilled Public Works Department employees received between two shillings three pence and three shillings a day. Carpenters, joiners, and boat-builders received between three shillings six pence and one pound three shillings six pence a day.

Social problems abounded in the mining communities: "Alcohol consumption, gambling and prostitution were quickly taking hold of the community," conditions that "aggravated rather than alleviated the stresses stemming from a harsh work routine, poor wages and congested living conditions."[3] These problems were compounded even further as wages stagnated. After a fight broke out among native Fijian mineworkers from Tailevu and Ra provinces at the Vatukoula mine in February 1936, mineworkers began to organize in an effort to improve their conditions of employment.

In September 1936, workers asked the management to recognize a committee that would be responsible for making submissions concerning working conditions, and the following year the workers made a demand for increased wages. The lack of response from Emperor Gold Mining's management to these petitions resulted in several hundred workers going out on strike in 1938. As it had done to quell the 1936 riot, the company called on the ranking chiefs from the two provinces concerned, the Roko Tui Tailevu and the Roko Tui Ra, to convince the strikers to go back to work, largely through communal appeals. Strategies to control labor through ethnic divisiveness thereafter were institutionalized, with native Fijian chiefs playing a prominent role. The use of communally-based committees, in particular, was employed as a means of thwarting unionization.[4]

In addition to the Tavua and Yanawai mines, gold also was produced for a while before the war in the Vuda Mining Area in western Viti Levu. Alluvial gold was discovered at Vuda in the early 1930s. Interest increased in 1935, when an auriferous lode was found by the Natalau Gold Prospecting Syndicate. The site was taken over by Whitehall Explorations Ltd., but Whitehall withdrew from Fiji after nine months. The government proclaimed the Vuda valley a Mining Area (comprising 4,470 acres) in December 1937. The Natalau Syndicate took out a lease on fifty acres of the area the next month and, in April 1940, another fifty acre lease was given to the Lautoka Mining Syndicate, which began to work the Vatutambua Mine. The majority shareholder in the Vuda syndicates was local attorney M.D. Richmond.

During the Second World War, gold exports were seen by colonial authorities as crucial to the Fijian economy and to the war effort in general. The industry was threatened, however, by increasing prices for agricultural commodities and opportunities to work in defence and related services, where the pay and conditions were much better. The threat posed to the industry as workers deserted in greater numbers led to state intervention. Government officers were instructed to take a variety of steps to help mobilize native Fijian labor for the mines and mineworkers were required to receive official permission before leaving the mines to enlist in the armed forces.[5] But labor was not the only problem facing the gold mines. The mines also had difficulty in securing machinery and other supplies.

The colonial authorities did what they could to help the mining industry, but wartime conditions limited what could be done. While the Tavua mines suffered some hardships during the war, the Mount Kasi mine had an even worse time. Restrictions made it difficult for the mine to obtain needed supplies until it was forced temporarily to close in December 1943. The mine was reopened in February 1944, but production ceased again in May. The remaining payable ore was recovered in 1946 and the mine was dismantled. Between 1932 and 1946 the Mount Kasi mine produced 63,592 ounces of gold and 4,850 ounces of silver, worth about £550,000.

Gold production at the Tavua gold field increased after the war. It peaked in 1947 and remained relatively high through 1950. Mining profits increased in 1949, after the price of gold rose as a result of revaluation of the pound. Production declined after 1950, however, and the companies prevailed on the colonial administration to offer them tax relief. The administration responded by exempting gold and silver bullion from port and service taxes and took other means of assisting the industry under consideration.

Interest in the Vuda goldfield increased around the end of the war. To increase work at the goldfield, M.D. Richmond of the Vuda syndicates arrived at an agreement in 1945 with Pioneer Gold Mines of British Columbia to form the South Pacific Mining company. The company found little additional gold, however, and reserves at its two mines were soon exhausted: the Vatutambua Mine was dismantled in 1949 and mining ceased at the Natalau mine in 1952. The Natalau mine had produced 692 ounces of gold and 163 ounces of silver, valued at £6,536, between 1938 and 1952, while production at the Vatutambua Mine was considerably less. Seven additional prospecting licences in the Vuda goldfield were awarded to various parties in 1946, but little gold was found and all were allowed to lapse.

The role of Indo-Fijians in the gold mining industry was never a large one, but some individuals with experience as goldsmiths carried out prospecting in western Viti Levu after the war. The only significant discovery was that by P.B. Sharma in 1946. His Mistry Mine commenced production in 1947 and was closed in 1958, after producing 821 ounces of gold and 234 ounces of silver, worth £10,100 (along with five tons of lead).

Having exhausted their reserves, production ceased at the Dolphin mine in 1955, and at the Lomaloma mine in 1957. Emperor Gold Mining's Vatukoula mine, essentially the colony's sole remaining gold mine, had depleted its open-cut reserves by 1956, and was forced to rely on more costly production techniques. In an effort to assist Emperor Gold Mining, in 1957 the colonial administration exempted the company from payment of royalties and income tax for two years. Emperor Gold Mining continued to plead financial difficulty in meeting exploration and development expenses and the government decided to remove the royalty and tax exemption and replaced them with a subsidy for three years. Emperor Gold Mining's gold production increased in 1963, and remained at relatively high levels throughout the remainder of the 1960s as Fiji moved toward independence, but production costs remained high. Emperor Gold

Mining asked the government for financial assistance again in 1965, this time to help cover the cost of further exploration. Around the time of independence, the mine was said to be operating at a loss, but its foreign owners gave no indications of being interested in pulling out.

Emperor Gold Mining's relationship with the colonial administration was an intimate one. It was a pattern similar to that existing with the colony's other large foreign enterprises such as Colonial Sugar Refining and Burns Philp.[5] Like these companies, Emperor Gold Mining also maintained close and important links with the Fijian Administration, which was the primary institution of the structure of indirect rule for the native Fijian community. In particular, relations between Emperor Gold Mining's management and the leading chief of the day, Ratu Sukuna, were extremely close.[6] While the administration in general sought to create a financial environment that benefitted the larger foreign companies, Sukuna and his chiefly associates concerned themselves with keeping the work force in line.

Between the end of the Second World War and independence in 1970, the work force in the gold mining industry averaged around 1,300. It reached a low of 1,148 in 1953 and a high of 1,972 just prior to independence. The communal pattern of recruitment remained much the same as it had been before the war. What changed was the degree of proletarianization of the work force as people came to be employed on a more permanent basis. This change emerged clearly during the course of labor unrest in 1947. The disturbances began when a riot broke out during a labor dispute involving a group of young militant labor leaders. The police intervened on behalf of the company and forty of those who took part in the riot were charged: sixteen being sentenced to between six months and one year of hard labor and the rest were given two years bonded probation. The matter did not end with the police intervention. In protest over the actions of the management and authorities, more than one thousand workers, including those of different communities, went on strike. The native Fijian strikers resisted the pleas of the chiefs with immediate authority over them to break ranks and end the strike. The authorities then decided to call in two prominent chiefs of national standing, Ratu George Toganivalu and Ratu Lala Sukuna, who were able at last to break the strike.

Following the 1947 strike, the government, through Sukuna, and in keeping with its postwar policy of promoting "responsible" trade unions in an effort to reduce the threat of worker militancy, set about to encourage and supervise the formation of a mineworkers' union.

TABLE 2.1 Gold, Silver, and Manganese Production, Fiji, 1946-1972

	Gold		Silver		Manganese	
	'000 ozs	£'000	'000 ozs	£'000	'000 tons	£'000
1946	68.9	657.5	na	na	0.0	0.0
1947	134.8	1,288.8	34.9	7.3	0.0	0.0
1948	105.7	1,011.2	37.9	6.9	0.0	0.0
1949	104.1	1,123.2	30.3	6.9	0.0	0.0
1950	103.1	1,419.6	29.1	8.7	0.2	na
1951	93.7	1296.4	30.2	10.5	0.6	10.2
1952	80.2	1,170.2	22.0	7.5	2.0	36.3
1953	70.5	993.7	14.7	5.0	2.2	33.4
1954	78.4	1,081.9	17.8	6.0	5.7	78.5
1955	85.9	1,027.5	20.4	8.2	9.3	118.0
1956	67.1	937.8	na	na	19.3	280.4
1957	76.6	1,074.8	24.9	9.1	27.4	449.6
1958	81.1	1,140.3	25.4	8.9	22.5	402.4
1959	70.7	990.0	23.6	8.3	20.6	338.1
1960	71.7	1,002.7	31.3	11.0	1.8	24.9
1961	95.3	1,202.0	37.7	13.3	2.3	15.9
1962	84.9	1,189.0	38.9	13.6	10.3	134.3
1963	111.3	1,557.6	46.9	16.4	10.2	119.6
1964	100.2	1,385.7	60.6	21.2	1.1	9.4
1966	109.7	1,515.0	70.0	27.0	5.1	76.4
1967	112.7	1,573.5	61.3	70.3	4.4	69.4
1968	105.9	1,685.1	55.2	84.9	10.8	116.6
	F$'000		F$'000		F$'000	
1969	95.3	3,361.0	38.0	61.0	11.1	133.0
1970	103.7	3,165.0	26.6	40.9	24.0	295.0
1971	89.1	2,718.4	19.9	28.5	7.5	94.6
1972	81.6	4,046.1	23.7	34.1	0.0	0.0

Source: Annual Reports for Fiji, 1938-1972 (Suva: Government Printer).

Two key features of this union were its formation along exclusive communal lines, involving only native Fijians (who were considered easier to control), and exclusion of the militant leaders of the 1947 strike in conjunction with promotion of more moderate trade union leaders.

As with other large companies in the colony at the time, Emperor Gold Mining did not support the idea of promoting even "responsible" unions, preferring to continue suppressing all attempts by workers to organize. Intimidation by the company resulted in declining union membership, from about one thousand in 1948 to five hundred by 1950. But the union did not disappear. Moreover, in 1949 its native Fijian members moved to open membership to all non-Europeans. Also, while the union leadership was relatively moderate, this did not bring about complete industrial peace. There was a strike involving one hundred and fifty mill workers in 1950 over wrongful dismissal. In this instance, the strike was concluded through conciliation involving the government labor officer. Deterioration of the quality of rations led to a strike by two hundred and seventy-five workers in 1951. The next year, demands by the Fiji Mineworkers' Union for wage increases and the abolition of food rationing was accompanied by a strike threat. In an unprecedented move, the management agreed to refer the dispute to a formal conciliation board, which awarded a six pence per day wage increase. The union also received government recognition at this time, although, by and large, Emperor Gold Mining continued to ignore it.

A ten day strike in 1955 over wage rates involved 1,138 workers. Once again, Emperor Gold Mine called in two prominent chiefs, Sukuna and George Cakobau, to try to break the strike. This time the chiefs' appeal to the striking workers, asking them to return to work pending the outcome of a tribunal award, failed. Moreover, for the first time, the union's submission included Rotuman and part-European workers.

During the 1950s, there was a marked increase in the use of state conciliation and arbitration machinery in labor relations. This was accepted by the union, which was also willing to allow indexation as a means of determining wages. In its submissions during the latter half of the decade, the union came to include all non-European workers and pushed for parity of wage rates, a system of job evaluation, and, in general, a greater say in conditions of employment.

Emperor Gold Mining's strategies for containing workers' demands were becoming more subtle by the end of the 1950s, with less overt reliance on force. The company was able to use indexation and claimed inability to pay as a means of keeping wages down. In fact, there were no wage increases between 1955 and 1963. As a result, workers saw their incomes decline in real terms. In addition, the company was still able to promote communal differences:

> The accelerated promotion of Rotumans and half-castes to supervisory positions had the desired effect of rekindling communal hostilities and curtailing union membership among these two groups. Their integration into the structure of management—usually to shift boss level—required them to renounce their union membership. The

formation of a separate staff association in the late 1960s marked the success of this initiative.[7]

The thirty year old assistant secretary to the Fiji Stevedoring Union, Sakiasi Waqanivavalagi, was elected general secretary of the Fiji Mine Workers' Union in 1962. Under his conservative leadership, the union began to lose credibility among the workers. This did not, however, stand in the way of his being elected to the Legislative Council in 1966. Thereafter, his political fortunes rose along with those of the Alliance Party, which was led by Sukuna's replacement as leader of the chiefly oligarchy, Ratu Kamasese Mara. Rather than benefitting the mineworkers' union, Waqanivavalagi's political activities meant that he identified increasingly with the chiefly oligarchy and with its tradition of support for the management of the mining company.

Although gold dominated the mining industry in colonial Fiji, to the point that few today are aware that anything else has ever been mined, during the 1950s and 1960s very active exploration for base metals took place and some manganese (along with smaller amounts of copper and iron) was exported. In addition to foreign interests, manganese mining also attracted Indo-Fijians from the Nadi area, some of whom had backgrounds as goldsmiths and were also involved in gold exploration, and a few native Fijians. The leading companies involved in manganese exploration and mining were Akhil Mines Ltd., Consolidated Manganese and Mining Company of Fiji Ltd., Vunamoli Mining Syndicate, Vunamoli Mining Company Ltd., and Banno Oceania Ltd.

Initial prospecting began in 1949, centered in western Viti Levu. The following year about 700 tons of manganese was mined in the Nadi area and 200 tons were exported to Britain. The industry got off to an erratic start, but by 1954 there were five mines in operation and ten mines were in production by 1955. Around seventy per cent of the ore was exported to the United States, with the remainder going to Japan. The mines were relatively small and most employed only ten to twenty workers.

While the majority of manganese mines were located in western Viti Levu, there were a few elsewhere in Fiji. The Masomo mine on Vanua Levu was worked briefly in 1959 and 1960 and the mine's licence was cancelled in 1962 for non-payment of rent. The Nubu mine, also on Vanua Levu, produced about 200 tons of ore in 1958 and 1959, but poor access and the high cost of shipping resulted in none of the ore being sold. A mine on the island of Nayau (in the Lau Group) was worked by Banno Mining Company. A lease was taken out in 1957 and the reserves were estimated to be around 10,000 tons. The mine produced 2,691 tons of ore from 1959 until 1962 (valued at £26,910), when the mining ceased in the face of low manganese prices in relation to high shipping costs.

In 1958 the price of fifty per cent grade manganese ore dropped from £18 to £12 a ton. The larger producers were able to continue, but many smaller operations found it impossible. The more accessible areas already having been explored and with the price down, the pace of exploration declined. When the price of manganese fell to £10 10s per ton in 1960, many of the remaining mines became idle. Disputes over title closed a few others. By 1962, exports consisted mainly of old stocks of ore and these were largely depleted by 1964.

Manganese production in Fiji was not quite finished, however. The Nubu mine was reopened in late 1964 and, in 1968, Manganex Ltd., a subsidiary of Great Southern Land Mining Company Ltd. of Australia, took over the operations of Akhil Holdings Ltd. with the aim of increasing production of low-grade manganese ore for export to Japan. Manganex's efforts resulted in a rise in manganese exports for another couple of years, but, by 1971, Fiji's manganese "boom" came to an end.

The best documented, and perhaps the most interesting, manganese mining venture was that of the Vunamoli Mining Syndicate.[8] The Vunamoli case illustrates many of the problems that continue to exist in relations between native Fijian villagers, foreign capital, and Europeans and high ranking chiefs who are members of the Fijian oligarchy. Vunamoli in located in the Sigatoka Valley of western Viti Levu. The origins of mining in the area can be traced to a local man who worked for the government savings bank as a clerk from 1941 to 1946. During this time he took an interest in minerals and learned the basics of prospecting. He returned to Vunamoli in 1947 as the village chief and began prospecting around the village. By 1953 he was confident that there were paying deposits of manganese in the area.

It took the villagers three visits to Suva to convince the Mining Board to grant them a licence to work the deposits. The board at first was skeptical that a group of native Fijians were capable of running a mining operation, even a small one. After changing its mind, the board offered assistance, including an agreement by the mining inspector to spend time with the villagers. Six villages near the deposit co-operated and by 1955, employing a continuous labor force of thirty men out of a total adult male population of 170, they had cleared the site and found a sizeable deposit. Having recovered a stock of about 250 tons of manganese by 1956, the group now turned to the Fijian Affairs Board (an arm of the colonial administration controlled by the chiefs supposedly to assist native Fijians) for additional assistance. When their request for a bulldozer to transport the ore was turned down, the villagers went ahead on their own using horses and bullocks pulling sleds to carry the ore down to the nearest road, at which point they contracted with an Indo-Fijian truck-owner to take the ore to Lautoka for storage.

The enterprise of the group gained the support of local European colonial officials, who helped them arrange to sell the ore to Metal Traders Inc. of New York, the largest manganese exporting firm operating in Fiji, for £13 a ton. The sale allowed them to pay off their debts, complete a road to the mine site, and purchase further explosives. Enthusiastic about the developmental prospects of the project, the mining inspector had quit his job with the government to work as an adviser to the villagers. A full-time work force of about twenty men was employed at eleven shillings a day. In 1956 two organizations were formed to handle the mining operation—the Vunamoli Syndicate, and the Vunamoli Association. The syndicate consisted of the association and Metal Traders, each with a fifty per cent interest.

The villagers were not entirely happy about the partnership with Metal Traders, even though the company had indicated that it intended to be a "silent partner." The involvement of Metal Traders had been promoted by the legal adviser to the Fijian Affairs Board, a resident European named John Falvey, who was closely associated with the chiefly oligarchy as well as being on the board of the Metal Traders subsidiary in Fiji. Problems came to a head in 1958 as the cost of selling the ore rose, unsold ore piled up in Lautoka, and profits declined. A dispute arose between the partners over the accounts. At the heart of the controversy were different expectations by the villagers and the mining company. The villagers were intent on using the mining enterprise to provide for broad-based development. They were anxious to develop the mine slowly to ensure that they could learn the appropriate skills needed for mining and stretch out the money to provide for other developmental goals. The association had been using its profits to provide for agricultural development, prepare for commercial tree planting and building a saw mill, launch a program of house construction, and for social welfare purposes (especially educational).

Metal Traders had become impatient with the running of the mine and now suggested that its local subsidiary take over the mining function. This seemed to confirm the villagers' initial fears and led them to complain once again about Falvey's dual role. They were particularly worried since the Metal Traders subsidiary operated a large mine nearby at Nasaucoko, Navosa, where it had sought to remove the ore as quickly as possible and had not involved the local population in a meaningful way. The Vunamoli people refused to accept the suggestion and before long the enterprise collapsed. Writing shortly after the events, Cyril Belshaw, in assessing the failure of the Vunamoli venture, does not blame Metal Traders, but, rather, points to the "negligence" of the Fiji Affairs Board.[9] Pursuit of the reasons behind such negligence, however, leads to a critical assessment of the manner in which the local oligarchy has used institutions such as the Fijian Affairs Board for its own ends and how this has often worked to the detriment of the majority of native Fijians. Moreover, the case is illustrative of the way in which corporate and class interests have served to ensure the maintenance of the enclave nature of the mining industry in Fiji.

Copper mining in Fiji dates back to 1906, when a shaft was sunk at the Kingston mine in western Viti Levu and samples were sent to Australia. The samples contained thirty-three per cent copper as well as some gold and silver. The site was worked by the Fiji Prospecting Syndicate until 1908, when mining ceased after passage of the 1908 mining ordinance. The licence was cancelled in 1911, and over the next few years the mine was worked on a limited basis by a few resident Europeans (J. Malcolm, P. Costello, and A.C. Winning). In total, only a couple of tons of copper ore were produced. The area was looked over again in 1934-35, but this time only for gold. Copper was found in 1912 at Namosi, near Suva, by J.B. Tarby. A licence was taken out on the site by the partnership of McGeady and McCrae in the late 1930s, but not worked.

Small-scale copper mining got underway again in the 1950s. The Wainivesi mine near Nadi was reopened for copper and zinc in 1953, and in 1956 Emperor Gold Mining took an option on the mine. Emperor Gold Mining's interest in base metals increased during the late 1950s as its profits from gold declined, but little actually came of this interest. Kennecott Exploration (Australia) Ltd. took out a prospecting licence over 360,320 acres in southwestern Viti Levu in 1956, but poor results led the company to surrender most of the licence the following year. R.L. Govind discovered copper at Mouta on Vanua Levu in 1957. A small shipment worth £772 was exported in 1960, but the ore grade was not considered sufficient to continue. A small quantity of copper was exported to Japan from the Nukudamu mine on Vanua Levu in 1958. After spending an additional £13,000 on further drilling, production was halted in 1959. Banno Mining Company carried out exploration for copper deposits at several sites and began to work the Udu mine in 1965. Shipments of ore to Japan began in 1968, but by the next year deposits were depleted and the mine was closed and dismantled. Additional exploration was conducted between 1969 and 1971 by United Mining Exploration Pty. Ltd. (Australia), Longreach Metals Ltd., Falconbridge (Australia) Ltd., and Southland Mining Ltd., but with no significant finds.

Iron ore was discovered at Tuveriki in Viti Levu in 1933, but reserves were considered uneconomical. Samples were taken again in 1943 and 1953, and mining commenced in 1957. Production in the first year was 1,300 tons and an additional 3,000 tons were produced in 1958, when a trial shipment was made to Japan. Mining continued until 1963, when all of the economic ore had been collected. Interest in iron ore mining in Fiji resumed in 1968, when Bauxite Fiji Ltd. began exploring the Wainunu area. In 1970, the company announced plans to open a mine with a 250,000 ton processing capacity and the following year invested F$750,000 in the mine. Production was due to start in mid-1972, but was delayed by damage caused by heavy rains, a dock strike in Japan that interfered with the delivery of equipment, and various managerial problems. Momentum having been lost, the company decided to pull out of the project and the mine never opened.

Base metal mining during its brief span had but a minimal impact on the colony. At various times hopes were raised that the industry would generate considerable wealth, but little was actually realized.

TABLE 2.2 Copper and Iron Ore Exports, Fiji, 1959-1969

	Copper		Iron Ore	
	tons	£	tons	£
1959	180	1,800	11,692	57,171
1960	97	1,275	23,396	93,584
1961	150	645	10,280	41,120
1962	128	1,360	6,229	24,816
1963	30	543	1,062	4,248
1964	50	500	0	0
1965	20	200	0	0
1966	10	100	0	0
1967	3	24	0	0
1968	3,619	473,968	0	0
1969	2,000	350,000	0	0

Source: *Annual Reports for Fiji*, 1960-1972 (Suva: Government Printer).

A few Indo-Fijian entrepreneurs made money on manganese, but most came away with little or nothing. Emperor Gold Mining's attempts to diversify in this direction were unsuccessful and other overseas interests failed to find much to sustain their efforts. A few jobs were provided, but most of the mines did not last long enough to provide stable employment. The workers were not organized and wages and conditions of work do not appear to have been very good. Such mining development occasionally met local resistance. Thus, in 1958 the people of Cikobia (in the Lau Group) managed to halt further searches for manganese ore. But by and large the industry never developed sufficiently to cause too much trouble.

Mining in Independent Fiji

Mining in Fiji since 1970, generally, has meant Emperor Gold Mining Company, although recently there has been increased gold exploration around the archipelago. Gold was Fiji's second highest export earner until 1978, when the industry went into a slump. Overall, the decade following independence was a difficult one for Emperor Gold Mining, which had been taken over largely by New Zealand interests around the time of independence. Production declined sharply from 3,235 kilograms in 1970 to a low of 774 kilograms in 1980, and the relatively low price of gold throughout most of the decade limited the mine's financial returns. In the face of such economic problems, Emperor Gold Mining's management became increasingly anti-union at a time when the union itself was becoming more militant. Sakiasi Waqanivavalagi was rewarded for his loyalty to the chiefly oligarchy with a seat in parliament as a member of the Alliance Party.[10] Under its new leader, Navitalai Raqona, the union became increasingly militant.

The mid-1970s were marked by considerable labor unrest, and relations between the Alliance Party government and the unions became very strained.[11] In the case of the mineworkers, the deterioration of labor relations culminated in a strike which assumed national importance. In 1977, as a bargaining ploy with the government and labor, Emperor Gold Mining threatened to close down the Vatukoula mine and lay off its 1,300 workers. The union, with the backing of the Fiji Trades Union Congress, responded by calling a strike. The government intervened and, in the end, some 700 workers lost their jobs. Those most active in the union were not among the 600 workers rehired and the union was broken, being finally deregistered in 1979.

TABLE 2.3 Gold Production, Fiji, 1975-1986

Year	Quantity*
1975	2,138
1976	1,700
1977	1,535
1978	873
1979	923
1980	774
1981	960
1982	1,423
1983	1,246
1984	1,676
1985	1,888
1986	2,856

*Kilograms.
Sources: *United Nations Statistical Yearbook, 1985/86;* British Geological Society, *World Mineral Statistics, 1982-1986.*

By the end of the 1970s, Emperor Gold Mining's financial health had improved considerably. The work force had been rationalized and the price of gold had risen sharply between 1978 and 1980. Having had its way with the government and its work force, the company responded to improved gold prices by increasing production—to 1,415 kilograms by 1982. The value of gold exports from Fiji increased from F$6.5 million in 1979 to F$15.3 million by 1982. By this time, however, the mining operation was badly in need of new capital, which the company had been unwilling to invest during the 1970s.

In the wake of renewed interest in gold mining throughout the southwest Pacific, an important change occurred for Emperor Gold Mining in April 1983, when Western Mining Corporation of Australia took a ten per cent share in the company and assumed managerial responsibility for the mine. Western Mining and Emperor Gold Mining also established a fifty-fifty joint venture to pursue further gold exploration in the Tavua basin, where the government granted the consortium a new exploration licence over 6,123 hectares. The new partners, operating under the name of Vatukoula Joint Venture, announced that F$30 million would be invested in the Vatukoula mine and that ore extraction would rise from 360,000 tons a year to 500,000 tons. Renewed activity resulted in increased gold production at the mine to 1,893 kilograms by 1985 (valued at F$22.5 million). In

1985-86, the consortium sank a new shaft at the Vatukoula mine at the cost of F$10 million. The royalty payments made by Emperor Gold Mining during this period speak for themselves: F$27,124 for 1980-81, nothing for 1981-82, F$250,399 for 1982-83, nothing for 1983-84, and F$10,686 for 1984-85.[12]

Following the launching of the Fiji Labour Party in July 1985, Emperor Gold Mining's activities in Fiji came under increasing public scrutiny. Emperor Gold Mining's expatriate manager, Jeffrey Reid, had long been closely associated with Prime Minister Mara and other leading figures in the Alliance Party, and Emperor Gold Mining now became embroiled in the national political struggle between the Alliance Party and the Fiji Labour Party. The front page of the *Fiji Times* on 7 July 1985, reporting on the launching of the Fiji Labour Party the previous day, carried the headline: "Labour Party Makes Call: Nationalize the Gold Mine." While this was only a minor point in the hour-long speech delivered by newly-elected party president Timoci Bavadra, it was considered sufficiently sensational by the press to warrant such attention.[13] The point was reiterated in Bavadra's address at the Fiji Labour Party's first annual convention on 19 July 1986. In outlining an overall plan for forming a mining council as part of a larger structure of producers' and workers' councils, Bavadra stated:

> Our reasons for calling for the nationalization of Emperor Goldmine are perhaps too obvious, but I will mention some of them nevertheless. They include stopping the repatriation of profits overseas (and here I would include both recognized and hidden profits); the need to improve industrial relations (here I would mention the dismal record of the company in its treatment of workers in terms of unionization and worker safety and health); and relations of the company to native landowners such as those of Nasomo.[14]

The Nasomo case was only the most recent of a long series of disputes by native landowners with Emperor Gold Mining over land used for mining in the Tavua goldfield. In March 1983, a block of 1,062 acres belonging to the Nasomo landowners was leased to Western Mining for twenty-one years by the director of mines. The villagers were not happy that their land had been leased with no prior consultation, nor were they happy with the terms of the lease, and in February 1986 they approached Bavadra, who himself was from western Fiji, for assistance.[15] The following month, with the backing of the Fiji Labour Party, the villagers filed a F$10 million writ against Emperor Gold Mining and Western Mining.[16]

The Alliance Party leadership was well aware that its control of the native Fijian vote was vulnerable in western Viti Levu and saw the Nasomo situation as a manifestation of this problem. In response to the Fiji Labour Party threat in the west, the Mara government stepped up public spending in this previously neglected area. In addition, to consolidate its control over native Fijians throughout the country, the Mara government had begun a restructuring of the Fijian Administration and taken other steps to enhance chiefly power and communal loyalty. Its drive to consolidate its position in the west began at a secret meeting in February 1986, hosted by Emperor Gold Mining manager Jeffrey Reid at his home at Vatukoula.[17] Mara himself was present. Among those invited were the primary Alliance Party local bosses in the west, including a number of ranking western chiefs. Following the meeting, the Alliance Party opened offices in the western towns of Nadi and Ba as part of its "groundwork" for the general election to be held early the following year.

The situation heated up further in early April as Nasomo became the scene of a political battle between pro-Labour and pro-Alliance forces. The close relationship between the mining company and the Alliance Party is revealed in a *Fiji Sun* account of a meeting held in Nasomo to form a Fiji Labour Party branch:

> According to villagers working in the mines, a number of workers have lost their jobs since the news of the writ and meetings got to their bosses. "A lot of people I have talked to are scared to show up today because they fear losing their jobs," a man who said he was a miner told the meeting...Several families from the village are staying in company quarters. They fear attending the meetings, which are now being held weekly, other villagers said. The villagers also claimed that some villagers are being "bought" by the companies to spy on workers.[18]

With the assistance of the mine's management, the Alliance Party next had a group of Nasomo villagers petition the local district officer, expressing their lack of support for those who had filed the writ against the mining companies and formed the Labour Party branch. Those who had signed this petition, it was claimed by one of the village leaders, did so "because they were told that if they did not sign then they would be sacked from their jobs."[19] The Alliance Party and Emperor Gold Mining also took steps to reward loyal workers. Thus, using funds from the workers' own pension fund, the company management initiated a housing scheme for designated company workers. The Nasivi Housing Estate, as it was called, was opened officially by Mara in August 1986.

The Nasomo case against the mining companies came to court in May 1986. Around one hundred villagers attended the opening, which was adjourned until the following month to allow the companies' lawyers further time to prepare their defence. A public meeting was held by the villagers after the adjournment, at which five villagers claimed that they had been fired from their jobs at the mine because of the writ. A short time later, the lawyer representing the villagers applied for an injunction to prevent the companies from carrying out any further work on the land in question until the matter was settled.

Jeffrey Reid decided to respond to the Nasomo landowners and the Fiji Labour Party through a paid statement in the country's two daily English-language newspapers. The statement appeared on 8 June, under the title "The Truth About Nasomo," stating that the companies had paid compensation for exploration work on the land in question, including F$260 to the village chairman. The Nasomo villagers replied that they had received only a small amount of money, and that it did not equal what they had been promised nor had anything been paid to the village committee. Emperor Gold Mining also sought to undermine support for the writ through traditional means. It sent a two-member delegation consisting of a native Fijian chief who was employed as an accountant by the company and the Tui Nadrau, a high ranking chief from the area with close links to the company and the Alliance Party, to the governor general, Ratu Penaia Ganilau, who was a friend of Reid's, in early June to ask him to intervene in the dispute on behalf of Emperor Gold Mining. The governor general declined to become involved, however, giving as his reason the need "to preserve the dignity, respect and neutrality of the Governor-General's office."

Reid also supported efforts to revitalize the Vatukoula branch of the Fijian Association (the native Fijian wing of the Alliance Party) in response to the Labour Party's activities at Nasomo. To keep the Fiji Labour Party out of Vatukoula, Reid had banned political meetings from the community, but this ban was lifted in June to allow Alliance Party parliamentarian Apisai Tora to hold a meeting of the Fijian Association, which was attended by an array of prominent Alliance Party leaders who promised to help sort out problems with the mining companies.

During the latter part of 1986, talks were held between the Fiji Labour Party and the older opposition party, the National Federation Party, which was on the verge of collapse, about forming a united front against the Alliance Party. A tentative agreement was arrived at in October to form a coalition for the period of the campaign. In preparing a draft manifesto[20] the Fiji Labour Party had its way on most matters, but was willing to compromise in several instances with the more conservative National Federation Party. The most noticeable item missing from the document was nationalization. Not all members of the Fiji Labour Party were happy to see this go, but most considered it a small price to pay in return for a united opposition.

The two parties became even more integrated in the course of negotiations and by the end of November had agreed to campaign jointly under the Coalition banner. Mara dissolved Parliament a short time later and the election was set for April 1987. The Coalition unveiled its election manifesto in February. On nationalization, the moderates had won: "We will not Nationalize any business or industry in Fiji."[21] But Emperor Gold Mining had not escaped entirely: "We will set up an inquiry into the Emperor Gold Mines with a view to advising the Government on the best way of operating the mines, whether through private sector; joint venture with Government; or worker participation."[22] On balance, it was a document aimed at assuring voters and overseas powers and interests that a Coalition government would be a moderate one and Fiji would not be turned into another Cuba.

The Alliance Party issued its election manifesto a couple of weeks later, promising a stable government and greater economic prosperity, taking credit for all that was good and ignoring problems for the most part. Not surprisingly, the manifesto made note of the Alliance Party's opposition to nationalization and, instead called for selective privatization.

The campaign was a very heated one. The Coalition focused on such "bread and butter" issues as unemployment, crime and corruption, and on the Alliance Party's failure to deliver on its promises, while the Alliance Party emphasized communalism and the "communist threat" posed by the Labour Party. The Nasomo land claim and Emperor Gold Mining featured prominently in the campaign. Something of the controversy surrounding the mining company can be seen from an exchange between Bavadra and Reid two weeks before the election—an exchange that is particularly interesting considering that it is between the head of one of the country's leading political parties and an expatriate manager of a foreign company. It began when Coalition leader Bavadra published a large newspaper advertisement, titled "An Open Letter to the People of Fiji—The Truth About Nasomo," charging the Alliance government of abandoning "the Nasomo people to the dubious dealings of the Vatukoula mining companies."[23] Reid responded with a half-page advertisement in which he accused Bavadra of having "grossly and unfairly maligned the companies, and in doing so manipulated people's minds for cheap political mileage."[24] Reid warned that "your tactics of winning votes by falsely maligning companies like ours does not augur well for the future of our country and its people." Bavadra's replied with another advertisement in which he stated: "You have at last been smoked out...You are doing a sterling job as a henchman for the Alliance government."

After the Alliance Party lost the election, it immediately began to take steps to keep the Coalition from assuming office and, once the Bavadra government had been installed, to destabilize it. While Mara remained in the background, Alliance Party members such as Apisai Tora became involved in destablization efforts largely through a group named the Taukei Movement. Members of the Coalition government were highly suspicious of Reid's involvement in these actions.

A few days after the election, a group of native Fijians led by the Tui Tavua, erected a roadblock near the gold mine outside Tavua and near Ba at Tunuk and displayed placards critical of the new government. The government was concerned about Reid's possible involvement because of his close relation with the Tui Tavua and the fact that he had been seen near the Tavua roadblock. Suspicions increased after Coalition supporters told the government of a meeting at Reid's house shortly after the election and just before the roadblocks attended by the Tui Tavua, Apisai Tora, and other prominent Alliance Party figures now active in destablization efforts. Bavadra asked the police to investigate and informed the governor general of his concerns for security and public safety.

The roadblocks were followed by a meeting of western chiefs addressed by Tora, at which he emphasized the need to maintain the paramountcy of native Fijian interests, which he claimed were being threatened by the new government. The Taukei Movement then prepared a petition to present to the governor general, asking him to intervene in order to protect native Fijian interests. The Taukei organized a march in Suva to present the petition. When the Taukei were able to bring a large contingent of supporters from the west by bus, the government became curious about the Taukei Movement's source of funds. It was rumored that the fund had come from a prominent expatriate businessman who was deeply involved in the destablization campaign.

By the second week of May the Bavadra government felt confident that the situation was being brought under control. Charges had been brought against some of those involved in the destablization campaign, with the promise of more charges to come, and the campaign itself seemed to be running out of steam. In Tavua, the hearing into the roadblocks was adjourned following an agreement to pursue "traditional customs" to defuse the situation. A short time later, however, the Bavadra government was overthrown in the South Pacific's first military coup.[25] The relationship of Fiji's gold mining industry to the overthrow of the Bavadra government remains a question.

Removal of the Bavadra government did not mean an end to Emperor Gold Mining's problems. Union bans on shipping of goods to Fiji from Australia and New Zealand presented the mine with some difficulties in securing needed machinery. A partial solution was found by relying on airlines that were willing to attempt to get around the bans. The initial postcoup crisis came to an end once the bans were lifted, but another potentially more serious one emerged a few months later, following Fiji's second coup in September. After the second coup, military strongman Sitiveni Rabuka formed an even more extremist cabinet in which communal zealots held the majority of seats. Specifically, to the dismay of expatriates in the mining industry, Sakeasi Butadroka, leader of the Fijian Nationalist Party, was given the portfolio for Lands and Natural Resources. In early November, Butadroka unveiled a radical program aimed at returning all land to native Fijian ownership.[26] Butadroka's plan brought a swift critical response from pro-Mara forces within the cabinet, however, and Rabuka himself failed to back the program.

Butadroka's excesses played a role in convincing Rabuka to return to a more moderate course and seek a deal to allow Mara to return to power. Mara's resumption of power in early 1988 did not put and end to Fiji's economic or political problems, but it did serve to create an environment that was more favorable to expatriate interests in the mining sector. Under the new regime, gold production at Vatukoula has increased—in part, as a result of spending on improved infrastructure starting in the mid-1980s. During 1989 the company produced 4,245 kilograms of unrefined gold, worth F$76.2 million, and in the first quarter of 1990 production was 831 kilograms of unrefined gold, worth F$16.3 million.

Fiji's trade union movement survived the political upheavals of 1987, and, despite considerable pressure from the governing regime, in 1989 launched a new bid to organize workers at Vatukoula. The Vatukoula Mineworkers' Union which had been registered in 1986 had not been functioning for some time. During the latter part of the year, the Fiji Trades Union Congress sent an organizer to Vatukoula to promote a new union known as the Fiji Mineworkers' Union.

Unable to use company facilities, initially the organizer had been granted permission to stay in Forestry Department quarters. The company responded to the FTUC's success in recruiting workers for the new union by putting pressure on the Forestry Department to evict the organizer. The Fiji Trades Union Congress accused the government of collusion with the mining company, while the evicted union organizer charged the company with treating the miners "like slaves."[27] The government also delayed registering the union on technical grounds since the Vatukoula Mineworkers Union had not been formally deregistered.[28] A short time later, the *Fiji Times* published two articles that were highly critical of working conditions at the mine.[29]

The mine's management responded to the articles with a four-page advertisement in which it sought to present a more positive view of the situation of its employees.[30] The company had also taken other steps to improve its image. Miners and their families had for a long time faced problems with debts that they had run up in local stores. There were also complaints about the inadequacy of shopping facilities in the immediate vicinity. The company made an arrangement with one of the country's leading retailers, Morris Hedstrom (owned by Carpenters Fiji Ltd.), to open a supermarket to serve the Vatukoula mine in January 1990.[31] The mining company contributed F$50,000 to the F$350,000 spent on the store and Morris Hedstrom installed a voucher system with specific spending limits to help solve the credit problem. In addition, the company management promoted establishment of the Koula Trust Society. Run by chiefs aligned with the management, and claiming 240 members, the society's professed aim was to help meet the health and educational needs of its members and to establish commercial ventures. One of its first undertakings was to invest F$40,000 (F$14,000 of which was provided by Emperor) in Fijian Holdings Ltd., a body with a rather checkered history that had been sponsored by the Great Council of Chiefs to promote native Fijian involvement in business. The society also announced plans to invest in a fifty acre cane farm on land that was to be used by the company "for storing ore residue from the mine."[32]

Despite continued harassment from the company, the Fiji Mineworkers' Union held its first meeting on 11 August 1990.[33] Two previous attempts to hold meetings had failed and this meeting had to be held in a hall in Tavua since the mine's management refused to provide a meeting site for the union. The meeting was chaired by Ema Druavesi of the Fiji Trades Union Congress and attended by over 300 miners. Samuel Sanday, a mechanic, was elected president and Alifereti, the organizer who had been expelled from the mining area earlier in the year, was elected secretary. Plans were announced to draw up a log of claims and a proposal for a health and safety scheme with the assistance of the Miners' Federation of Australia.

Before concluding the chapter on Fiji, mention should be made of other mining activities during the independence period. Considerable excitement was aroused in Fiji in 1975, when a consortium headed by Amax (in conjunction with Anglo American, CRA, and Preussig) expressed interest in a site in the Namosi area where copper deposits had been pinpointed by Barringer of Canada, raising hopes of a discovery comparable to the one on Bougainville, in Papua New Guinea. After the consortium announced, in early 1979, that exploration efforts would be intensified, Alliance Party government ministers indicated that a large copper mine probably would be in production in the area within a few years. A short time later, however, Amax reported that the deposits appeared to be small. Some exploration continued, but lower copper prices after 1980 effectively put an end to any hope of a mine being opened. During the exploration period there had been a good deal of discussion about the possible impact of a mine on the people living in the Namosi area and Amax commissioned a social impact study.[34] Debate arose over the environmental and cultural impact of the mine and concern was expressed that adequate compensation and employment be provided for the local population.

Finally, following intensified gold exploration in Papua New Guinea (see chapter 3), Fiji experienced a boom in gold exploration in the early 1980s. There were twenty-five prospecting licences at the end of 1984. Nine of these expired during 1985, but an additional seventeen were issued during the year. This represented the highest level of activity since the manganese boom in the 1950s. Most of the new gold exploration has been carried out by foreign interests.[35] So far there have been no major discoveries, although tests at a few sites have indicated the possibility of mineable deposits.[36] Thus, in December 1990, Placer Pacific, which had been prospecting in the northern part of the country since 1984, announced that results from drilling carried out in August and September at Nakelikoso, in Macuata, were "quite promising."[37] The company indicated, however, that it intended to continue prospecting for another two years before deciding whether to develop a mine. In addition, in late 1989, two Australian mining companies, Newmont Pty. Ltd. and Range Resources Ltd., applied to reestablish a prospecting licence at Mt. Kasi in hope of finding new gold prospects suitable for open-pit mining. Despite these possibilities, for the time being Vatukoula remains the country's only significant mine.

Notes

1. Among the relevant works providing background reading on Fiji are: Michael C. Howard, *Fiji: Race and Politics in an Island State* (Vancouver: University of British Columbia Press, 1991); Simione Durutalo, *The Paramountcy of Fijian Interest and the Politicization of Ethnicity* (Suva: University of the South Pacific Sociological Society, 1986); Ernst Utrecht, ed., *Fiji: Client State of Australasia?* (Sydney: University of Sydney, Transnational Corporations Research Project, 1984); R.A.Derrick, *A History of Fiji* (Suva: Government Press, 1950); N. Thomas, *Planets Around the Sun*, Oceania Monograph 31 (Sydney: University of Sydney, 1986); David Routledge, *Matanitu* (Suva: Institute of Pacific Studies, University of the South Pacific, 1985); Peter France, *The Charter of the Land* (Melbourne: Oxford University Press, 1969); Timothy Macnaught, *The Fijian Colonial Experience*, Pacific Research Monograph 7 (Canberra: Australian National University, 1982); R.R. Nayacakalou, *Leadership in Fiji* (Melbourne: Oxford University Press, 1975); J.D. Legge, *Britain in Fiji, 1858-1880* (London: Macmillan, 1958); O.H.K. Spate, *The Fijian People*, Legislative Council Paper 13 (Suva: Government Printer, 1959); Michael Moynagh, *Brown or White? A History of the Fiji Sugar Industry 1873-1973*, Pacific Research Monograph 5 (Canberra: Australian National University, 1981); K.L. Gillion, *Fiji's Indian Migrants* (Melbourne: Oxford University Press, 1962); Brij Lal, ed., *Politics in Fiji* (Sydney: George Allen & Unwin, 1985); Michael Taylor, ed., *Fiji: Future Imperfect?* (Sydney: George Allen & Unwin, 1987); and Robert Norton, *Race and Politics in Fiji* (St.Lucia: University of Queensland Press, 1977).

2. Material on mining in colonial Fiji is drawn largely from: 'Atu Bain, "Labour Protest and Control in the Gold Mining Industry of Fiji, 1930-1970," in *South Pacific Forum*, Vol. 3, No.1, 1986, pp. 37-59; R.F. Duberal and P. Rodda, *The History of some Mines and Prospects of Fiji* (Suva: Mineral Resources Division, Ministry of Lands and Mineral Resources, 1978); and *Annual Reports for Fiji, 1938-1972* (Suva, Government Printer).

3. Bain, "Labour Protest," p. 41.

4. On industrial relations in Fiji during the 1930s, see Michael Howard, "The Evolution of Industrial Relations in Fiji and the Reaction of Public Employees' Unions to the Current Economic Crisis," in *South Pacific Forum*, Vol. 2, No. 2, 1985; and Michael C. Howard "The Trade Union Movement in Fiji," in Taylor, *Fiji*, pp. 108-21.

5. On CSR, see Moynagh, *Brown or White*. On Burns Philp, see Kenneth Buckley and Kris Klugman, *The History of Burns Philp* (Sydney: Burns, Philp & Co. Ltd., 1981); and K. Buckley and K. Klugman, *"The Australian Presence in the Pacific": Burns Philp 1914-1946* (Sydney: George Allen & Unwin, 1983).

6. On the Fijian Administration and Ratu Sukuna, see Macnaught, *The Fijian Colonial Experience.* Historian Deryck Scarr has written extensively on Ratu Sukuna, but his work should be treated with caution for its lack of objectivity. Interesting insights into Sukuna's relations with Emperor Gold Mining and other elements of the colonial business and administrative

community can be gleaned from his correspondence as reprinted in Deryck Scarr, ed., *The Three-legged Stool: Selected Writings of Ratu Sir Lala Sukuna* (London: Macmillan Education, 1983).

7. Bain, "Labour Protest," p. 55.

8. The Vunamoli case is documented in Cyril Belshaw, *Under the Ivi Tree: Social and Economic Growth in Rural Fiji* (Berkeley: University of California Press, 1964), pp. 64-73.

9. Belshaw, *Ivi Tree*, p. 72.

10. Sakiasi Waqanivavalagi remained in parliament from 1970 until 1982. He was appointed minister for commerce, industry, and co-operatives in 1973, and, in 1981, he became minister for lands. He ran again for the Alliance Party in the 1987 election against a candidate backed by the Fiji Labour Party.

11. See Howard, "Evolution of Industrial Relations," and "The Trade Union Movement."

12. "Emperor's Promise," in *Islands Business*, December 1985, pp. 14-15. Also on Western Mining investing in Emperor, see John Richardson, "How Gold in Fiji's Valley," in *Islands Business*, June 1983, pp. 14-17.

13. The full text of the speech is reprinted in *South Pacific Forum*, Vol. 2, No. 1, 1985, pp. 70-81.

14. "Presidential Address," *Fiji Labour Party, First Annual Convention, 19th July, 1986, Conference Papers, Girmit Centenary Centre, Lautoka*, p. 4; also see "The Lands Commission Plan and Why Labour Wants It," in *Fiji Sun*, 4 September 1986.

15. "Landowners Seek Help from Labour," in *Fiji Sun*, 17 February 1986.

16. "$10m Writ on Gold Firms," in *Fiji Times*, 29 March 1986, p. 1.

17. *Fiji Times*, 19 February 1986.

18. "'Intimidation' Claim Against Goldmines as Villagers Join Labour," in *Fiji Sun*, 23 April 1986, p. 1.

19. *Fiji Sun*, 23 April 1986, p. 1.

20. The mimeographed document was prepared under the name of National People's Unity, a title later changed simply to the Coalition.

21. *Fiji Sun* and *Fiji Times*, supplement, 28 January 1987.

22. *Fiji Sun* and *Fiji Times*, supplement, 28 January 1987.

23. *Fiji Sun* and *Fiji Times*, 2 April 1987.

24. *Fiji Sun* and *Fiji Times*, 4 April 1987.

25. Relevant events surrounding the coup are discussed in more detail in Howard, *Fiji*, chapter 6.

26. *Fiji Times*, 5 November 1987.

27. *Fiji Times*, 19 January 1990, p. 2.

28. *Fiji Times*, 13 January 1990. p. 2.

29. The two articles were by reporter Asha Lakhan: "Rumblings in the Golden Bowl," *Fiji Times*, 6 March 1990, pp. 12-13; and "A Goldminer's Life," *Fiji Times*, 7 March 1990, p. 11.

30. "The Facts About Vatukoula," *Fiji Times*, 9 March 1990, pp. 19-20, and 29-30).

31. *Fiji Times,* 31 January 1990, pp. 19-26. The two functioning co-operative shops at Vatukoula (one of which serves the Rotuman community) have not worked well. Stocking only minimal necessities, their resources have been limited, as has their support from the company (in contrast to its support for the Morris Hedstrom undertaking).

32. *Fiji Times,* 24 April 1990, p.8.

33. *Fiji Times,* 13 August 1990, p. 3.

34. See James P. Rizer, et al, *The Potential Impacts of a Namosi Copper Mine: A Case Study of Assimilation Planning* (Suva: Centre for Applied Studies in Development, University of the South Pacific, 1982).

35. A list of mining and petroleum licence holders in Fiji in 1985 is provided in Michael C. Howard, *The Impact of the International Mining Industry on Native Peoples* (Sydney: Transnational Corporations Research Project, University of Sydney, 1988), pp. 120-21. In addition, in August 1990, the Japanese government, through the Metal Mining Agency of Japan, signed an agreement with the Fijian government to provide F$3 million over a three year period for technical assistance in further mineral exploration in Viti Levu (*Fiji Times,* 3 August 1990, p. 13).

36. See "Gold Anger: Landowners Unaware of Mining Prospects" (*Fiji Sun,* 4 March 1987, p. 1), for a discussion of controversy surrounding a site near Labasa being explored by Paget Gold Mining Company of Australia. Two active exploration companies at the end of 1989 are Beta Ltd., a joint venture of Associated Gold Fields (forty-seven per cent) and Gold Resources Ltd. of New Zealand (fifty-three per cent), and Pacific Islands Gold NL, comprised of six separate joint venture partners. Both are exploring several sites around Fiji. Pacific Islands Gold has indicated the mining could begin at one or two of its site in 1990 (see *Pacific Islands Monthly,* October 1989, p. 32).

37. *Fiji Times,* 12 December 1990, p. 1.

3

Papua New Guinea

> Then I turned to one-eared Bill and said to him:
> 'You are all after gold, but do any of you here at Rabaul bar know
> exactly where gold is to be found?'
> 'No, Sir, not yet....But a friend of ours left four months ago for the
> Markam valley. As soon as he has struck anything he will send us a
> message, and then we shall go to join him. We are waiting....'
> Waiting! That is what everyone is doing at Rabaul. For a sign, for
> a miracle, for gold!
>
> Edmond Demaitre, *New Guinea Gold*, p. 23

Although the indigenous inhabitants of Papua New Guinea had no
use for it, it was gold, perhaps more than any other substance, that
drew Europeans to the island. Shortly after the Portuguese explorer
Jorge de Menses landed on the island's northwestern corner, the
Spanish conquistador Cortes sent three ships from Mexico in 1527,
under the command of Alvaro de Saavedra, to the spice islands of
Indonesia. Two of the ships were lost on the way, but Saavedra
himself reached the Moluccas. Attempting to return to Mexico in
1528, he was wrecked along the northern coast of New Guinea,
where he discovered traces of alluvial gold and gave the island the
name of "Isla del Oro." Despite the name, neither the Spanish or the
Portuguese undertook any serious attempts to search for gold on the
island, the Portuguese concentrating their efforts on the spice trade
to the west and the Spanish on commerce, and to a lesser extent on
the search for gold, in the Philippines to the north.

As the Dutch began to move into Southeast Asia, they heard
rumors of the gold and spices of the "Papuas" from Indonesian
traders. In November 1605, the ship *Duyfken* was sent from Bantam
to look for gold. It sailed along the western and southern coast of
Papua New Guinea as far as Torres Strait before turning around. The

ship arrived home in June 1606, with a very unfavorable report that did little to excite a further search for gold. There were other European explorers over the next couple of centuries, but no settlement or conquest took place and there was virtually no more allusion to the golden riches of an island that had gained a reputation as disease-ridden and occupied by fierce and poor savages.

The Gold Rush—I

European interest in New Guinea increased during the 1870s, as the pace of colonial expansion across the Pacific intensified. The Australian colonies urged Britain to assume control of the eastern portion of New Guinea to keep it from falling into the hands of another European power. Britain failing to act, Queensland decided to annex the southeastern portion of the island in 1883 on behalf of the empire, but Britain refused to agree to the annexation until the Australian colonies agreed to meet a portion of the administrative costs the following year. The protectorate was proclaimed in 1884, and the territory was annexed in 1888. A short time later, in 1901, Australia agreed to take over the colony, known as Papua. The transfer was finalized in 1906, and Papua became an Australian colony.

Gold mining was the most important industry in Papua prior to the First World War. Gold was discovered near Port Moresby in 1877, by a prospector recently arrived from New Caledonia, but it was not until after annexation that extensive exploration began. The initial development of the gold mining industry took place in the wake of the decline of blackbirding in Melanesia, which was being suppressed by the British, and centered on the smaller eastern islands and coastal regions of the mainland.

The "gold rush" began on Misima Island, in the Lousiade Archipelago, in 1888. By the end of the following year, around 400 European prospectors along with 1,200 indentured workers were active on Misima and some of the neighboring islands in the archipelago. During the first two years of mining, almost £27,000 worth of gold was exported from the Lousiade goldfield. As alluvial gold became more difficult to find, miners left to look elsewhere. By 1894-95 there were only thirty miners and ninety indentured workers left in the Lousiades and the value of gold exports had dropped to £2,565. The next important discovery was on Woodlark Island in 1895. The Murua goldfield on Woodlark quickly attracted 230 miners, who brought with them almost 900 indentured workers. During the first year, the value of gold production on Woodlark reached around £45,000.

Other discoveries followed: the Gira goldfield in 1898, Milne Bay in 1899, the Yodda goldfield in 1900, the Kereni goldfield near Cloudy Bay in 1904, the Astrolabe goldfield near Port Moresby in 1906, and the Lakekamu goldfield along the Lakekamu River in 1909. The industry employed around 200 European miners and about 1,000 indentured workers and almost entirely entailed alluvial mining. In 1909-10, gold accounted for £54,927 of the colony's total exports, worth £100,599. Attempts by prospectors to move further inland proved unsuccessful in the face of strong opposition from interior tribes.

Mining activities in the smaller eastern islands, in particular, had an important impact on the local tribal economy. The Melanesians found themselves saturated with trade goods and came to demand traditional forms of wealth, especially so-called "shell-money." To meet the growing demand, the shells were provided to the miners in increasing quantities by traders who bought them in the Solomon Islands. As the trade grew, the Solomon Islanders, in turn, began to demand more for the shell money, adding to inflation.[1]

During and immediately after the First World War, alluvial gold mining declined sharply in Papua. By 1925, there were only eighteen European miners and 262 indentured workers left. Plantation-based copra production assumed primary importance in the colonial economy, spurred on by government support, including land laws that were "probably the most liberal in the tropics."[2] The center of gold mining now was to shift to British New Guinea (formerly German New Guinea).

The Germans annexed the northeastern part of the island in 1884-85, which came to be known as German New Guinea. The initial German presence, however, was a precarious one. The New Guinea Kompagnie sought to establish a settlement at Finschhafen in 1885, but it was abandoned in 1892. After a few other unsuccessful attempts, they finally settled at Rabaul, on New Britain. Around the same time, Lutheran missionaries managed to establish a presence on the mainland coast, and slowly European settlement spread. The New Guinea Kompagnie sent a party to explore for gold along the western tributaries of the Ramu River in 1896, under the leadership of a Dr. Lauterbach. Despite an intensive search, nothing came of the effort. Likewise, subsequent prospecting expeditions in 1896 and 1901 also failed. The company gave up its search in 1902, and closed its Ramu

Goldfields Station. The German minerological expert Dr. Schlentzig continued to explore the Gulf of Huon region until 1906, when he left after contracting malaria.

Rumors spread of rich veins of gold in the Bulolo valley and a few private syndicates sent search parties up the Marobe valleys to explore for gold. Hampered by hostility from the local inhabitants and the difficult terrain, most of the parties met with no success. Then, in 1913, Australian prospector Arthur Darling, came from Papua with a group of armed men to search for gold in New Guinea. He discovered gold at Koranga Creek, but died of wounds shortly after returning to the coast. The First World War interrupted further exploration. The British assumed control of German New Guinea in 1914, and by 1919 the colony's plantation-based economy had begun to recover (total exports in 1919-20 were valued at £849,422, with copra accounting for £745,056 of this amount).

In 1921, an adventurer known as "Shark-Eye" Park arrived in Morobe to search for Darling's gold. He crossed the Bulolo valley in 1922. Wounded and ill, he reached Koranga Creek, near Wau, where he discovered an extremely rich site known as the Rocks of Gold. As word spread, prospectors arrived from Papua, Australia, the New Hebrides, and as far away as California. The Kukukuku, who inhabited the region, quickly gained a reputation for violence, but prospectors continued to arrive.[3] The journey from the coast to the goldfield took up to two months and an output of ten ounces a day was considered minimal to meet transportation costs. But those who survived could make thousands of pounds. By 1925, there were around fifty prospectors working in the Morobe area, with more on the way.

A group of prospectors known as the Big Six, led by Bill Royal, discovered even richer veins at Edie Creek (about twenty kilometers above Wau) in 1926. Their discovery precipitated a stampede of prospectors headed toward the Morobe Mountains. Gold hunters arrived at the port of Salamua, from where they struggled for eight days up the fifty kilometer track to Wau. Most were Australians, but the goldfields were attracting people from around the world. Opposition form the Kukukuku grew and many of the fortune hunters were killed. By the end of 1926, arrows and disease had thinned the numbers of prospectors to the point that it looked as if the rush was over.

Australian Cecil J. Levien, after serving in the army during the First World War, had taken a job as a patrol officer on Buka, in the Solomon Islands, in 1918.[4] From Buka he transferred to New Guinea.

After recuperating from wounds received in an ambush in the Bulolo valley in 1923, he left government service and returned to Australia to raise money to undertake gold mining in the Bulolo valley. He raised a few thousand pounds and came back to the Bulolo valley with a crew to work alluvial deposits he had discovered at Edie Creek through his newly formed company, Guinea Gold NL. Levien introduced air transport to the goldfields, which allowed for the intensification of mining on an unprecedented scale. Levien, Mustar & Co. started flying heavy mining equipment to the goldfield from the coast in April 1927, while Levein's New Guinea Airways Ltd. carried miners to the goldfield for £100 apiece. Further development of the goldfield was to be left largely to others and Levien himself died in 1932.[5]

Guinea Gold's leases at Bulolo were sold to Placer Development Ltd., which was based in Vancouver, with most of its capital being Australian. After very favorable testing of the ore, Placer sold the leases to Bulolo Gold Dredging Ltd., also based in Vancouver. Placer owned a large share of Bulolo, with the remaining shares being divided among British, South African, and other Australian interests (its capital in the late 1930s amounted to C$4 million). The Bulolo enterprise invested a large amount in building mining infrastructure at the goldfield. This included 2,500 ton dredges, a cyanide mill, and two hydroelectric powerhouses. The first dredge began operation in 1932, and three more were installed by 1934, by which time they were recovering over 10,000 ounces of gold per month. During the remainder of the decade, the company installed four more dredges. Bulolo's operations were very profitable and, by 1935, the value of its shares had risen from £1 to £9.

While Bulolo was the largest company operating in the area, there were other major interests as well and a host of smaller concerns. The largest of these was New Guinea Goldfields Ltd., formed in 1929 (capital of £1.1 million), by Mining Trust Ltd. which was associated with Russo-Asiatic Consolidated Ltd., chaired by Leslie Urquhart. Urguhart was quoted at the time as saying: "Since the opening of the Rand, no goldfield exhibiting such potentialities as that in New Guinea has been discovered."[6] New Guinea Goldfields worked valuable sites on the Upper Bulolo, Koranga, Namie Creek, and Edie Creek. The most significant of these was at Golden Ridge on Namie Creek, with 100,000 tons of rich ore, where a crushing mill and cyanide plant went into operation in 1930. The dispersal of the company's activities among several sites caused problems during the early part of the 1930s, as its operations failed to produce gold in sufficient quantities to cover its outlays. After reorganization in 1935, the company began to recover financially and, by 1937, it had become profitable and was able to pay a dividend.

The third largest company operating in the area was Day Dawn Ltd., which operated the Day Dawn mine at Edie Creek between 1930 and 1935. During its brief history the mine was very profitable, but the vein ran out in 1935, and the mine was closed.

During the first few years, the output of gold from Morobe accounted for between ten and twenty per cent of the value of the colony's exports and contributed only an insignificant amount to colonial revenue. After 1930-31, however, the level of production increased substantially. During the 1930s gold came to account for from sixty to over eighty per cent of the value of New Guinea's exports and around one-third of government revenue, relegating copra, which had been hurt by the depression, to a much less important role in the colonial economy.

TABLE 3.1 Gold Production & Revenue, New Guinea, 1924-41

	A	B	C	D
1924-25	18.5	03	na	na
1925-26	25.2	00	na	na
1926-27	195.4	18	1.2	00
1927-28	256.2	17	5.8	02
1928-29	179.4	16	7.8	02
1929-30	96.3	10	4.6	01
1930-31	132.2	14	6.6	02
1931-32	398.9	36	34.7	11
1932-33	933.9	59	63.6	20
1933-34	1,367.6	77	85.2	na
1934-35	1,897.2	81	109.8	28
1935-36	1,704.5	66	97.1	23
1936-37	2,020.7	60	116.7	24
1937-38	2,029.0	68	na	na
1938-39	2,129.3	72	121.8	26
1939-40	3,021.7	82	155.6	31
1940-41	2,797.2	86	130.8	31

A. Gold exports (£'000).
B. Gold as a per cent of total exports.
C. Government revenue from gold royalties and mining rentals (£'000).
D. C as a per cent of total government revenue.

The camps that grew up around the mining operations were rough places in which to live.[7] The camp at Edie Creek had about two hundred European miners and a much larger number of indentured workers. There were only a few European women. People lived in huts and tents. Hygienic conditions and the quality of the food were poor and diseases widespread. Work began at 5:00 a.m. and lasted until sunset. Most of the Europeans worked as "tributaries." A big company would work a site a couple of times and then would sublet it to the tributary. The tributary would employ indentured workers and would provide his own mining equipment. For the right to work the site he would pay forty to fifty per cent of his return on the sale of gold to the company that owned the reef. The presence of such a large community served to convince the Kukukuku to leave the miners alone and the mining settlements grew up as enclaves with limited contact with those living around them.

Indentured workers were recruited for the Morobe goldfields from various parts of New Guinea and Papua. Legislation dealing with indentured workers, primarily the 1922 labour ordinance, was intended to encourage maintenance of viable agriculturally-based villages and to avoid the creation of a permanent proletariat. Provision was made to repatriate workers to their homes upon completion of a three-year contract (individuals could sign on again after three months). To stop over-recruitment, limits were placed on recruitment in some areas and others were closed to recruiters altogether. Breaches of the rules were common, however, leading one writer in the 1930s to refer to the labor recruiters as "modern blackbirders."[8] While relations between miners and the Melanesians working for them were perhaps better than those prevailing elsewhere in the colony, they were far from good. When Patrol Officer John McCarthy asked another official with longer experience in the area about this difference, he responded:

> Generally, you're right... But it isn't as easy as that. You haven't seen the shocking death rate among the carrier lines that walk from here to Wau. And maybe you haven't seen the cold-blooded bartering that goes on for likely carriers, who are paraded in a ring and auctioned to the highest bidder.[9]

Later McCarthy was moved to comment: "Before my term in Morobe came to an end I was convinced of one thing—that little benefit comes to local natives when gold is found in their country."[10]

Growing demand for labor as gold production increased did little to improve the wages paid to indentured workers or the conditions of their employment, but recruiters were able to charge more for their efforts. Thus, it cost only about £3 10s to recruit a worker in 1926, while the amount that miners paid to recruiters rose from £5 to between £20 and £25. Village headmen, who assisted labor recruiters, shared in the profits, making enforcement of regulations even more difficult. Nor did employers always adhere to rules regulating conditions of work and desertion was relatively common (several hundred workers were convicted of desertion on the mid-1920s).

Labor requirements changed in the 1930s as a result of mechanization. Mining companies became less interested in temporary indentured workers, and more interested in skilled and semi-skilled labor. At first, such positions were taken by Europeans, but Melanesians gradually moved into semi-skilled jobs as mining companies began to see the advantage of a more skilled Melanesian workforce:

> By 1935, New Guinea Goldfield Ltd., to save on labour costs, began to experiment with a policy of replacing expensive expatriate workers with trained New Guineans. This resulted in two strikes by expatriate workers, followed by intervention by the Administration, which was worried about the example of the strikes for indentured labourers.[11]

State intervention was motivated in large part by the fear that labor militancy would spread from the European miners to the Melanesian mineworkers and then to Melanesians working on the plantations, and thereby threaten the entire colonial economy. Government intervention served to put a halt to further attempts to train Melanesians for more skilled work.

As the gold industry grew, those who serviced the industry also prospered. By the mid-1930s, there were seventeen planes serving the Morobe District, bringing the cost of the flight down to £5. During the early 1930s, more airfreight was lifted in New Guinea than in any other part of the world—in fact, the amount was greater than the rest of the world's total.[12] Two Australian companies that assumed a prominent place in serving the mines were Burns Philp and W.R. Carpenter.[13] Burns Philp entered the Morobe area in 1927, when it bought shares in Bulolo Goldfields Aeroplane Service Ltd. and became the booking agent for the airline's passengers and cargo. The following year, a company ship called at Salamaua to supply miners and later Burns Philp opened a store in the town. For the remainder of the period before the war, most prospective miners and mineworkers were transported on Burns Philp ships. The ships also carried supplies from (especially rice) and gold to Australia (with insurance being provided by Burns Philp subsidiary Queensland Insurance Co.). Burns Philp opened stores in Lae and Wau in the early 1930s, and installed a large refrigerator in Madang. Rival W.R. Carpenter & Co., which was already well established in Rabaul, was more successful than Burns Philp in developing its interests in air service. Carpenter initiated flights to the goldfields in 1933 and secured the government contract to carry mail and cargo. Profits generated by their gold-related activities were extremely important to both companies and served to balance against losses being made on the plantation side as a result of the depression.

The Morobe goldfields remained productive until the Second World War and miners continued to push further inland beyond the Ramu River toward Mount Hagen. The 1930s also witnessed a revival of gold mining across the border in Papua. This was motivated in part by activities in the Morobe goldfields, as well as by the increased price of gold, and by government assistance and encouragement (which was related to developments in Morobe). The value of Papuan gold production increased from £34,043 in 1931-32 to £150,198 in 1938-39 (64,622 ounces).

Gold mining in Papua in the 1930s was centered in the Lakekamu, Yodda, and Louisiade fields, and to a lesser extent the Astrolabe field. In general, after an initial burst of activity, significant mining only continued on Misima (which was to produce some £2 million worth of gold between the late nineteenth century and the Second World War). The Tiveri Gold-Mining Company began operating a small dredge in the Tiveri area of the Lakekamu field in 1932. Its operation was very profitable but only lasted for a couple of years. New Misima Gold Mining Ltd. (owned by a Mr. Cuthbert) had access to very rich ore and operated a cyanide and crushing plant. It was an extremely profitable operation, paying up to ninety per cent per annum on its capital, and, by the late 1930s, it was Papua's leading gold company. Not all companies on Misima did well. Gold Mines of Papua Ltd., which began operating on Misima in 1937, collapsed in 1939 and its shareholders lost their entire investments. Mandated Alluvials NL sought to bring the Astrolabe field into production again in 1938, but the operation did not become a large one.

There were also prospecting expeditions into new areas. The Oroville Co., using a seaplane, explored the upper Fly River in 1935, and J.G. Hides and D. Lyal explored the Strickland River between 1935 and 1937. None of these activities were successful. Hides and Lyall did find traces of gold, but both men died from diseases in 1937, after abandoning further searches.

Although gold dominated mining in New Guinea and Papua before the Second World War, there were also occasional attempts to mine other minerals—none being particularly successful. New Guinea Copper Mines Ltd. began developing the Laloki and Dubuna mines in the Astrolabe field in 1920. The mines were estimated to contain around 300,000 tons of ore, capable of producing over 13,000 tons of copper and over 32,000 ounces of gold. Fires in both mine shafts led the company to shift to open-cut mining. Additional problems with the smelting plant caused a further delay and when the mine finally did commence operation, the company was confronted with a declining world price for copper. The company decided to suspend its operation in 1927, after having produced £200,000 worth of copper. Closure of the mine put 100 Europeans and 1,000 Melanesians out of work.

The Second World War brought a halt to most gold mining activities in Papua and New Guinea. Morobe was the site of intense fighting during the war. In January 1943, the Japanese attacked Australian troops at Wau. The Japanese were repulsed, but the campaign to push them out of the area took six months. Lae, Salamaua, Wau, and Bulolo were all destroyed during the fighting and Salamaua was never rebuilt. As roads were repaired and built towards the end and immediately after the war, the region was opened up for coffee and tea production. While agriculture increased in importance in the Morobe district, gold mining failed to recover to its prewar levels. The cost of rebuilding the infrastructure was considerable and the recovery rate of the ore in most of the sites was substantially less than it had been during the early 1930s. With the price of gold pegged at a low U.S.$35 an ounce, there was not much incentive for mining interests. Gradually the dredges were closed down (the last one in 1965) and the mining companies diversified into timber and other businesses. New Guinea Gold Company alone continued to carry out some mining, while the working of most sites was left to small-scale local miners (Europeans and Melanesians).

Bougainville—I

Mining activity in Papua New Guinea (united and under Australian administration since the war) did not pick up again until the 1960s. This time the focus of attention was the island of Bougainville and copper rather than gold. Goldfields around Kieta on Bougainville had been worked in the 1930s, but production was not very significant. A small amount of gold was mined again between 1949 and 1955.

Copper deposits were known to exist, but no attempt was made to exploit them.

A survey of the Pumkuna goldfield on Bougainville in early 1960 reported that copper deposits on the island would be difficult to exploit.[14] However, as world market conditions improved, Australian mining interests were attracted to the site. In 1963, the colonial authorities gave Conzinc Riotinto (Australia) Exploration Pty. Ltd. (CRAE), a subsidiary of CRA, permission to search 630 square kilometers inland from Kieta.[15] In addition to skilled expatriates, around three hundred islanders were employed to assist in the work. Local opposition grew as the pace of exploration increased. CRAE had relied on the support of one outspoken Nasioi man who, it turned out, had little support within the community. As Momis and Ogan have noted, the people of the region had a long history of suspicion and antagonism to the colonial administration.[16] The fact that fees paid by CRAE for exploration rights went to the national government, with no provision for payments to the local administration or population, did not make matters easier.

Opposition on Bougainville was sufficient by 1966 to be perceived by elements within the government as a threat to further exploration. Pressure was placed on the local administration to bring matters under control by those in the national government "who feared that CRAE might feel compelled to withdraw from an operation which was being talked of as the most important economic venture in the country."[17] The central government finally recognized the need for some form of compensation, but local opposition continued among those who wanted exploration stopped altogether.

The ore body at the Panguna site, where exploration was concentrated, was estimated to be 900 million tons, containing an average of 0.48 per cent copper and 0.36 dwt. gold per ton. This allowed for an average potential annual production of 150,000 tons of copper concentrate and 500,000 ounces of gold (as well as a million ounces of silver). Such huge reserves meant that the Panguna mine had the potential of becoming one of the largest open-pit copper mines in the world. The prospects of such vast wealth also served to closely link Papua New Guinea's economic future to the copper mining industry.

Bougainville Copper Pty. Ltd. (BCL) was formed in June 1967 to exploit the site. Two Australian companies held an eighty per cent share in BCL through Bougainville Mining Ltd.: CRA held a two-thirds share and New Broken Hill Consolidated Ltd. one-third. The remaining portion was divided between the government and a small percentage of ordinary public shares offered to the public. Out of the total 180 million shares in BCL (worth A$90 million), about nineteen million ordinary shares were offered for subscription. Of this amount, only one million shares were reserved for "bone fide Territory residents." Eventually, 1,114,000 shares were sold in Papua New Guinea: 893,000 to "indigenous or largely indigenous groups" and the rest to missions, long-term expatriates, and the like.[18]

Construction of the mine was to be carried out under the direction of two San Francisco-based firms, Bechtel International and Western Knapp Engineering, together referred to as Bechtel-WKE. An investment of A$400 million was called for—an unprecedented amount for the country. The Bank of America assumed responsibility for arranging finance and served as head of a consortium of twenty-seven banks to raise the initial A$246 million. Its primary partner in raising capital was the Commonwealth Trading Bank of Australia. An additional U.S.$60 million was raised in Japan. In February 1969, a fifteen year sales agreement was reached with the Japanese Smelter Group for 1,025,000 million tons, starting in 1972. A second fifteen year agreement was made in July with Nordentische Affinerie of West Germany for 787,500 tons and with Rio Tinto Zinc of Spain for 180,000 tons. Later, smelters in the United States agreed to purchased smaller amounts as well.

The Panguna mine began production in early 1972. The total value of production for the first six months of 1972 was A$31.8 million, while production and financing costs amounted to A$23.3 million. Bougainville Mining Ltd. recorded earnings of A$6.6 million and the government received A$309,000 in payment as royalties and A$1.6 million from its interest in BCL. Production during this period amounted to 42,954 tons of copper, 3,524 kilograms of gold, and 10,819 kilograms of silver.[19]

Production of copper doubled during the first six months of 1973, and production of gold nearly tripled. The total value of mine production for 1973 was A$98.1 million, with production and finance costs amounting to A$47.9 million. Bougainville Mining Ltd.'s net earnings were A$38.3 million. In contrast, the government earned A$1.1 million in royalties and A$10.4 million from its share in BCL.[20] The high level of profits being earned by foreign interests from the mine in relation to what the government was earning became a political issue at a time when Papua New Guinea was moving closer to independence. A new House of Assembly had been elected in 1972, and internal self-government was proclaimed in December 1973. The changing political environment led the Australian mining interests and the government to renegotiate the mining agreement in 1974.[21] Under the new arrangement, taxes were increased and shares of the joint venture were altered: CRA's portion was reduced to 53.6 per cent, the government's share became 20.2 per cent, and public ownership was increased to 26.2 per cent.

As the mine came into production, relations between BCL and the local communities continued to be strained as a result of disputes over compensation.[22] Between early 1969 and early 1971, BCL requested a total of 12,500 hectares of land to lease in order to develop the mine. After a dispute with local landowners arising from claims that provisions for compensation were inadequate, a new schedule of compensation for subsistence crops, animals, and trees was agreed to in 1970. The company also had underestimated the number of people affected by development of the mine. Between 1966 and 1974, about four hundred people were rehoused and around 1,500 received some form of compensation. The total amount paid out for compensation during this period was around A$1.8 million. The individual payments were mostly small (usually under A$1,000) and were unevenly distributed.

Beyond the immediate issue of compensation, there was more general disagreement over distribution of the income generated from mining between the national government and local governing bodies. During 1972 and 1973, BCL had made all of its tax and royalty payments directly to the national government. The national government, in turn, was opposed to spending any of the money that it received from BCL specifically on Bougainville. The feeling at the national level was that Bougainville was to be treated like any other part of the country in terms of public spending. A bitter struggle erupted and the national government finally was pressured to allocate A$2 million for public works in Bougainville for the 1974-75 fiscal year. With independence only a few months away, the national government of Michael Somare reversed this decision in April 1975, and reverted to its previous practice. Tension built to the point that Somare suspended the Interim Provincial Council on Bougainville in September. Local political leaders responded with a threat to secede.[23] At issue was a much larger debate over the relative degree of decentralization that was to be permitted in the newly independent state. A compromise was achieved in which the wealthier provinces such as North Solomons (of which Bougainville was a part) were able to receive a relatively higher share of the revenue available from developments like the Panguna mine. But it was to remain an uneasy compromise as both the national and provincial governments found themselves increasingly in need of funds to pay for administrative expenses.

Labor relations comprised the remaining point of tension for the new mine. Peak employment during the construction phase was 10,189. This included 3,861 expatriates, and 6,328 Melanesians. The vast majority of skilled workers were expatriates, whereas all of the unskilled and almost all of the semi-skilled workers were Melanesians. The number of employees was reduced substantially once the construction phase was completed. It was anticipated that the number of workers would average around 3,000 to 3,500 after 1971, making BCL still one of the largest private employers in the country. The breakdown of Melanesian employees according to status in 1972 was thirty-six per cent at the supervisory and skilled levels, four per cent at the sub-professional level, and one per cent at the managerial and professional level. To improve this situation, BCL established training programs to increase localization at all levels.[24] Some progress was made (in the Mining Department, for example), but the overall management of the mining operation remained expatriate.[25]

Australian workers brought their trade union organization with them and were represented by nineteen different Australian unions as well as by the Australian Council of Trade Unions. Melanesian workers were represented by two local unions, the Bougainville Construction and General Workers Union (BCGWU) and the Bougainville Mining Workers Union (BMWU), as well as in some ways by the Australian Council of Trade Unions. The BCGWU was registered in August 1970, with 428 members. The union was suspended twice, in 1971 and 1972, and faced a rapid reduction in potential members as the construction phase of the mine ended. Its membership had declined to 151 by 1974. The BMWU was registered

TABLE 3.2 Employment at Panguna Mine, 1972

Job Category	Expatriate	Melanesian	Total
Pit Operators	36	318	354
Mine Engineers	18	11	29
Geology	8	9	17
Pit Maintenance	<u>181</u>	<u>225</u>	<u>406</u>
Total	243	563	806

Source: R.L. Kay, "Mine Operations at Bougainville," in H.E. Stephensen, ed., *Bougainville: The Establishment of a Copper Mine* (St.Kilda: Construction, Mining, Engineering Publications, n.d.), p. 81.

in December 1969, and its membership remained relatively constant, at around 200, until 1973, when the mine began full operation. With the decline of the BCGWU and the reduction of the expatriate workforce, the BMWU became the primary union at the mine after 1973.

The first action by organized labor took place in January 1970, when an Area Committee approached Bechtel-WKE with a log of claims. No agreement was reached after several meetings and a strike was called in March. The Australian Council of Trade Unions was asked to mediate and afterwards industrial relations were put on a more regular footing. Out of a total thirty million working hours during 1971, only 90,000 were lost as a result of disputes (there were 106 disputes, sixty of which were over wages and general conditions).[26] There was relative labor piece for the next couple of years as the mine moved into full production, with disputes centering around problems facing workers in the construction sector.

Relations between the BMWU and the management deteriorated during 1974 and early 1975, at the same time that tensions were in evidence in virtually all other levels of the mining industry. Finally, in May 1975, the BMWU called a strike. Good and Fitzpatrick have commented that, although the direct causes of the strike were unclear, there were several underlying factors: "the issue of alterations in differentials for skill, and...the remoteness of the expatriate management from the workers and, more generally, the alien nature of the enterprise within the agricultural communities on the island."[27]

The strike lasted only two days and was met with the heavy use of police force and the arrest of a large number of workers, following the evacuation of expatriate women and children. The reaction of the authorities was reminiscent of the worst of colonial rule, only this time it was Melanesian against Melanesian. Chief Minister Michael Somare was especially critical of the workers and of the union leaders, in particular. Later in the month, charges were brought before the Supreme Court against six leaders of the union. The Somare government was in no mood to tolerate what it perceived as a threat national economic development. The BMWU was able to withstand this attack from the government and responded the following year by proposing to join the Soviet-aligned World Federation of Trade Unions—a move that received considerable criticism from the more moderate Papua New Guinea Trade Union Congress and from the premier of the North Solomons Province (who had no more sympathy for union militants than the chief minister).

Following independence, both the North Solomons provincial government and the national government initially spent a large amount of the revenue from the Panguna mine on infrastructure. Before long, however, a growing proportion was being spent on administration, and, especially, on white collar salaries. Thus, the direct contribution of mining to national development, in a broad sense, declined, as funds were used to support national and provincial bureaucracies that had more and more to do with political patronage than with nation-building. As Premdas has argued: "Papua New Guinea's 50,000 public servants in a country of only 2.5 million people appear to be engaged less in developmental change and more in wasting public resources."[28] This desire for ready cash from mining to pay for administrative salaries was reflected in government mining policy. As O'Faircheallaigh has pointed out, the government has viewed mines mainly as being useful for the revenue that they bring, not for more complex benefits: "This emphasis on revenue generation has been accompanied by a relative lack of interest in trying to maximize the direct economic impact of mineral development, especially employment and linkage (i.e. input-supplying and processing) industries."[29]

Copper production from the Panguna mine peaked in 1978 at almost 200,000 tons. The price of copper, while down from its 1973-74 high, was still at a relatively profitable level. The declining quality of the ore, however, contributed to a sharp decline in production over the next two years—to less than 150,000 tons by 1980. This loss was offset to some extent by a rise in the international price of copper (the LME price climbing from U.S.$0.62 in 1978 to U.S.$0.99 in 1980). BCL recorded a profit of K71 million in 1980. Profits were especially good for BCL's foreign mining interests. Thus, Rio Tinto Zinc, which held a 57.2 per cent interest in CRA, made a before tax profit on its Bougainville investment of £103.7 million in 1979 (representing 22.9 per cent of its total worldwide profits).[30]

BCL responded to the problem of declining ore quality by taking steps to increase production by processing more ore. As a result, by 1982 copper production had climbed to 170,000 tons.[31] A further problem was added, however, when the price of copper began to decline in 1982 (the LME price dropped to around $0.67), and BCL's profits for the year were only K11.2 million. RTZ was able to compensate for this decline through higher profits elsewhere (for example, in Namibia), but government revenue from the mine suffered. Some optimism returned the following year, when production increased by another 10,000 tons, and BCL was able to record a profit of K54.6 million. Moreover, the government earned a total of K62 million from the mine in 1983.

What followed over the next few years, rather than a period of sustained profitability, was one of continuing uncertainty. Production declined again in 1984 and the price of copper fell even further (the LME price going to around U.S.$0.62). Fluctuating prices in 1985 allowed periods of encouragement, but BCL's profits dropped markedly for the year, to A$13 million, and, overall, it was clear that there would be no major improvement in the international copper market in the immediate future. Despite a further fall in the price of copper in 1986, BCL's profits rose once again (to A$37 million for the year). This was possible because of a drop in the value of the Australian dollar and in the price of oil (thus reducing financing and operating costs, respectively) and a rise in the price of gold. In addition, BCL was able to increase copper and gold production. The situation reversed itself during the first half of 1987. The value of the Australian dollar rose and other factors served to increase production costs. World demand and the price of copper remained relatively low and production of copper, gold, and silver was down, reflecting a decline in the quality of ore.

The international copper market finally began to improve by mid-1987, with world copper stocks at their lowest point since 1973. The LME copper price stood at U.S.$0.63 in April and then began to climb, reaching $0.76 by mid-July. It seemed as if the only dark cloud on the horizon was the state of the mine's reserves. BCL's strategy to weather a period of historically low prices had been to increase production. One result of this was to hasten the day when the mine would run out of ore, and by mid-1987 the mine was estimated to have reserves sufficient to last only another ten years at the current rate of production.

Declining revenue from Bougainville's copper during the late 1970s was compensated for, in part, by the dramatic rise in the price of gold—from U.S.$147 an ounce in 1977 to U.S.$607 in 1980. Actual gold production in Papua New Guinea (a good deal of which came from the Panguna mine) declined from a high of just under 24,000 kilograms in 1978 to 14,532 kilograms in 1980, but this was more than offset by the fourfold increase in the price of gold. The price of gold subsequently dropped, but it and the generally improved international metals market during this period were sufficient to stimulate new prospecting and mining ventures elsewhere in Papua New Guinea.

An increase in the value of contained gold in the Panguna mine by thirty per cent in 1986, while welcomed, did not alleviate the central

problem of declining reserves overall. Out of a desire not to upset
local landowners, BCL had long been faced with a moratorium on
further exploration on Bougainville. At various times, BCL had
raised the possibility of lifting the moratorium, and in 1986 proposed
establishment of a second mine. This suggestion generated
considerable debate that ended inconclusively with the central
government unwilling to pursue the matter, primarily out of fear of
antagonizing the population on Bougainville. The following year,
tension between the central and provincial governments generated
by the Bougainville government's desire to renegotiate the royalty
agreement led to a delay in the scheduled review of the BCL agreement
and precluded any further discussion of a second mine.

Ok Tedi: The "Pot of Gold"[32]

The most important new mining venture after development of the
Panguna mine was the Ok Tedi mine, on Mt. Fubilan near Ok Tedi
River in the Star Mountains, and close to the Indonesian border.[33]
The site is reached by air or by boat up the Fly River to Kiunga and
then overland. Some twenty thousand Min, divided into various
subdivisions, live scattered in small settlements in the area along the
border between Papua New Guinea and Indonesia surrounding the
Ok Tedi mine.[34] The Min living immediately adjacent to the mine site
itself are known as the Wopkaimin. The tailings dam is on land of a
neighboring group, the Ningerum, who live at a lower altitude than
the Min and are more densely settled. Still further to the south,
where the port of Kiunga is located, live the Awin. The Min and
Ningerum have been exposed intermittently to outside contact since
the 1920s, but remained relatively isolated prior to the coming of the
mine when compared to the Awin, who were involved in commercial
rubber growing in the 1960s.

The mountainous region behind Kiunga had been briefly explored
for gold in 1936-37, while more thorough exploration of the Star
Mountains themselves did not take place until 1963, with the Fitzer
patrol. The discovery of copper at Bougainville in 1964 and the
relatively healthy world copper market during the latter half of the
1960s, prompted Kennecott to look for other large copper deposits in
Papua New Guinea. Kennecott discovered an interesting deposit at
Yandera, near Madang, and established a base at Goroka, from
where it carried out further exploratory work. In 1968 the Ok Tedi
deposit was discovered. Preliminary drilling took place in 1970-71,
and Kiunga became the site of a busy airfield as personnel and

freight were airlifted to the isolated site. In an effort to avoid problems nationally and the develop a stable workforce for the mine, Kennecott sought to reduce the duality in pay that was prevalent in the colony at the time and instituted scholarship and training programs to promote localization. The national government, for its part, was far more concerned with Bougainville and paid relatively little attention to Ok Tedi.

Exploration activities came to a virtual halt in the middle of 1972, for a variety of reasons. One immediate reason was that a drought in the upper Fly region was making river transport difficult. But more important was the February 1972 electoral victory of Michael Somare's Pangu Pati and the party's pledge to work toward early independence. Kennecott decided to stop further exploration until the new government had clarified its mining policies. Behind this decision were international problems for Kennecott. Its mines in Chile had been expropriated by the Allende government in 1971, and the Whitlam Labor government in Australia, elected in 1972, was putting pressure on foreign mining companies, like Kennecott, to increase local participation and to reduce environmental damage.

Kennecott became very nervous during the latter part of 1972, as members of the Somare government and their advisers were seen to have adopted a hostile attitude toward BCL. As Kennecott delayed the start of negotiations with the new government, the government solicited the advice of countries like Chile and Zambia about how best to negotiate with Kennecott. Negotiations between Kennecott and the Somare government finally got under way in August 1973. Local sentiment against Kennecott grew the following month when the Allende government was overthrown in Chile, an act that many in Papua New Guinea believed had involved Kennecott.

Toward the end of 1974, the atmosphere surrounding the negotiations improved, but, among other things, the price of copper had begun to fall sharply. In an effort to make this "marginal" operation viable, Kennecott had managed to interest Mitsui and Newmont in the possibility of taking it on as a joint venture. Periodic negotiations continued during the latter part of 1974 and into early 1975, until they finally broke down in March. While many factors contributed to the failure of the talks, essentially it reflected Kennecott's inability to come to terms with the political realities of a developing country on the verge of independence. Its approach, a mixture of hostility, paternalism, and condescension, combined with an overly pessimistic attitude about the future of Papua New Guinea, was seriously out of touch with the time. Reviewing the negotiations, Jackson comments: "Bad luck...was compounded by a considerable

degree of bad management."[35] After spending nearly A$16 million
on exploratory work, Kennecott left Ok Tedi before discovering the
true magnitude of the reserves.

Following the collapse of negotiations with Kennecott in March
1975, the government assumed control of the prospect and the site
facilities and established the Ok Tedi Development Company (OTDC)
to carry out further exploration. To compensate Kennecott for its
losses, the government offered the company bonds that would be
issued with the commencement of construction of the mine. OTDC
engaged American consultants Behre Dolbear to conduct further
drilling. After spending an additional U.S.$4 million, OTDC
announced in February 1976 that the size of known reserves had
been greatly expanded. While these tests were in progress, the
government was actively engaged in efforts to secure new foreign
investment to develop the site. Negotiations were conducted with
two parties: a group headed by Alusuisse and with Broken Hill Pty.
Ltd. (BHP). A draft agreement was made with the Alusuisse group,
but negotiations collapsed when one of the parties in the group,
Pennaroya, pulled out. A short time later, in March 1976, an agreement
was reached with BHP to conduct a feasibility study and to try to
form an investor consortium. BHP's motivation for becoming
involved in the project appeared to be a combination of a sense of its
corporate role in Australia in relation to Australia's interests in
Papua New Guinea as much as a general desire to extend its overseas
mining activities.

BHP succeeded in forming a consortium in October 1976 with
Standard Oil of Indiana subsidiary Amoco Minerals Inc. (37.5 per
cent), and a group of four West German companies (led by
Metallgesellschaft) under the title of Kupferexplorationsgesellschaft
(twenty-five per cent). Amoco's involvement in the project reflected
moves by oil companies in the 1970s to diversify, while the West
German group was concerned primarily with greater security of
copper supplies for West German industry and its involvement was
sponsored by the West German government. The Papua New Guinea
government used these negotiations as a basis for establishing a new
structure to tax mining ventures in 1978.[36]

The consortium's development proposal was completed in 1979.[37]
The plan divided development of the mine into three stages:
production of gold bullion only, production of gold bullion and
copper concentrates, and, finally, production of copper concentrates
alone. The consortium also proposed that the government take up its
twenty per cent equity option and provide infrastructural and
concessional assistance worth some A$180 million. The government

responded with a counter-proposal that included provision of a maximum of A$50 million in the form of a long-term loan for construction of an access road that would be secured against the project's assets and cash flow. The government also indicated that it would not decide on the extent of its equity share until it had finalized approval of the overall financing package for the project.

A joint-venture to develop the mine was formed in 1981 under the name of Ok Tedi Mining Ltd. (OTML). OTML was a joint-venture between BHP (thirty per cent), Amoco (thirty per cent), the West German companies (twenty per cent), and the government of Papua New Guinea (twenty per cent). Construction was to be carried out by Bechtel-WKE. Development of the mine did not go smoothly. A huge landslide and a drought delayed construction and led to substantial cost overruns. In fact, costs were U.S.$300 million over the initial estimate of U.S.$700 million and there was still considerable work to be done. As a result, relations between Bechtel and OTML became strained. In addition, there was squabbling among the OTML partners, related in part to the drop in the international price of copper. And a heated argument developed between the foreign partners and the Somare government. The foreign companies, especially Amoco, which more than the others was anxious for a quick return on its investment, wished to push ahead with gold production at the expense of copper. The Ok Tedi mine contained the country's largest known gold reserve: the cap alone containing an estimated 125 tons of gold. Somare argued: "My government fears that they will take out the gold on top of the mountain, and then leave the copper mine no longer viable."[38]

Gold production commenced on a limited scale in May 1984, but doubts soon emerged over obtaining the U.S.$200 million additional funding needed for completion of the second stage of construction.[39] Working with Bank of America, Metallgesellschaft announced that it would arrange the needed finance in Europe. But negotiations between the government and the foreign partners, centering on the gold versus copper issue, remained tense. Amoco indicated that it wanted out of the venture and, in January 1985, talks broke down completely. After the government stated that it would shut the project down on 1 February, an agreement was finally reached. Although problems remained, work now went ahead. A group of banks headed by the Bank of America, and including Westpac, agreed in May 1985 to provide A$288 million to finance the remainder of the project.[40]

Mining initially was concentrated on the mountain's leached cap, where the highest grade of gold ore was located, before the consortium commenced digging into rest of peak for gold and copper. Two used copper plants were purchased in the United States (resulting in a considerable savings) and copper production commenced in late 1986. Copper concentrate from the mine is sent by a 135 kilometer slurry pipeline to the Fly River, where it is dried and then taken by barge 500 kilometers down river to a floating off-shore terminal. In 1988, the operation produced 52,680 tons of copper, 381,360 ounces of gold, and 198,770 ounces of gold bullion. Gold bullion production ended in September 1988, and the mine came to be characterized as a long-term supplier of copper concentrate. Ok Tedi was expected to reach its ultimate average processing rate of 70,000 tons of ore per day by end of 1989, at the end of which year it would yield around 120,000 tons of copper and more than 450,000 ounces of gold. Profits for 1987, the last full year of the initial period of gold production from high quality ore, were K77 million. Profits for 1988 dropped to K20.7 million, despite a rise in sales revenue from K297 million to K331.5 million. This was, in part, due to disruptions caused by a strike in September, but also because of the changing nature of the mining operation. Labor and mechanical troubles and a disruptive landslide, led to a loss of K8 million during the first half of 1989.

Relations between the consortium partners were not the only problem facing the Ok Tedi mine. The mine has been plagued by environmental problems since its inception. The 1978 Environmental Planning Act required mining projects to liaise with the Department of Environment and Planning and, if necessary, to prepare an environmental impact plan. The act reflected growing concern in Papua New Guinea about the impact of mining on the environment, but, as Ok Tedi and later projects were to demonstrate, the act alone was far from adequate to confront the considerable environmental problems relating to mining.

During the construction phase of the Ok Tedi mine, pollution of the Fly River, resulting from dumping untreated chemical pollutants into the river, led the government to insist that Bechtel build facilities to dispose of the tailings and treat the chemical pollutants. There was also concern expressed from many quarters following the massive Okma landslide, which temporarily halted construction. Once the mine began operation, environment problems continued. At the outset, on two occasions, in June 1984 and May 1985, a number of cyanide drums were spilled in the Gulf of Papua while on their way to the mine, raising further alarm about the impact of the mine on the Fly River and the twenty thousand people living on or near its banks.[41]

Environmental problems along the Fly River soon became evident, as silting and pollution led to the death of trees and other forms of vegetation. In response to environmental concern about the disposal of mine wastes, OTML commissioned an independent environmental report. The report concluded that the river and its fish would indeed be harmed by dumping the waste in the river. But the company estimated that construction of a tailings dam would cost around U.S.$380 million—an amount that would threaten the mine's financial future. In October 1989, the government gave permission to allow OTML to dump up to 150,000 tons of waste a day into the Fly River, despite its effect on the environment. By way of compensation, it also announced a K2.5 million annual grant to the people living along the river. Opposition parliamentarian and former minister of the environment, Parry Zeipi, sought a court order to close the mine temporarily to allow more time to study plans. In addition, a few days later, hundreds of students protested against government decision in Port Moresby and presented the prime minister with a petition asking him to reconsider, but the government was in no mood to allow such concerns for the environment to stand in the way of the potential revenue from this large undertaking.[42]

TABLE 3.3 Ok Tedi Labor Costs, 1981-1983

Country of Origin	1981 Budget Est. (K million)	1983 Actual Cost (K million)
Manual Laborers		
Papua New Guinea	15.1	21.0
South Korea	5.8	3.9
Philippines	4.0	12.1
Australia	19.0	20.2
Non-manual Employees		
Papua New Guinea	1.8	2.0
Philippines	3.6	5.6
Australia	6.9	10.9
North America	7.7	19.7
Total	63.9	95.5

Source: Times of Papua New Guinea, 14 June 1984, p. 9.

Labor relations at the Ok Tedi mine have also been the subject of controversy. Two issues arose during the construction phase in response to Bechtel's decision to employ a large number of Asians: (1) the traditional favored position of Australians as skilled workers in the country and (2) the fear that nationals would be denied jobs. Bechtel's argument was that Asians would be used instead of more expensive Australian and North American skilled workers to cut costs and that the workers brought in would only occupy skilled posts. A 1983 report by the Institute of Applied Social and Economic Research was sympathetic to Bechtel's position.[43] The report found that the Asian laborers hired since 1980 had been exclusively in the more skilled categories and, therefore, posed no threat to employment opportunities for nationals in the less skilled categories. It argued in favor of continuing the policy since employment of more skilled nationals would be disruptive to other areas of the economy and skilled Asians were much cheaper to employ than expatriates from Australia and other developed countries. A *Times of Papua New Guinea* article the following year (see table 3.3), responding to Bechtel's cost overruns, made the point that part of the problem was that still too many expensive Australian and North American workers had been hired and that Bechtel had not gone far enough in hiring Asians.[44]

The mine also experienced three strikes in 1988. The last of these took place in September 1988 (around time bullion production ceased) and flared into violence when a mob went on a rampage in the local mining town of Tabubil. One of the issues involved a claim by Melanesian workers that thirty jobs which were to be set aside for nationals had been given to expatriates. The violence surrounding this strike led to production being halted at the mine, resulting in a sharp drop in profits for OTML for the year. Industrial relations stabilized somewhat after this strike, but there were further industrial disputes in early 1989.

Initially, the Ok Tedi mine was spared some of the difficulties faced by the Bougainville mine relating to the local population because of the relatively small population and isolation of the Star Mountain area. OTML was careful to initiate policies to ensure that the local peoples, the Kiunga and Teleform, received economic benefits from the mine. The IASER report pointed to the success of a vegetable growing project to provide food for the mine workers. It also noted that since 1980 around 1,500 people from the North Fly region had been hired and that 1,300 of these were Kiunga and Teleform.[45] Two other factors bear consideration in regard to the relative lack of local opposition to the project at the outset when compared with Bougainville. One is the absence of business and political interests seeking to maximize benefits from the mine at the provincial level comparable to those in Bougainville. The other is a lack of a similar history of opposition to colonial rule.

The Gold Rush—II

Once Bougainville's Panguna mine went into full production, mining became the country's main export earner. In 1973-74, the Panguna mine was responsible for sixty-four per cent of the value of Papua New Guinea's export earnings. But, as noted above, the mine's productivity began to decline in the late 1970s, and, by 1982, mining accounted for only fifty-one per cent of exports. Gold production in Papua New Guinea, mostly from the Panguna mine, reached a low point of 16.9 million tons in 1981—a fact compensated for only by the relatively high price of gold at the time. Ok Tedi resuscitated faith within the country that the mining sector could pave the way for the nation's development, but problems in getting the mine into operation in the mid-1980s, and subsequent difficulties with the mine once production began, muted enthusiasm for mining-led growth.

Gold production had risen to 36.7 million tons by 1986, far above previous postwar levels, but the nation's economy as a whole at the time was in poor shape.[46] When Paias Wingti displaced Michael Somare as prime minister in 1985, his government inherited an economy suffering from low commodity prices, a large government salary bill, mismanagement, and corruption. Employment was depressed, there was very little new private-sector investment, and inflation rose to six per cent in 1986. The national budget in 1986 was K930 million, only K500 million of which was generated internally. The balance came largely from Australian aid and overseas loans, and Australian aid was being cut. The national debt was over K1 billion by 1986, and debt servicing amounted to K176 million per year. Public debt was not limited to the national government, for the provincial governments also were increasingly in debt. The International Monetary Fund issued a warning that debt servicing could reach thirty-five per cent of current receipts by 1988.

Julius Chan, who had been prime minister from 1980 to 1982, and who was closely identified with the business sector, became finance minister in the Wingti government in March 1986. Chan cut the budget and redirected government spending away from health, education, and other social services to focus on the "economic sector," with priority being given to agriculture.

TABLE 3.4 Copper and Gold Production, Papua New Guinea, 1976-1986

Year	Copper[a]	Gold[b]
1976	176.5	27.2
1977	182.3	22.4
1978	198.6	23.4
1979	170.8	19.7
1980	146.8	14.1
1981	165.4	16.9
1982	170.0	17.7
1983	183.2	18.3
1984	164.4	20.1
1985	175.0	31.3
1986	178.6	36.7

a)   Thousand metric tons.
b)   Metric tons.
Sources: World Bureau of Metals, *World Metal Statistics Yearbook, 1986;*
British Geological Survey, *World Mineral Statistics, 1982-86.*

Agriculture, however, was soon to take a backseat to mining once
again. While attention had been focused on Panguna and Ok Tedi,
less publicized prospecting activities around the country were setting
the stage for a new gold rush of unprecedented proportions.[47] The
new search had been motivated, in part, by technological innovations
which allowed the mining of previously difficult or impossible sites.
Initial interest also had been spurred on by the rise in the price of
gold in the late 1970s, but the subsequent drop in the gold price in the
early 1980s did little to dampen the pace of exploration.

At the end of 1982 there were thirty-six prospecting authorities
being actively worked in the country, most of which were primarily
concerned with gold. There were an additional fifty-four applications
by the end of 1983, and by the mid-1980s there were about a dozen
significant foreign companies carrying out exploration for gold.
Among these were Niugini Mining Ltd., Kennecott, Newmont, Esso
Exploration, Nord Resources, City and Suburban Properties (later
changed to City Resources Ltd.), Mount Isa Mines, Placer PNG, and
Renison Goldfields Consolidated Ltd.

The new gold rush began in earnest in 1986-87. In 1986 alone, over
A$200 million was spent on mineral (largely gold) exploration. The
principle sites of the new gold rush were: Wau, Porgera, Mt. Kare,
Misima, and Lihir. By 1987, it was estimated that, once production
began for the new sites being developed as mines, mining revenue

TABLE 3.5 Principal Gold Mining/Exploration Sites, Papua New Guinea

Mine	Start-up	Ownership	Reserves	Production
				(ozs., 1986)
Bougainville	1972	CRA[a] (54%)	625 mt	526,211
		PNG (20%)	0.46 g/t	
		Public (26%)		
Ok Tedi	1984	BHP (30%)	38 mt	630,000
		Amoco (30%)	2.6 g/t	
		BRD Cons. (30%)		
		PNG (10%)		
Wau	1985[b]	Renison (100%)	3.1 mt	24,000
		2.6 g/t	Expect. Prod.	(ozs/year)
Porgera	1992	Placer (30%)	84.4 mt at	1,000,000
		MIM (30%)	4.9 g/t	for initial
		Renison (30%)		six years
		PNG (10%)		
Mt.Kare		CRAa (100%)	3-5 g/t	
Lihir	1993	RTZ (80%)	300 mt	850,000
		Niugini (20%)	4.5 g/t	
Misima	1989	Placer (80%)	56 mt	200,000
		PNG (20%)	1.38 g/t	

a) CRA is a 49 per cent-owned affiliate of RTZ.
b) Wau first began operation in 1933; it is to be closed in 1990.

would reach between K3 billion and K10 billion annually—more than Papua New Guinea's entire gross domestic product at the time.[48] In addition to gold, there was also considerable exploration for petroleum, which also led to significant discoveries. The prospects of a boom in gold and petroleum production revived hope for faster economic growth based on mineral production. Interest in other sectors did not disappear, but their future, too, was seen to be linked to the minerals sector.

Wau

Renison bought New Guinea Goldfields in 1982, with the intention of reworking the old Wau goldfield. The company spent K8 million on a gold refining mill in 1984 and then began extensive exploitation of the site. These actions elicited local opposition from environmentalists, who formed the Wau Ecology Group, and from small alluvial miners (numbering some 500) who had worked deposits in the area for a number of years and felt threatened by the new development. A group of some 200 people staged a demonstration at the Wau site in May 1985, calling for a proper social, economic, and environmental impact study to be carried out before further development was allowed to proceed. The response of the secretary for minerals and energy was: "I think there are a few people in Wau who are out just to cause trouble, but I see no reasons for any argument against New Guinea Goldfields."[49] New Guinea Goldfields commissioned an environmental plan and began enhanced mining of the site,[50] but in late 1989, hurt by low gold prices and a strong Australian dollar, Renison's New Guinea Goldfields decided to close the mine by June 1990.[51]

Porgera

The Porgera deposit, located at an altitude of 2,300 meters inside a mountaintop in Enga province, 130 kilometers west of Mt. Hagen, is likely to be one of the world's largest gold mines. Until recently, the site was accessible only on foot or by helicopter. The area around it is occupied by twelve thousand people belonging to seven tribes. First located in 1938, the scale of the deposit only began to emerge in 1984, after a few years of work by a joint venture between Placer Pacific, Renison Goldfields, and Mount Isa Mines (in which Placer is to serve as the mine operator). Tests indicated that the site contained around fifty-nine million tons of various grades of gold and silver bearing ore, potentially making it one of the larger gold mines in the world. The partners indicated that a mine could be operational by 1989, provided that successful negotiations could be completed with local landowners and the various arms of government. The central government, for its part, announced in late 1985 that it would take a ten per cent share in the venture.[52]

As with most mines, relations with the local population were not entirely smooth, especially as activities at the mine site progressed. In January 1987, Placer requested police assistance to deal with about three hundred villagers who had gathered near the mine site after gold was discovered in a tunnel to cart away rock. The company feared that there might be injuries because of the large mining trucks operating in the area. Since the mine was not yet operational, the site still technically belonged to the government, and the government response was that there were not enough police available.[53] A few months after this incident, a group of local residents formed the Porgera Land Owners' Association to press claims for compensation payments and infrastructural improvements.[54] The infrastructure requested included a high school, a primary school, an agricultural research station, and improved health centers and roads. Three submissions sent to the government by the group received virtually no official response—the officials' minds seemed to be focused on negotiations with the companies over their own share of the venture.

The center of attention was on a proposal by Mount Isa Mines (MIM) for a A$160 million share float by a new subsidiary, Highlands Gold, to represent its thirty per cent interest in the mine. The amount of money involved was large, but the Porgera mine now looked as if it could indeed be one of, if not, the largest gold mine in the world. By late 1987, estimated ore reserves had risen to 76.8 million tons. The average grading of the ore was 3.8 grams per ton, with the site including a high grade zone which brought the total estimated quantity of recoverable gold to 387 tons—worth around A$7 billion. Production was expected to be around 800,000 ounces of gold a year for the first six years of the mine's nineteen year life.[55]

As negotiations between MIM and the government got underway in February 1987, there was disagreement over equity for Papua New Guinea investors, the share price, and stamp duty charges. MIM's initial proposal was to keep sixty per cent of the shares for itself, while reserving the balance of the remaining shares for its own shareholders, and setting aside only four per cent for the government. Prime Minister Wingti and Minister for Minerals and Energy John Kaputin were not happy with certain aspects of the float, and wanted a thirty per cent share for the government, with a further ten per cent reserved for citizens. The negotiations became politically sensitive when Deputy Prime Minister Julius Chan and Forestry Minister Paul Torato openly disapproved of the way that Wingti was handling the negotiations. Torato describing the prime minister's handling of the float as "deplorable."[56] An agreement finally was reached toward the end of 1987, in which the government retained an option for a ten per cent interest in the Porgera project (half of its entitlement) but decided not to take shares in the Highlands float at the time, and MIM retained about sixty per cent of the shares.[57] A further issue surrounding the negotiations arose when it became public that some politicians and senior government officials had made large purchases of shares in the company, in what had become a typical pattern of apparent corruption in the mining industry.

The joint venture completed a draft feasibility study in May 1987, which placed the cost of the mine at K660 million, and an environmental impact study in early 1988.[58] A plan was also announced to use the nearby Hides gas field (ninety-five per cent owned by British Petroleum) as a source of cheap power for the mine. Government approval hit a snag in February 1988, however, when the minister of the environment insisted on a tailings dam being built, despite the project's claim that the land was too newly formed and that some alternative was needed to avoid a disaster. Progress was further delayed when the government changed in July, and Rabbie Namaliu replaced Paias Wingti as prime minister.

Talks began again in September 1988, this time under the Namaliu government's new "Development Forum" structure, whereby all parties (landowners, developers, provincial governments, and the national government) all met to discuss problems jointly at some point. The question of the tailings dam became a crucial issue and the project manager announced that the mine might not be developed if the dam, which he considered too costly and too unstable, was required, adding that the mine could begin operations quickly once this obstacle was out of the way. Jim Waim, the minister of environment, withdrew his insistence on the dam and gave his permission to the project in February 1989. Still outstanding, however, were settlements with the provincial government and the Enga landowners. After nine months of intense negotiations between these two parties and the national government, a final agreement was achieved in May, the first under Namaliu's forum process.

The May settlement was the first agreement by which landowners and the provincial government were given equity in a project. Each were to receive a 2.45 per cent share, to be administered through a trust by the Department of Finance on a non-transferable basis. In addition, the landowners won a twenty per cent royalty instead of the originally offered five per cent; an amount that will translate into about K10 million over the life of the mine. Further payments included K15 million for compensation, K16 million for relocation, and K4 million for construction of community facilities. Provision was also made for employment of about five hundred Porgera people. In addition to its equity share, the Enga provincial government would receive some K40 million in royalty payments and K39 million in a special support grant. As for the national government, its eventual take from the project was estimated to be: K589 million from taxes, K49 million from royalties, and K70 million from other taxes relating to the project. All of this to come out of a total production of an estimated K3,900 million worth of gold.

Shortly before the agreement was reached, further drilling into the high-grade core raised the reserve estimates by twenty-six per cent. Mineable reserves now stood at 84.4 million tons of ore, grading an average of 4.9 grams of gold per ton, and extending the life of the mine to twenty years. It was also decided to mine the high-grade underground deposits directly before moving to open-pit mining, thereby raising the annual output during the first five years of operation to one million ounces (production would then fall to 640,000 ounces per year for the next five years). For the government, the revised reserve estimate meant about another K7 million, an important addition since, with the May agreement, it had to share more of its profits with the provincial government and landowners.[59]

One other hitch during the negotiation period had to do with thirty per cent shareholder Renison. Renison Goldfields Consolidated was forty-eight per cent owned by Consolidated Gold Fields of Australia, which became the object of a takeover bid by South African controlled Minorco. Because of the South African connection, the Papua New Guinea government announced that Renison would have to pull out of Porgera if the Minorco bid was successful since national laws and international obligations prohibited such relations with South Africa.[60] The Minorco bid failed, however, and Renison was able to remain as a partner.

During the prolonged negotiations, MIM's Highlands Gold float had stalled. With all major negotiable matters settled, the float was revived in November 1989. There were to be a total of 565 million shares, with a market capitalization of K282.5 million (U.S.$352 million) in Highlands Gold, and 198 million of the shares were to be involved in the float (170 million to be sold in Australia and twenty-eight million reserved for Papua New Guinea citizens and residents).[61]

As a result of inflation, additional compensation expenses, and adjustments in the mine design, by January 1990, the estimated cost of the Porgera mine had risen by twenty-five per cent above the May 1987 figure, and now stood at well over K800 million. The added cost, however, would be offset by the higher level of gold production anticipated following the April 1989 revision of reserve estimates.[62] The first stage of the mine was completed during the latter half of 1990, with final work to be completed by 1992. The workforce at the mine site in early 1990 stood at 2,300, of whom 1,600 were either Porgerans or Engans.

Mt. Kare: PNG's El Dorado

With authority to prospect a large Highlands area, in 1985 CRA began exploratory work around Mt. Kare, a rugged jungle-covered 3,050 meter high mountain twenty-two kilometers from Porgera.

The discovery of colluvial[63] and alluvial ore grading three to five grams per ton touched off a massive gold rush in 1988. Having spent some U.S.$3.5 million on exploration, after word of the find leaked out, CRA employees watched helplessly as about four thousand Melanesian prospectors descended on a particularly rich one square kilometer site and in the course of the year carried off some ten metric tons of gold (mostly in coffee jars) valued at between U.S.$85 million and U.S.$120 million. Under Papua New Guinea's mining act, Melanesian landowners are entitled to take whatever gold they can remove from a site so long as they use only pans and shovels, whereas a mining company like CRA cannot remove any gold until it has completed environmental impact studies and gained government permission to start mining.[64]

Having been granted permission by the central government to start mining, CRA still had to come to terms with the local landowners over compensation.[65] Mt. Kare being near the border of Enga and Southern Highlands provinces, CRA also had to deal with conflicting claims by the two provincial governments. In addition, the problem of determining who were the rightful landowners was especially difficult in this instance since the land had been virtually unclaimed before the discovery of gold. Thus, in May 1988, a disturbance broke out at the airstrip between rival claimants as CRA sought to fly a group of landowners out for discussions. Because of the ambiguous situation, the journey proved a waste of time, with a number of people who were not landowners getting a free trip. As the situation began to settle down, a group of landowners formed Mt. Kare Investment Corp. Pty. Ltd., and began talks for a stake in the mine. Throughout the period, CRA remained anxious to discover the identities of the true landowners and to develop a working relationship with them.

The prospectors arriving at Mt. Kare either walked in or took a helicopter from Porgera or Tari. The miners' camp that grew up around the site was extremely rough. People slept under plastic sheets hung over branches or in crude bush shelters. There were no sanitation facilities and little water. Disease became common among miners, including dysentery and even typhoid. Government services were minimal, consisting, essentially, of a health worker and a policeman (with most police from outside the area taking leave to work for gold). This was a point of contention with some local landowners, who wanted the government at least to provide a school or clinic.

Tension among the miners was exacerbated by the fact that they were drawn from a variety of tribal groups. Thus, in August 1988, a virtual war broke out between Hulis and Engans. The fighting lasted about a week and the goldfield was deserted. Peace returned after the Hulis made an offering, and people once again turned their attention to mining. CRA employees, working in the midst of this, also were sometimes confronted by suspicious Melanesian prospectors, but actual violence usually was avoided. In general, it was a typical gold rush scene, with a degree of lawlessness, while people devoted most of their energies to the search for gold.

Initially, large nuggets (some very large) were relatively easy to find, and even later in 1988, as gold became more scarce and the number of prospectors increased, individuals could still find good sized quantities of gold dust in relatively short periods of time. The gold was either sold to buyers who set themselves up at the camp or some prospectors would spend the A$450 for the helicopter fare to Mt. Hagen, where they could sell their gold to a bank or white businessman for more than they would receive at Mt. Kare. The need to provision the prospectors and the amount of money circulating at the goldfield led to the establishment of a market where the items sold ranged from Cokes and biscuits to frozen chickens brought by helicopter and sold for A$60 apiece. Among those engaged in flying in goods to sell at Mt. Kare was the local member of Parliament. The helicopters also brought prostitutes and a range of other people interested in finding ways to part the miners and their money.

As in all gold rushes, not everyone made their fortune, but many were able to make thousands of kina:

Nat Koleala, national director of one of the helicopter companies, Nationair, said an eight-year-old boy heaved a bottle of 21 kilograms of gold, worth about $A250,000, on to his desk at Mt.Hagen airport. He bought it, and the boy went straight off to the local Toyota dealer, accompanied by his driver. Where once coffee was king in Mt. Hagen, now most of the new car purchases are gold-related; and most go for cash.[66]

Those who were not so lucky sometimes went hungry in the face of the high prices charged for food at the camp and the scarcity of game.

By the end of 1988, the Mt. Kare gold rush had succeeded in putting a huge amount of money directly into the hands of many Melanesians. While much of this was spent in ways that did little long-term good, it remains to be seen, as the "dust settles," whether at least a portion of the wealth will contribute in a more lasting way to the development of the region. For its part, CRA had nothing to show for its efforts, but in December 1988 it announced that it still wished to develop a mine at Mt. Kare, starting with a small operation that would handle about one million tons of ore a year.[67] The gold rush was largely over by the end of 1989. Meanwhile, plans had gone ahead for CRA to mine gold on the surface and underground in a joint venture with local landowners.

Lihir

The small eastern island of Lihir, off New Ireland, has produced two important goldfields that constitute "the world's richest undeveloped gold deposit."[68] The first was the Lienetz gold field, discovered in 1983 by Niugini Mining, estimated to contain 11.5 million ounces of gold: reserves of 88.9 million tons of ore, grading an average of 0.8 grams of gold per ton, and an additional 8.1 tons of ore, grading an average of 0.6 ounces of gold per ton. Niugini Mining (twelve per cent) and Kennecott Explorations (Australia) Ltd. (eighty-eight per cent) formed a joint venture to explore the site further. In 1985, the companies announced plans to spend an initial A$5 million on preliminary work. Feasibility studies began in 1986, and the amount to be spent was raised to A$22 million. A second site, the Minifie goldfield, was discovered in late 1986, containing 22.5 million tons of ore, grading 0.14 ounces of gold per ton. The Lihir sites, being located on an active volcano, presented considerable technical problems. The rock would have to be cooled with piped sea water to be mined and then the rock would require heating to very high temperature to release the ore. Despite the difficulties, indications were that gold could be produced for a cost of around U.S.$132 an ounce; making it an expensive mine to develop but, once in operation, potentially a very profitable undertaking.

The Lihir deposits received worldwide attention in 1987, when it was revealed that they contained as much as an estimated fourteen million ounces of gold.[69] By the time feasibility studies were completed in mid-1988, Lihir had known reserves of 130 million tons of ore, grading an average of 3.4 grams of gold per ton, and including a twenty-five million ton surface deposit grading around eight grams of gold per ton.

In 1987, the companies announced that they hoped to commence mining in 1989, with production reaching one million ounces per year within two years of startup. The mine did not start in 1989, although progress was made in obtaining official permission to mine a site that was now seen as a likely to produce even more gold than Porgera. Further feasibility studies were conducted and the amount of recoverable gold in the site was revised upward in early 1989 to a possible 42.74 million ounces. With proven reserves of 24.45 million ounces, Lihir was possibly the largest single deposit of gold outside of South Africa.[70]

One reason for the delay was the decision of British Petroleum, announced in January 1989, to sell BP Minerals to RTZ. British Petroleum had the largest stake in the Lihir site through Kennecott and it took time for RTZ to assume control of the former BP assets. Meanwhile, Niugini Mining, which had been looking for a rich partner to help pay its way in developing the site (and perhaps even raise its share to thirty per cent), worked out a deal with Houston-based Battle Mountain Gold. Battle Mountain initially had taken a thirty-two per cent share of Niugini Mining for U.S.$82.8 million, and now increased its stake to 50.5 per cent, for a total investment of U.S.$165 million, as well as agreeing not to raise its share above seventy-five per cent over the next five years.[71]

By late 1990, the final feasibility studies were not finished, and about U.S.$65 million had already been spent on the site. Negotiations with the government were not complete, but it was expected that the government would take a twenty per cent share in the project. Plans were to commence mining in 1993, with an annual output of 850,000 ounces by the mid-1990s. With known reserves of forty-three million ounces of gold, production was anticipated to last thirty-five years. Once the final go-ahead is given by the government, the remaining finance for capital equipment and other expenses, estimated to be U.S.$750 million, remains to be raised. While there was some worry about raising this amount in light of problems at Bougainville, backers of the project pointed to the fact that Misima and Porgera had been able to raise large amounts of money in late 1989.[72]

Misima

Placer Pacific Ltd. (fifty per cent) and CRA (fifty per cent) formed a joint venture to undertake gold exploration on Misima Island, with the government having an option to assume a twenty to thirty per cent share. Misima Island is forty kilometers long and ten kilometers wide, with the deposit located at the eastern end of the island, in an area where mining took place before the Second World War. The island is inhabited by around 9,000 people, concentrated along the coast. The joint venture's exploratory work discovered a deposit with estimated reserves of 62.1 million tons of ore , grading at 1.35 grams of gold per ton and twenty grams of silver per ton. During

1986 and early 1987, Placer drew up plans to develop the site at a cost of A$278 million.[73] The mine was to have a life of ten years, producing 400,000 ounces of gold the first year and 200,000 ounces a year thereafter.

In an initial share offer in 1986, Placer made 11.7 million shares available to Papua New Guineans at A$1 each. A scandal emerged when word leaked out in October 1986 that a number of prominent people in the country had bought these shares under questionable circumstances and subsequently sold them on the Sydney stock exchange for A$2 to A$3 a share. Among the prominent public figures identified with the share purchases were Julius Chan (deputy prime minister and finance minister), Charles Maino (chief ombudsman), Michael Somare (former prime minister and then opposition leader), Henry ToRobert (governor of the Bank of Papua New Guinea), four judges (including the chief justice), and a number of cabinet ministers. Julius Chan had been involved in questionable share purchases in relation to the Bougainville mine in the early 1970s, and now he was linked to a K1 million loan from the Papua New Guinea Banking Corporation to himself and fourteen of his associates in the People's Progress Party to purchase Placer shares, again under questionable circumstances. The shares were bought in violation of Papua New Guinea's leadership code, which requires such persons to obtain the permission of the Ombudsman Commission before investing in a foreign business.[74]

Under pressure to take action on the matter, Prime Minister Wingti commissioned an inquiry at the end of 1986. The confidential report of the inquiry was leaked to the press in March 1987, during the national election campaign, and proved to be highly critical of the behavior of many politicians and government officials in the affair—including Wingti himself (who had, however, not bought shares), nine cabinet ministers, and fifty-nine members of Parliament. Among those receiving particular criticism were Julius Chan and Paul Torato, the minister for forests. Trading through his family and family companies, Chan had made a profit of A$1.44 million on the shares, while Torato had approached Placer's managing director in an effort to obtain favorable treatment in the allocation of shares. The report also criticized Chief Ombudsman Charles Maino, since, by purchasing shares through his family company, he had placed himself in a position where he could not investigate the behavior of the others.[75]

Approval of the Misima project had been delayed by the election. Once it was over and Wingti was back in as prime minister and interest in the shares scandal had faded, things moved ahead once again. The project's environmental plan was approved in April, and overall approval for the project came in June, granting Placer Pacific subsidiary Misima Mines Pty. Ltd. a twenty-one year lease to mine.[76] The government had the option of acquiring a thirty per cent stake in the project, but indicated that it would probably take a twenty per cent share. Assuming such a portion of the venture would entail providing the equivalent share of the exploration and mine development costs. The next month Placer announced a new share float to raise an additional A$83.6 million for Misima.[77]

Matters were not completely settled, however. In October there was a disagreement between the government over housing for expatriate employees. The original plan had been to house expatriate workers in Cairns, Queensland, and to use a "fly-in, fly-out" model similar to the one used by Placer for its Kidston mine in Australia (that is, flying workers in to the mine at the start of the week and out at the end of the week). The government now requested that Placer build a town to house all married and single personnel at Alotau, on the Papua New Guinea mainland about 275 kilometers west of Misima. Placer responded that this plan would cost more and that the additional expense would force the company to reassess the project, which it argued was marginal because of the low ore grade and, therefore, highly dependent on the price of gold and construction costs.[78] The other outstanding issue, how the project was to be financed, was settled in November. With the cost of the project now estimated to be A$270 million, Placer agreed to finance eighty per cent of the project, while the government agreed to assume a twenty per cent share.[79] The housing issue was settled in December, with Placer agreeing to build permanent accommodation at Misima and to abandon the fly-in, fly-out plan.[80]

Both the accommodation and the finance issues were subject to considerable debate within the Wingti cabinet. The decision to take up a twenty per cent share led to disagreement over whether the government should invest in such a high risk venture and over the question of whether it was appropriate for the government to be both a shareholder and environmental regulator.

Construction of the open-pit mine began in January 1988. In mid-1988, the cabinet agreed to provide guarantees for loans totalling U.S.$42 million to secure the government's twenty per cent equity in the project. Reserves at the time were estimated to be 55.9 million tons, grading 1.38 grams per ton of gold and 21 grams per ton of silver; producing about 77.2 tons or 2.48 million ounces of gold and

1,175 tons of silver, worth a total of around U.S.$935 million. The life expectancy of the mine was ten years, but there was the possibility of its being extended because of the potential for finding more ore. The mine began operation in May 1989, and, for the final quarter of 1989, production figures were above estimates (86,890 ounces of gold and 533,370 ounces of silver).

One hundred years of mining on the island had already left a good deal of debris and environmental pollution. Cooktown Creek, on the coast near the present mine, contains a build-up of waste from mercury and cyanide from previous mining activities, although reefs and palm trees had fully recovered during the forty-five years since mining ceased. Following population and land use studies, the present mine and its infrastructure was build on land with low agricultural potential as much as possible.[81] The exceptions are the processing plant and accommodation compound, which were built on freehold coconut plantations, and the haulage road and low-grade ore stockpile, which occupy village-owned land that was agriculturally productive. More than half of the solid rock waste from the mine will be stored in stable dumps in the interior of the island, with the rest used for back-fill in the open pit. The primary source of environmental pollution will be oxidized rock and treated chemicals which will be dumped into the sea at a depth of one hundred meters. The chemical slurry will be dumped through an outfall pipe and will flow down a steep underwater slope. Once mining ceases in the late 1990s, sea-life is expected to recover in the area. The impact of this dumping is to be monitored in an effort to assess its impact not only for Misima, but also since a similar system is planned for Lihir and Fergusson islands.

Villagers living in the area of the mine are to be paid compensation for loss of marine resources and discoloration of usable water. Landowners decided against ten per cent equity participation in the venture, which was offered to them by the national government in early 1990. Instead, they decided to ask for infrastructural development; including improved schools, hospitals, and roads.

Other Sites

In addition to these more prominent sites, during the 1980s, foreign mining companies were engaged in the search for gold in dozens of other locations across Papua New Guinea. In some instances they were going over areas that had been worked previously, but many of the sites were new. As with the first gold rush of the late nineteenth century, considerable attention focused on the small eastern islands. Kennecott, Niugini Mining, and Nord formed a joint venture to explore a prospect on Tebar Island, near Lihir. Esso and City Resources joined together to look for gold on Ioma Island. City Resources already had advanced projects at Wapolu on Fergusson Island and Wild Dog near Rabaul, when it announced, in July 1987, that it had found seven new epithermal gold prospects, the most significant one being at Sehulea on Normanby Island.[82] And, in late 1988, a joint venture was formed between MIM's Highland Gold (fifty-one per cent) and City Resources to explore a site on Basilaki Island, in Milne Bay. At around the same time, Highland Gold acquired eight other prospecting authorities in Papua New Guinea.[83]

Among the more important "other" prospects on the mainland in the late 1980s are Mount Victor, Bulgao, and Hidden Valley. The Mount Victor Mine, located in Chumbu Province near Kainantu, has been developed by Niugini Mining. The site contains an estimated 314,000 tons of ore, grading 0.13 ounces of gold per ton. Production began in late 1987, and is expected to average 15,000 ounces a year. The life of the mine, based on proven reserves, initially is only four years, but it is anticipated that additional reserves might be found.[84] The Bulgao prospect, located in the southern Highlands between Porgera and Ok Tedi, is held by Equitorial Gold NL, which is twenty-three per cent owned by Niugini Mining (with option to control thirty-four per cent). Preliminary tests were not very exciting, but a more thorough sampling across the width of the zone during the latter part of 1987 revealed a very rich ore body—a nine meter wide interval averaging 87.98 grams of gold per ton.[85] CRA completed evaluation of three years of exploratory drilling at Hidden Valley, an isolated prospect south of Wau, in August 1988, indicating that the ore body contained about seventy tons of gold and seven hundred tons of silver. The company announced that it intended to proceed with development of a mine at the site, which it characterized as medium tonnage and low-grade. The mine would take two years to build, at a cost of A$200 million, and will last for ten years.

One final site to mention is Lakekamu, where City Resources began exploratory work in 1987. In late 1988, City Resources announced plans to commence mining at Lakekamu in 1991, in partnership with American-based Ludgate Holdings Ltd. The site was expected to produce some 35,000-40,000 ounces of gold a year.

The Initial Impact of the Gold Rush

In 1989, it was anticipated that Papua New Guinea would be producing between ninety and one hundred and thirty million tons of gold a year by the mid-1990s. The prospect of such wealth is certainly enough to generate a good deal of optimism about Papua New Guinea's future, but what about the immediate impact of the gold rush? The onset of the gold rush coincided with another change of government, when Rabbie Namaliu, who had replaced Michael Somare as head of the Pangu Party after the 1987 national election, ousted Paias Wingti as prime minister in July 1988.

The startup of the Ok Tedi mine in 1986 led to predictions of an improved gross domestic product for 1987. Such predictions proved to be overly optimistic, and increased mining and exploration activities led to a sharp rise in the current account deficit—a condition then expected to persist until at least 1990. Finance Minister Julius Chan sought to reduce the deficit with higher duties on imported foodstuffs and further encouragement of agricultural development and food processing. The government also decided to cover some of its costs by drawing on the Mineral Resources Stabilization Fund (into which all of the government's mining and oil income revenue flows). In 1986, the fund stood at K74 million and was subject to a maximum twenty per cent drawdown. Having taken only K14 million from the fund in 1986, in 1987, the government removed the twenty per cent limit and withdrew K55 million—effectively, transforming the fund from a reserve to a revenue earner. The decision was tied, in large part, to the feeling that once the new mining projects came into operation in a couple of years there would be plenty of money, and, in the meantime, there were immediate pressing needs for the money currently in the fund.

Other important issues arose in 1987 in relation to the mining sector. The first had to do with the question of the government assuming equity in the new mining ventures and, if the decision was made to do so, where to find the cash. In August 1987, Wingti suggested selling the government's twenty per cent shareholding in BCL to raise some A$400 million for new investment in mining as well as to provide for cash loans to small farmers and fishermen and to repay some overseas borrowing.[86] As was discussed above, such participation in these new mining ventures received some criticism, as did the proposal to sell its BCL shares. As a result, the government did not move immediately on either issue. The government also found itself under pressure to increase the amount of mining-derived revenue going directly to the provinces and villages. In October

1987, Wingti stated that his government planned to review gold taxes in order to give villagers a greater share in the gold boom. But, again, there was no immediate progress on the matter.

When Namaliu assumed the prime ministership in mid-1988, the country's economic performance had improved since 1986, helped, in part, by the continued recovery of the international metals market. Also, confidence had returned that the mining boom would bring major benefits to Papua New Guinea in the years ahead. It was now estimated that by 1995 gold would contribute K400 million to government revenue, equal to about forty per cent of current expenditure, and that oil revenue could reach another K250 million. The new finance minister, Paul Pora, proclaimed that on the basis of forthcoming mineral wealth: "We'll be self-reliant by the late 1990s. We won't be seeking aid, we may be investing in Australia and elsewhere—we might be a donor country to the rest of the Pacific."[87]

In the meantime, real growth for 1988 was expected to amount to four per cent, slightly below the average of 4.8 per cent for the period since 1985. But inflation was down to five per cent, foreign reserves stood at a healthy K400 million (the Mineral Resources Stabilization Fund was K77 million), and the external debt had declined to U.S.$2.2 billion. On the negative side, most of the long-term problems remained: the country was still saddled with a large and not always efficient bureaucracy, there had been only limited growth in the country's infrastructure (roads, power, etc.), over half of the nation's electricity went to the enclave industries (mostly mining), there had been little progress in localization and many sectors of the economy continued to be highly dependent on expatriates, the population growth rate remained very high (as the total population approached four million), only one-eighth of the labor force was formally employed (and one-third of this was in the public sector), and law and order problems related to joblessness and breakdown of customary lines of authority were on the increase. The new finance minister increased the budget in 1988, but felt compelled to reorient spending in ways to deal with the immediate problem of law and order (especially training and recruitment of enforcement personnel).

The economy was dominated to even a greater extent than before by mining. Thus, during first six months of 1988, receipts from agricultural commodities were down from K117 million for the previous corresponding period to K106 million, while receipts from mining had risen from K440 million to K453 million. The total value of exports in 1988 was K1.23 billion. Copper accounted for K424 million of this, gold K411 million, while agricultural exports amounted to only K255 million, and forestry K88 million. But, although mining was putting more money than ever into the national economy, its contribution to national development remained problematic.

Efforts to increase earnings from minerals and other natural resources continued to be aimed largely at short-term gains, and, in many ways, mining remained an enclave industry. Enhancing input supplying and processing linkages had been neglected. Most mining remained in foreign hands, with public or even local participation being quite limited when compared with many other Third World countries. Mining directly had created relatively little employment, it had contributed little to improvement of national infrastructure, and the industry was still heavily reliant on imports. There was also the danger that without careful management, the money supply could get out of control and that the money accruing to governments, rather than being well and invested for development purposes, would be squandered by elites on themselves, on patronage, and on prestige projects that contribute little to improving basic infrastructure. The ease with which the Wingti government altered the rules governing use of the Mineral Resources Stabilization Fund was a warning of how plans to regulate mining revenue for long-term benefits could be changed to serve the immediate needs of the government in power. Moreover, the money generated by mining had served to exacerbate tensions between provinces and the national government, among provinces, and between governments and local populations.

The problems of corruption and unequal distribution of wealth were seen by many critical observers in Papua New Guinea in the 1987-88 period as especially serious and likely to grow worse unless substantial efforts were made by the government to alter the existing situation. Some cynics commented that the only growth industries in the country were crime, corruption, and compensation.

The problems facing the industry led Papua New Guinea's ambassador to the European Economic Community, Peter Peipul, in mid-1987 to call for a halt to further mining development until the country was in a better position to handle the wealth derived from such non-renewable resources, citing the need specifically to train managers and improve expertise: "Let's learn from Africa. There are big holes where mines used to be. Look at Peru, Chile and other South American countries. All they have now are big holes where once gold and copper was flowing."[88]

The Namaliu government expressed its awareness of the problems surrounding the mining industry, but indicated its desire to press ahead with increased mineral production, while seeking to overcome existing and potential difficulties. The most concrete steps taken by the new government were initiation of the Development Forum structure for negotiations and establishment of the Mineral Resources Development Company to take up state equity in mining projects. The forum brought together all interested parties in a mining project to hold discussions, while the company had as its directors heads of government departments as well as representatives from the primary mining provinces. The government made a point of emphasizing its commitment to seeing to it that natural resource development would benefit as wide a spectrum of the population as possible and that mineral and petroleum wealth, in particular, would be used to increase agricultural production. These were pledges that differed little from those of previous governments. What remained to be seen was whether it could do a better job of acting on its promises.

Pressure on the government was considerable from the provinces and local landowners on one side and from the mining companies on the other side. Provinces with oil and mineral prospects were anxious to reconstruct the royalty system, as were the landowners. But the government was worried that any substantial change in the system might undermine the confidence of the mining companies. And there was evidence that at least some foreign mining concerns were becoming frustrated with the problems they were encountering. One consortium official is quoted as commenting that: "the landowners, bankers and national and provincial governments have benefitted most so far, not the shareholders."[89]

The success of the government's new Development Forum structure in the case of Porgera, indicated that a formula seemed to have been found for overcoming many of the problems in the negotiation process and in dividing the spoils. But, just as the new approach seemed to be working, the situation on Bougainville took a turn that threatened to undermine any progress that had been made elsewhere, when islanders launched a campaign of sabotage against the mine in November 1988.

Bougainville—II[90]

Despite widespread optimism that Papua New Guinea had a golden future, there were growing signs of trouble. In his budget speech in late 1987, Minister for Minerals and Energy John Kaputin warned that the country's potential gold and oil boom was threatened by "unreasonable compensation demands" and "outrageous statements by politicians," and that this was making potential investors nervous.[91] Trouble erupted in March at Ok Tedi, when landowners, angered over the death of a clansman, blocked the access road with fallen trees and damaged some property; actions that forced the mine to suspend operations briefly.[92] And mining was not the only source of trouble from landowners. A month after the incident at Ok Tedi, elsewhere in the country, members of a landowning clan disabled a repeater station on Mount Takaniat, causing a communications blackout in the area, after demanding greater compensation from the Posts and Telecommunications Corporation.

But the most serious trouble was to come from Bougainville. There had been indications that all was not well on the island for some time, but nothing to indicate the dimensions of the crisis that was about to erupt. The immediate source of the problem in the late 1980s, was dissatisfaction among younger, more educated Bougainvillians with the conservative leadership of their landowning elders. One particular source of discontent was young males who were not in a direct line to benefit from mining royalties because of the matrilineal nature of Bougainvillian society. In 1987, a group of younger militants led by Francis Ona and his sister tried, unsuccessfully, to take over the corporation representing the landowners. Ona, a graduate of the University of Technology and onetime surveyor for BCL, seemed to chafe under the necessity of depending on his matrilineal uncle Matthew Kove for benefits from mining—after the outbreak of hostilities, Kove was kidnapped by Ona's men and is believed to be dead.[93]

These issues were not, however, taken seriously by BCL or the national government, whose attention was focused narrowly on the need to find new bodies of ore suitable for mining on the island. The Panguna mine had only ten to fifteen more years of operation remaining and BCL needed time to try to develop an alternative mine. In his budget speech, Kaputin had suggested holding talks on Bougainville to allow lifting the moratorium on further exploration which had been in place since the initial agreement in the 1970s.[94]

Discussions were not to go smoothly and, in April 1988, Ona and his followers presented BCL with a demand for K10 billion in compensation for environmental damage and disruption to the people of Bougainville. The demand was quickly dismissed, but a short time later the national government commissioned the Auckland-based consulting firm Applied Geology Ltd. to prepare an independent environmental and social impact study as part of its effort to overcome resistance to further mining on the island. In fact, the report came to serve just the opposite function—becoming a catalyst for Ona and his militant followers to act. The report was prepared over a three month period as the militants sought to stir up opposition to the mine, blaming mining for everything from driving away the island's fruit bats to causing girls to menstruate earlier.

At a September 1988 meeting held by the consultants on Bougainville, Ona threatened to kill the team leader, environmentalist Martin Ward. In November, Ona and his followers walked out of a meeting held to present the consultant's report, claiming that the report was a whitewash and that it did not adequately address environmental questions. On his way out, Ona proclaimed that the only course of action remaining "is for us to shut the mine."[95] In fact, the report was critical of BCL and the national government and did deal extensively with environmental questions, but the militants were not really interested in its contents, referring to the report as "white man's trickery" and caring little for scientific argument. Moreover, later evidence indicted that the militants already were well advanced with plans to launch a guerilla offensive against the mine.

The situation deteriorated quickly.[96] On 22 November, a group of Ona's followers stole explosive from BCL and on the twenty-forth they attacked company facilities, burning an administrative block, a guest house, and a helicopter and its hanger. There were further attacks on the twenty-sixth, with the cost of the damage caused during these two days estimated to be K700,000. A few days later, BCL chairman Don Carruthers flew to Port Moresby, where he issued a warning that CRA, BCL's largest shareholder, would "seriously reconsider" future investments in Papua New Guinea in light of what he described as the "acts of terrorism" on Bougainville resulting from "unrealistic expectations" on the part of landowners.

The threat by Carruthers was a serious one for the national government since the company spent some K10 million a year in Papua New Guinea on exploration, was in the process of reinvesting K250 million in the Panguna mine over a three year period, and had plans to invest K200 million in its Hidden Valley project. Prime Minister Namaliu responded by calling the statement a "regrettable over-reaction" and reminded CRA that such problems were not unique to Papua New Guinea, as CRA knew from its experience with Aboriginal landowners in Australia. The North Solomons' most prominent national political figure, Minister for Provincial Affairs John Momis, issued a statement saying that the landowners on Bougainville had been ignored for too long and now needed to be taken seriously. Likewise, provincial politicians in the North Solomons, while not supporting the acts of violence, generally expressed sympathy for the militants.

The militants continued their harassment of the mine, and on 1 December stole more dynamite. The following night a power transmission tower was destroyed, cutting off power to the mine site. As BCL employees sought to restore power, militants destroyed a repeater station providing communication for the mine and another power transmission tower, forcing the mine to shutdown for six days. Prime Minister Namaliu delegated a committee, led by Deputy Prime Minister Akoka Doi, to go to Bougainville and to try to meet with the various parties concerned. At the same time, Police Commissioner Paul Tohian issued orders for his men to shoot and kill saboteurs if necessary, and Defence Force soldiers were mobilized and placed on stand-by. Ona's group refused to talk to Doi's committee and on 7 December blew up a BCL maintenance building (causing an estimated K350,000 worth of damage).

When Doi's committee and Ona's group finally met on 8 December, Ona gave the committee assurances of peace. Despite these assurances, and even though power had been restored to the mine, BCL refused to reopen the mine because of the large quantities of explosive remaining in the hands of the militants. The government gave the militants until 12 December to hand over the explosives in their possession, and, after a quantity of explosives were turned over to security forces, the mine resumed production on 11 December. A few days later, the government appointed a new committee, also headed by Doi, to renegotiate the Bougainville Copper Agreement, and Namaliu held a cordial meeting with Carruthers, at which he received an assurance of CRA's cooperation in the negotiations. The worst of the crisis seemed to be over.

The situation on Bougainville, however, remained tense, prompting the government to impose a dusk-to-dawn curfew for communities near the mine site, to be enforced by 400 heavily-armed police. Security forces had been unable to capture Ona and on 24 January he sent North Solomons Premier Joseph Kabui a message that he would not surrender. The issue of amnesty for Ona in exchange for an end to his campaign was broached, but this was ruled out by the justice minister, who did, nevertheless, state that the cabinet could direct the police not to prosecute Ona.[97]

In mid-February, a new dimension was added to the crisis, when Ona issued a letter advocating secession for Bougainville, referring to a "white mafia network" that had subverted the national government.[98] The following month, communal violence broke out between Bougainvillians and non-Bougainvillians, resulting in two deaths and numerous casualties and leading to the removal of hundreds of workers and their families from the island. There were also armed clashes between villagers and police, in which one villager was killed and several wounded.[99] The military, too, had suffered casualties, with two soldiers killed. The escalation of violence prompted the government to fly in an additional one hundred police and to call out the Defence Force to help enforce the curfew, which had been extended for another two months. Authorities also banned foreign media and diplomats from Bougainville.

Ona failed to meet an ultimatum from Premier Kabui that he come out of hiding by 23 March and support for Ona among provincial authorities was starting to wane. In particular, Kabui, who had been sympathetic up to this point, now gave up further efforts to liaise with Ona. While local authorities and many Bougainvillians had been supportive of Ona's efforts to strike a better deal in relation to the mine, they now seemed to feel that the situation had gotten out of hand. A provincial committee report on the crisis noted widespread support for secession in the province, but the committee itself advocated a federal system, with the role of the national government limited to such areas as defence and foreign affairs.[100] In addition to felt political and economic injustice, support for secession was linked to the views of the people of Bougainville and neighboring islands that they were ethnically closer to neighboring Solomon Islanders, with whom they also shared common physical features, such as very dark skin, than to other Papua New Guineans, who they refer to as "red skins," in reference to their lighter complexions.

In the face of militant demands for secession, provincial officials and national politicians from the North Solomons found themselves in a difficult position. Peter Larmour, sees the degree of "solidarity between the provincial and national governments" in the crisis as being related, in part, to party ties.[101] Thus, John Momis was leader of the Melanesian Alliance, which was part of Prime Minister Namaliu's governing coalition, and was himself a minister in the national government. Premier Kabui had been estranged from the Melanesian Alliance, but, subsequently, had rejoined the party. In addition, several leading business and political figures in the province had been involved in the initial 1976 Bougainville agreement (among them, John Momis and former Bougainville premiers Alexis Sarei and Leo Hannett), which the militants now sought to attack—Rabbie Namaliu had been the head of the central government's negotiating team for the agreement.

The national government was growing increasingly frustrated by its inability to bring about a negotiated settlement, especially in light of the extent to which Namaliu's government had shown itself to be sympathetic to provincial interests. Evidence of its commitment to bringing about a better deal for the provinces was considerable. Thus, in February, the national government had revised financial arrangements for the overall distribution of funds in favor of the provinces, and its new mining policy was much more favorable to provincial governments and landowners. But none of this seemed to matter to Ona and his followers. John Momis had been given a free hand by the government to find a solution, but without result. Namaliu next sought to form a premiers' committee, headed by John Kaputin, to pursue negotiations, but Kaputin was reticent to become involved, claiming that the terms of reference for the committee were unclear.

On the military front, initially security forces and the national government had been hampered by a lack of reliable information about Ona and the militants' armed wing, the Bougainville Revolutionary Army. By early 1989, this situation had begun to change, and, in March, Namaliu claimed that the government had learned that Ona was receiving assistance in the form of high-powered weapons from unspecified outside sources. On 6 April, a patrol of twenty soldiers was ambushed about six kilometers from the mine by some thirty militants armed with automatic weapons, leaving two soldiers dead and one wounded and two militants dead and two wounded. The militants attacked the mine again on 15 April, destroying a power transmission pole and forcing the mine to close for two days. These attacks led to growing unease elsewhere in the country and, specifically, to increased anti-Bougainvillian feelings and prompted Namaliu and Michael Somare to issue appeals for restraint.

It finally looked as if a breakthrough had been made in early May, when a provincial committee produced a report, known as the Bougainville Peace Package, that seemed to offer a workable solution. Responsibility for the negotiations had been given to John Bika, a Nasioi with a history of community work and sympathy for the aspirations of the landowners, who recently had been named provincial minister for commerce. Bika was made chairman of the Panguna Crisis Provincial Select Committee, which was empowered to examine the causes of the crisis and to offer possible solutions. The report called for a settlement package for the landowners and the provincial government that included a K200 million development program spread over a five year period and a special unconditional grant to the provincial government, to be paid for largely from the national government's share in BCL; an increase in the royalty rate for the landowners; and the right of the landowners and provincial government to purchase about half of the central government's 19.1 per cent equity in BCL, 4.9 per cent at cost, and 5.1 per cent at current market value.[102] The report also advocated greater autonomy for the North Solomons, giving the province full powers over all areas except defence, foreign affairs, and currency and foreign exchange. For its part, to support the peace initiative, BCL came up with an K40 million package over seven years. In promoting the settlement to the Bougainvillians, Bika appealed to them not to be "fooled anymore by the militants with their propaganda and trickery."[103]

The response of Ona and the Bougainville Revolutionary Army to the Peace Package initiative was to step up their attacks until BCL was forced to close the Panguna mine on 15 May. The following week, there were further acts of sabotage against the mine's electrical pylons and eight BCL employees were wounded. In addition, Premier Kabui revealed that he and other political leaders in the province had received death threats from the militants. Later in the month, Ona told an intermediary that he wanted the national government to agree to a referendum on secession and on 1 June Bishop Gregory Singkai met with Ona in a further effort at mediation, but the bishop met with no success.[104]

With the Panguna mine still closed, on 7 June, the cabinet instructed four top public servants to draw up contingency plans should the mine remain closed for a prolonged period.[105] The report was presented three weeks later and its findings were far from encouraging. A three month shutdown of the mine, which contributed twenty per cent of the national budget, would result in a loss of K30 million in foreign reserves and K46 million in direct revenue, while a six month shutdown would increase losses to K70 million and K140 million respectively. If the mine were to remain closed until August, the report called for: (1) a cut in the national budget by K25 million, (2) a reduction in lending by the Bank of Papua New Guinea, (3) the implementation of cost-cutting measures for the public service, (4) deferral of a pending decision by the Minimum Wages Board, and (5) allowing foreign reserves to decline by an additional K20 million. The report drew up three more drastic scenarios should the mine remain closed longer; including cutting the public service by twenty-five and reducing the work week for those remaining, and allowing the International Monetary Fund to manage part or all of the economy.

Meanwhile, Namaliu visited Australia to sign an aid agreement with Prime Minister Hawke and to try to calm Australian investors.[106]

His task was made more difficult when an Australian was wounded on Bougainville shortly before the visit, but Namaliu sought to dispel concern by referring to successes elsewhere in the country such as with the negotiations at Porgera. The Australian cabinet strongly endorsed Namaliu's efforts to find a solution, but the actual aid agreement, which had been negotiated earlier in the year, did little to help his government through its current crisis. The agreement, which was designed to decrease Australian aid as mining revenue increased, called for a total aid package of A$1.5 billion over five years, representing a sixteen per cent decline from the previous five year period. On the positive side, and of more immediate concern, Australia pledged four Iroquois helicopters for surveillance and troop deployment (Papua New Guinea having no helicopters of its own at the time), which Prime Minister Hawke was quick to describe as part of Australia's normal aid program and not directly related to the Bougainville crisis.

Namaliu's assurances and the Labor cabinet's support did not completely convince Australian mining interests that all was well in Papua New Guinea. Because of the terrain, Papua New Guinea was already one of the costliest areas in the world to explore for minerals (for example, a jungle seismic survey costs A$60,000 a kilometer versus A$7,000 in Australia). In addition, even before the Bougainville crisis, mining interests were becoming increasingly nervous about the national government's ability to regulate the demands of landowners. And the Porgera negotiations had done little to reassure miners, who saw them as setting a costly precedent. Australian mining interests now were extremely worried about the implications of Bougainville and Porgera and likelihood that landowners throughout the country would ask for even more in the future. One mining executive, around the time of Namaliu's visit, was quoted as complaining: "We won't know how much the landowners will ask for until each deal comes up for negotiation."[107] By June, several prospecting companies were believed to have scaled down exploration plans and some mining firms already had begun winding down operations. The implication was that, while projects such as Hidden Valley and Lihir would go ahead, it was unlikely that there would be new major exploration until the political situation became more stable.

Back home, while awaiting release of the contingency plans, Namaliu proclaimed a state of emergency on Bougainville on 22 June, to take effect on 26 June, and increased security forces on the island from 600 to 2,000. Over the next few weeks, security forces under the command of Colonel Lima Dotaona launched attacks against rebel strongholds, resulting in a number of casualties and dozens of arrests. The troops put the rebels on the defensive but failed to capture any of the principal leaders (one of the casualties was a younger brother of Ona's, who was killed on 18 July). In mid-July, Colonel Dotaona sounded optimistic: "The security forces are closing in fast and it is only a matter of time before the armed resistance is crushed."[108]

Anxious to demonstrate that the situation was improving on Bougainville, in August, the national government put pressure on BCL to announce that it was about to begin repair work on the mine in preparation to reopening it. BCL had its own reasons for wanting the mine back in operation. Its reported profits for the first six months of 1989 were down to K37.77 million, a decline from K51.8 million for same period the previous year, with the company having to spend K9.6 million to cover costs for repairs, redundancies and related items.[109] Meanwhile, there were growing causes for concern on the government's part. As an indication of the extent to which foreign investors had become wary of Papua New Guinea, the country's electricity generating authority found itself unable to convince foreign banks to lend it U.S.$20 million. Controversy was also growing over the environmental pollution of the Ok Tedi mine. Given the fact that the Ok Tedi mine generated K100 million in foreign reserves, directly employed 4,500 people, and supported local companies with an annual turnover of K22 million, the government could not afford any additional worries from this direction. As further indication of the problems facing the mining industry, 1988 gold production figures indicated that total production in the country had declined to thirty-three tons. To make matters even worse, a parliamentary committee issued a report arguing that the original Bougainville agreement had overlooked important legal points and possibly should be renegotiated in its entirety.

One bright spot was Porgera,[110] where Ipili Porgera Investments Ltd. had been formed with 3,332 shareholders, including 2,600 members of landowning clans in the area, to represent landowners' interests in the project. The company secured rights over downstream alluvial gold deposits in an effort to eliminate illegal miners and reached an agreement with Australian interests to form Porgera Gold Dredging (PNG) Ltd. (to be floated on Australian Stock Exchange, with 11.4 per cent of the shares going to the Papua New Guinea public) to work the alluvial deposits. The agreement included a guarantee that up to fifty per cent of the mine's net proceeds would go to the landowners.

During the first week of September, Ona issued another letter. This one argued that the diverse customs of the people of Papua New Guinea did not allow them to live together peacefully and called, once again, for secession.[111] A short time later, in an interview with a local journalist, the Bougainville Revolutionary Army's commander, Sam Kauona, called for a complete withdrawal of security forces to be followed by discussions among Bougainvillians leading to a referendum on secession.[112] Kauona also accused government soldiers of torturing and killing two women on 25 August whom the military reported had been killed accidently in a shootout. Security forces responded to the interview by harassing the local media— clamping down even further on reporters and forcing the reporter responsible for the Kauona interview to go into hiding.

The recognized landowners, represented by the Panguna Landowners' Association and Road Mining Tailings Leases Trustee Ltd., also had been busy. They had presented the government with a list of demands in response to the proposal contained in the Bougainville Peace Package proposal. Among the demands were that they be given the entire 19.1 per cent state share in BCL, tax exemption for their company, permission for landowners to sell their shares at any time to national or foreign interests, increased representation on the BCL board, a new royalty sharing arrangement, and a new contract awarding system to favor the landowners. The economic demands were considerable, but the landowners were not insisting on secession, and at least they were talking. What had yet to be addressed satisfactorily were divisions between the landowners and the militants relating to the distribution of wealth and power.

A degree of calm having settled over Bougainville during the latter part of August, the Panguna mine was reopened on 5 September.[113] The same day in Port Moresby, the government sounded optimistic as it unveiled the details of the agreement that had been reached with the landowners. The optimism was shortlived, however, for within hours renewed violence on Bougainville forced the mine to be closed once again. Militants had ambushed two buses carrying workers and attempted to destroy another pylon, making it clear that they were not in sympathy with the peace package. A few days later, the situation deteriorated even further, when seven masked gunmen killed John Bika. Bika was assassinated at his home in Toboroi village on 11 September as he was preparing to leave for Port Moresby for the signing of the agreement between representative of the government and landowners. To the militants, Bika's primary sin had been to offer an alternative to the goal of secession.

Ted Diro, the minister for state and former head of the defence forces, responded to the assassination by issuing a K200,000 reward offer for Ona and seven of his deputies and empowering the commander of the forces on Bougainville, Colonel Dotaona, to use tougher measures against the militants, including planting landmines. Just how difficult it would be to arrive at a compromise became even clearer when Namaliu revealed that military intelligence had learned that the militants had begun preparing their military campaign in 1987, codifying district names and regional commands and digging trenches and tunnels in the jungle.[114]

Sporadic fighting continued throughout September and October. By late October, the total dead from the conflict had risen to around forty people. Also, more than three thousand villagers had been relocated to makeshift camps in order to create a military zone. While there was evidence that many people on Bougainville no longer supported the militants and the security forces had scored some military successes, it was clear that the fighting would continue for some time to come. Colonel Dotaona, who had been field commander since June, was recalled from Bougainville in mid-October.[115] Some politicians, in particular, considered Dotaona too moderate in his dealings with the militants and he was known to be critical of interference from politicians. His comments on the way politicians were handling the situation prompted Diro to order him disciplined "as a warning to all disciplined force personnel that future breaches of Defence Force rules and traditions in regard to public comment will not be tolerated."[116] The new commander, Colonel Leo Niua, was from East New Britain, and was considered a "no nonsense" soldier. Anxious to move quickly, with the state of emergency due to expire on 11 November, Niua's first actions included bringing in an extra two hundred soldiers and reimposing the dusk-to-dawn curfew which had been relaxed in recent months.

Finance Minister Paul Pora's K1,250 million 1990 budget, released in November, sought to encourage a sense that the situation still could be handled without too much difficulty.[117] Avoiding any serious budget cuts or tax increases, the budget's underlying assumption was that the Bougainville mine would be reopened soon. To help cover the anticipated deficit (privately predicted to be K117 million), the government planned to draw K80 million from the Mineral Resource Stabilization Fund which was anticipated to have a year-end balance of K144 million. Pora stated that the government was looking for ways to increase mining revenue (including taxation of contractors and landowners who received income from mining) while encouraging greater investment in non-mining sectors. Finally, in an effort to maintain the country's credit rating because of concern over future borrowing needs, the government intended to pay off K254 million of the country's K1.2 billion foreign debt.

The opposition was quick to criticize the budget. Opposition economic critic Julius Chan characterized the budget as "pinned together with panic and madness," for being based on the false premise of an early reopening of the Bougainville mine and containing no contingency plan.[118] While such political rhetoric could be ignored, the government felt more constrained to pay attention to warnings issued by Bank of Papua New Guinea Governor Henry ToRobert. In the Bank's *Quarterly Review,* ToRobert warned the government of the need to make more thorough adjustments should the mine remain closed.[119] The bank estimated that the country would end the year with a K50 million shortfall in foreign exchange earnings and that there would be zero real growth in the gross domestic product as a result of the mine closure and falling prices for agricultural exports. On the positive side, the bank estimated that even without Bougainville, the balance in the Mineral Resource Stabilization Fund should be adequate to cover budgetary needs for the next two years.

Responding to ToRobert's warning as well as to indications that the Bougainville mine would remain closed for a while yet, Namaliu conceded that it might be necessary to bring down a supplementary budget and Pora began to look for ways to cut government expenditure.[120] At the same time, however, the government was confronted with new demands for money. By the end of 1989, the Bougainville security operation had cost the government K18 million. Low prices for agricultural commodities meant that the government was facing pressure to provide financial support for coffee and cocoa growers.[121] In addition, following a decision in early December by BCL's directors to keep the mine in a state of readiness rather than mothball it, the government and CRA agreed to advance BCL K45 million to keep on most of the remaining 2,400 employees at the mine.

In the face of continued violence and the lack of progress in achieving a lasting solution to the crisis, BCL announced just after Christmas that it would mothball the Panguna mine on 7 January and lay off around two thousand workers, leaving only a skeleton staff of some three hundred.[122] Estimates of the time that would be required to reopen the mine varied from three to six months at a cost of between K75 million and K100 million.

Following the closure of the mine, the government instituted major financial adjustments in early January 1990. The adjustments began on 4 January, when Finance Minister Pora cut the budget by K100 million. All national departments and government agencies were told to cut their budgets by twenty-five per cent, provincial departments were ordered to reduce their budgets by ten per cent, and the government planned to seek an agreement on wage restraint with the unions. On 9 January, ToRobert announced drastic monetary policies that severely limited new bank lending, and predicted a three-year recession. The next day, Pora announced a ten per cent devaluation of the kina and urged people to show restraint and turn back to subsistence production. A few days later the government approached the International Monetary Fund and World Bank for U.S.$130 million in financial assistance.[123]

The economic measures coincided with a toughening of government policies toward the militants. Also on 4 January, Prime Minister Namaliu announced that the government had ceased efforts aimed at achieving a peaceful settlement with the militants and had decided to adopt an all-military solution. The opposition responded that the action had come too late and called for a withdrawal of security forces, but the next day Parliament voted sixty-two to eighteen to extend the state of emergency on Bougainville for a further two months. Now that he had "the green light from the elected representative of the people to pursue our military option on Bougainville," Namaliu pledged to "rid Bougainville of this terrorist scourge," and restore peace and reopen the mine.[124]

Government security forces launched Operation Footloose on 11 January, with the aim of destroying the Bougainville Revolutionary Army. The military claimed a number of successes during the early days of its campaign. The guerillas hit back and violence escalated during the last two weeks of January as militants killed seven people and freed several prisoners at Kuveria prison, burned a helicopter and several properties (including one government building on neighboring Buka island), killed the expatriate local manager of Bridgestone Tyres, and wounded two Australians. In early February, eight truckloads of guerillas attacked the Kuruwina plantation, where they held and robbed expatriate staff and burned buildings. The escalation of violence prompted BCL to prepare an airstrip at the mine site should expatriate civilians need to be evacuated. At the request of the Papua New Guinea government, Australia agreed to help fund, train, and equip an additional six hundred men for the defence force. The Australians also shipped a supply of small arms

to replenish depleted supplies and added K1 million to its aid
package for the country's police force.

Continued violence led CRA to withdraw all of its remaining
employees from Bougainville on 7 February and the Australian
government to urge the roughly six hundred Australian citizens
remaining on the island to leave.[125] On 9 February, security forces
launched a counter attack against the guerillas as a mass evacuation
of plantation workers, government workers, and expatriates,
including nearly all BCL employees, began. The bloodiest battle to
date occurred a few days later with security forces, using Australian-
supplied helicopters, killing as many as twenty guerillas.

As the fighting on Bougainville increased, the local economy of
the North Solomons ground to a virtual halt.[126] The cash flow within
the province had dropped to twenty per cent of previous levels as
cocoa and coconut trees were left untended and people stayed away
from markets for fear of travelling. People living in the main areas of
guerilla activity had run out of many commodities since the security
forces had restricted the flow of goods into these regions to keep
them from going to the guerillas. The provincial government was
virtually unable to govern and the national government was
considering suspending it (using the provincial government's K17
million budget to help pay for security forces). Meanwhile, the
recognized landowners associated with the Panguna Landowners
Association and Road Mining Tailings and Leases Trustees Ltd.
signalled to the government that they were prepared to try to end the
crisis and announced that there would be leadership changes.

Having announced that it would cut operating expenses, the
national government ran into difficulty implementing its cost-cutting
initiatives. Government ministers were resistant to plans to do away
with nine departments and retrench and redeploy 14,000 civil
servants. Faced with the prospect of having their annual slush funds
cut from K100,000 to K40,000, the country's 109 parliamentarians
were asking for the K100,000 in advance.[127] At the same time, the
Australians had proven less keen to increase assistance than had
been anticipated. There appeared to be a feeling on Australia's part
that Papua New Guinea needed to make further cuts and learn to
come to terms realistically with its problems. Evidence of other
financial dimensions of the problems were increasingly apparent.
BCL announced an operating loss of K2.89 million, and extraordinary
losses of K17.73 million, for the calendar year 1989, and the Central
Bank stated that it anticipated foreign reserves dropping from their
current K363 million to K150 million by the end of 1990. There were
social costs as well. Loss of government revenue combined with low

coffee prices were seen by government observers to be linked to increased poverty and violence in the highlands and, in general, to a deterioration of law and order throughout the country.

To make matters worse, there were troubles from other mines around the country. In January, landowners around the Misima mine threatened trouble if their log of claims, outstanding since June 1989, was not settled (especially their demand for construction contracts), and the Misima landowners were being supported by the Milne Bay Provincial government. In Enga Province, CRA was surprised when it was criticized by the Enga Provincial government for negotiating a "secret deal" behind the backs of the government and landowners over the recently announced settlement at Mt. Kare. The Enga Province premier called on the national government not to issue the licence for Mt. Kare Alluvial Mining, stating that the forty-nine per cent share offered to landowners was insufficient since the mining project only involved some "earthmoving" which the people could do themselves: "CRA will rip the gold out of this corner of the province and go, leaving behind them the sort of political and social disaster they have created on Bougainville." And he accused CRA of dealing only with selected landowners while ignoring the "real" leaders.[128] Then, in February, landowners again forced the Ok Tedi mine to shut down briefly, this time as a result of a protracted dispute with the government over a share-out of royalties and, in particular, over compensation for a road.[129]

In an effort to get peace talks underway, in mid-February the government agreed to a withdrawal of all of its forces from Bougainville on 16 March.[130] In preparation for the withdrawal, a ceasefire went into effect on 1 March and the government invited Commonwealth and Scandinavian countries to monitor the ceasefire. There were a few incidents, but generally the withdrawal went smoothly.[131] With all national government presence gone from the island (including air, telecommunication, and postal services), the Bougainville Revolutionary Army, under the command of Sam Kauona, established its headquarters at the Panguna mine site and took over all districts in the province. Although most already had fled, all remaining non-Bougainvillians with no legal proof of employment, including those married to Bougainvillians, were told to leave the island. The Bougainville Revolutionary Army issued local businesses letters guaranteeing their protection, but shortly after the withdrawal gangs began taking items from shops and car yards. At a 13 March press conference, Kauona insisted that the question of secession was not negotiable, and by the end of March negotiations had yet to begin.

Police Commissioner and Commander of the State of Emergency on Bougainville Paul Tohian had not approved of the government's decision to pull out so abruptly. Rather, he favored a phased withdrawal. Critical of the government's handling of the situation on Bougainville and angered over the withdrawal, on 14 March, Tohian attempted to stage a coup in Port Moresby.[132] The attempt failed and the government claimed that Tohian acted alone, but there was widespread speculation that this was not the case. It was also evident that there were many discontented soldiers in the defence force and that the feeling among the security forces was that Tohian had done a good job on Bougainville but that there had been too much political interference. Papua New Guinea's parliamentary system survived this crisis with relative ease, but it did serve as a reminder of just what could happen should the economic and political situation continue to deteriorate.

Attempts to hold talks between the national government and the BRA during the month of April met with no success. A proposal by the BRA to hold talks on Bougainville was rejected by the national government for reasons of security, the government arguing that it could not be sure of the safety of Foreign Minister Michael Somare and Attorney General Bernard Narokobe. Believing that talks effectively had collapsed, on 2 May the cabinet imposed an economic blockade around Bougainville. It imposed a 50-mile restricted sea zone and 20,000 foot restricted airspace zone around the island, threatening to fire on unauthorized craft. Only shipping and airline services carrying essential medical supplies and fuel for the island's hospital would be allowed to pass. The idea was to isolate Bougainville until conditions deteriorated to the point that support for the rebels waned. The government had no intention to land on Bougainville itself, but when nearby Nissan islanders pledged to break away from Bougainville, PNG Defence Force troops landed on the island in an exercise of "reconciliation, reconstruction, and rehabilitation."[133]

The Bougainville rebels responded to the national government's actions on 17 May with a declaration of independence.[134] Francis Ona was proclaimed president of the republic. Sam Kauona became defence minister. In addition, Joseph Kabui accepted the post of minister for police, justice, and peace in the new government, confirming allegations that he had collaborated with the BRA throughout the uprising. The declaration was rejected by the Papua New Guinea government and by the governments of the other Melanesian states. In a secret brief leaked to the press, the PNG Defence Force recommended re-taking the island and capturing or killing Kauona, but Defence Minister Benias Sabumei ruled out a military invasion of the island.[135]

Talks between the rebels and the national government resumed in late August, with the parties agreeing to meet aboard the New Zealand warship *Endeavour* off the coast of Bougainville. The delegation from the national government was led by Somare and Narokobi. The Bougainville delegation was led by Joseph Kabui, and included hardliner James Singko (from the BRA and chief of Ona's Supreme Advisory Council) as two important church representatives Gregory Singkai (Roman Catholic bishop of Bougainville and eduction minister in the rebel government), and John Zale (United Church bishop and health minister in the rebel government). Also present were three international observers: Tony Brown (from the New Zealand prime minister's department), Nick Etheridge (Canadian deputy high commissioner in Canberra), and Sela Molisa (Vanuatu's finance minister). Neither Ona or Kauona were present at the meetings, although they were in regular contact with their delegates.

After almost a week of extremely difficult talks, in which the group's shared Christianity played a significant role, an agreement was reached. The talks had almost collapsed, but at the last minute a compromise was achieved, formalized as the Endeavour Accord, by which the long-term political status of Bougainville was to be the subject of an on-going dialogue while the national government pledged to take steps to restore services to Bougainville.[136] Talks concerning the political status of Bougainville were to begin within the next six to eight weeks.

Problems re-emerged almost immediately after the accord. After community leaders at Buka issued a statement denouncing the rebel government and asking the national government for assistance, PNG Defence Force patrol boats landed supplies Over the next week around 300 troops and police landed. This was followed by clashes with the BRA in which twenty-seven rebels and an undetermined number of soldiers were killed. Following these clashes, Kabui made the withdrawal of government forces from Buka a prerequisite for the resumption of talks. Meanwhile, reports circulated of starvation, illness and some deaths on Bougainville as a result of shortages brought about by the six month blockade of the island. Supplies of medicines and consumer goods had been exhausted and, after heavy rains destroyed many gardens, even basic foods were scarce.[137] As of the end of September it appeared as if some progress had been made in finding a solution to the Bougainville crisis, but an end was still a long way off.

The national government, meanwhile, had been active in seeking to adapt to the new economic realities brought on by the Bougainville crisis and severe problems with the agricultural sector.[138] The Consultative Group for Papua New Guinea, comprised of the country's leading aid donors, met in Singapore 17-18 May.[139] The consensus of the group was that despite Papua New Guinea's immediate problems, its "medium-term external financial outlook and credit-worthiness remained strong as a result of a combination of policy actions by the government and support form donors."[140] As an expression of its support for the policies of the Namaliu government, the group announced a substantial increase in grants and concessional loans, up U.S.$280 million to a total of U.S.$710 million. A short time later, on 7 June, Namaliu announced a package of major reforms in keeping with the wishes of the consultative group. The reforms included plans for a substantial restructuring of the government—"The days of a bloated, inefficient and irresponsible public sector were not just numbered, they are finished"—and a further opening of the economy to foreign investment.[141] An additional step to encourage foreign investment was taken with the signing of the Promotion and Protection of Investment Agreement by Australia and Papua New Guinea.[142] According to the agreement, the Australian government would provide a range of guarantees to Australian companies investing in Papua New Guinea, including protection against nationalization, while the Papua New Guinea government agreed to ease restrictions on foreign ownership and the granting of visas for skilled workers.

By the latter part of 1990, it was clear that the loss of the Panguna mine had hurt Papua New Guinea's mining industry, but, overall, the industry had shown considerable strength. Bougainville Copper had been the big loser. Although helped by a K61.3 million insurance settlement, it recorded a net loss for the first half of 1990 of K69.3 million, in contrast to a profit of K37.7 million for the previous six months.[143] Ok Tedi Mining Ltd., however, reported a seventeen per cent rise in profits for 1989, from K20.7 million to K24.2 million, its best performance to date. This reflected high production during the second half of 1989, after a failure by the mine's ore delivery system during the first half of the year (resulting in a first half loss of K8.1 million).[144]

For newer mining projects, the situation seemed mixed—that is, difficult, but with room for optimism. Although not due to be operating at full capacity until the end of 1993, the Porgera project completed its first stage without incident and made its first shipment of gold bullion in September 1990. Moreover, the joint venture operator announced that it was revising the mine's resources upward by eleven per cent (to 900,000 ounces per year during the first six years of operation, at a cash cost of U.S.$105 per ounce, and U.S.$150 over the eighteen year life of the mine).[145] Keeping the Porgera project alive, however, had not been without its difficulties. The projects manager, Placer Dome (with a twenty-three per cent stake), found it difficult to secure financing for the mine and had to provide the development money from its own resources (which are substantial), with bank borrowing only possible once the mine was producing.

Placer Dome's exposure in Papua New Guinea has led some analysts to express concern about the security of investment in Papua New Guinea," but its president and chief executive, Tony Petrina, has stated, in reference to its interests in Misima and Porgera, that "we believe the risks are manageable and the potential rewards are considerable."[146] With twenty-two operations in seven countries, Placer Dome has indicated that it is willing "to go where the deposits are good and the risks are considered manageable."[147] The two largest sources of its overseas exposure are Papua New Guinea and Chile, where its combined investments amount to C$700 million. Part of its strategy for making the risks "manageable" in such countries is to take out political risk insurance on half of its exposure.

The most important setback in the country's mining sector has been a decision by Kennecott and Niugini Mining to put the Lihir project on hold. When previous owner BP Minerals was considering floating its interests in 1988, it offered only a potential fourteen per cent rate of return on investment. Since then the price of gold had dropped by some forty dollars an ounce and costs of project had gone from U.S.$700 million to over U.S.$1 billion. Cash costs of production, in terms of ounces of gold, had risen from an estimated U.S.$130 per ounce in 1989 to U.S.$180 in 1990. By mid-1990 financing for the project was proving hard to come by and the partners in the venture appeared to be in no hurry to proceed.

In May, Niugini Mining Ltd, chairman Geoffrey Loudon, stated that banks were not refusing outright to lend money for the project, they were "just being coy," and he noted that "there are not too many banks wanting to lend to Papua New Guinea at the moment."[148] Some executives from RTZ had come to view Lihir as marginal at present gold prices and the company was facing strong capital demands from other projects (such as the Escondida copper mine in Chile and the Bingham Canyon copper facilities in Utah).[149] There were also indications that RTZ was waiting to see how negotiations relating to Bougainville turned out before proceeding with such a large undertaking. For its part, the national government was in no rush to push ahead with the project since this would mean its having to pay for its twenty per cent stake in what might prove to be an unviable project.

After completion of the final feasibility study for the Lihir project, in late October Kennecott announced that it was putting the project on hold. Kennecott's president cited "relatively low, weak gold prices" and a resultant "return on investment which we thought was too low" as the primary reasons for the decision.[150] Despite this setback, Kennecott and RTZ indicated that they were still committed to the project. For the moment, they were pursuing new drilling to look for high-grade ore nearer to the surface in order to improve the potential cash flow from the mine. They were also looking into new technology to reduce production costs. Given the size of the deposits it is certain that it will be developed at some point, but precisely when depends on a number of factors, including the price of gold and the Bougainville negotiations.

Part of the long-term government economic planning includes replacing revenue lost from Bougainville with new earnings from petroleum—a plan given a substantial boost in the wake of Iraq's invasion of Kuwait in mid-1990 and the subsequent rise in the price of oil. The focus of attention has been on the Iagifu/Hedinia and associated fields in the Southern Highlands, known collectively as the Kutubu project. The project is a joint venture involving Cheveron Niugini (twenty-five per cent), BP Petroleum Development (twenty-five per cent), the Ampolex Group (21.23 per cent), BHP Petroleum Inc. (12.5 per cent), Oil Search (10.02 per cent), and Merlin Petroleum/ Bond Energy (6.25 per cent). Development of the project is expected to cost U.S.$1.3 billion, with production reaching 90,000 barrels a day by late 1992. Also involved is a U.S.$300 million 265 kilometer pipeline that will carry the oil thirty-five kilometers offshore in the Gulf of Papua.

Local opposition emerged to the way in which the field and the pipeline was being developed. In particular, a local business consortium, Monticello Enterprises, was formed in an effort to have the pipeline built by local business interests rather than by the foreign-owned joint venture.[151] Cheveron argued that it needed to retain control of the pipeline to ensure the overall viability of the project and pointing to the difficulties in developing in over very rough terrain. The Monticello bid was rejected and, in mid-July, the government announced its strong support for the joint venture project and its aim to sign an agreement by November. Despite such assurances, the bid and its appeal to economic nationalism served to make Cheveron nervous and to raise broader issues about foreign investment in the country. For the Namiliu government, the project, which will contribute an estimated K1.4 billion in revenues over ten years, is crucial because of the impact of falling commodity prices and the closure of Bougainville. From the government's perspective, every effort must be made to accommodate the interests behind the project and to overcome any obstacles that stand in its way.

Conclusions

The fighting on Bougainville has stopped, but the crisis remains unsettled. The question of Bougainville's future political status in particular has yet to be resolved and the implications of the Panguna mine's closure continue to be felt throughout the country. The Bougainville crisis has thrown into sharp relief many of the problems facing Papua New Guinea, not the least of which is the whole strategy of reliance on mineral and oil wealth.

Foreign mining interests have been left feeling very uncertain about the future of mining in Papua New Guinea—at least in the short run. The sentiment among many in the mining industry concerning Papua New Guinea seems to be that, while the immediate future is difficult and uncertain, things will probably be alright in a decade or so. It is a belief that could be expressed about the political and economic situation in Papua New Guinea as a whole. Essentially, the national government has shown itself to be unable to deal effectively with a sustained regional dispute over mining. It was a difficult situation, but many in the industry and outside it feel that the national government should have been able to handle things much better. To make matters worse, the mining industry feels that BCL has been a model corporate citizen in recent years, as indicated by its good record of training and the K1 billion it has contributed to government revenue since 1972. In short, from the perspective of the industry, BCL did the best that it could but fell victim to still very sensitive political quarrels related to decentralization.

The current government has made significant progress in reforming national-provincial relations, but its efforts may not prove sufficient to avoid further serious conflicts. For one thing, as Bougainville has demonstrated, simply giving more to the provinces does not necessarily resolve conflicts at the provincial level. More money or power to certain interest groups, in fact, may only serve to increase resentment among those who benefitted least under previous arrangements and who continue to be left out under new ones. In addition, by implication, the Bougainville crisis threatens to weaken even further the legitimacy of the national government at the regional level. Despite some alarmist predictions, Papua New Guinea does not appear to be on the verge of breaking up for the time being, but the state clearly is in trouble and the next few years should prove extremely tricky for those trying to carry out reforms to hold it together and to provide it with a firmer basis of national support.

Who or what manner of government will carry out these reforms? Tohian's attempted coup, while it had little chance of success, did raise the specter of the possibility of a more serious attempt by segments within the military to seize power in the future. The prospect of a military coup in Papua New Guinea has been the subject of speculation for a number of years, especially after the first Fiji coup in May 1987, and the Bougainville crisis certainly provided the type of incident which often sparks disgruntled soldiers to act against a civilian government. Namaliu's civilian government has survived the country's first attempted coup, but a weakened national government and further deterioration of law and order throughout the country means that conditions tempting military intervention are likely to persist.

Beyond the immediate threat of a military take over, there has also been support expressed in some circles within the country for doing away with the parliamentary structure that Papua New Guinea inherited from its colonial past in favor of some, as yet poorly defined, system more in keeping with its tribal or clan-based traditions. While one could argue that the current structure already reflects these traditional interests, appeals to traditionalism, undoubtedly, will feature prominently in future debate about political reform in terms of the nature of the national government and national-provincial relations.

Efforts to promote some form of quasi-traditional political structure has an immediate bearing on the mining industry. Nowhere is this more apparent than with questions surrounding the relationship between common law and customary law and, especially, the colonial legacy by which the Crown owns mineral rights. This land issue has featured prominently in much of the conflict between local landowners and the national government and was an important factor behind the actions of Ona and the Bougainville Revolutionary Army, who called into question the right of the national government to have made any deal for mining on Bougainville. Suggested compromises by provincial politicians and recognized landowners on the island generally have supported the notion that it is the people of Bougainville alone who have the right to negotiate mining rights and that the national government's role should be a very limited one. The Namaliu government's "forum process" sought to provide a means of articulating local interests in mining negotiations, but the Bougainville crisis indicates that this initiative may not have gone far enough in trying to satisfy local demands.

Another issue of concern to local populations has been environmental degradation caused by mining. The anxiety expressed by the militants on Bougainville over the environmental impact of mining and their distrust of the assurances by officials and experts that they had things well in hand are sentiments shared by many throughout the country. While it is apparent that the national government has taken steps to limit the environmental impact of mining, where the cost of environmental protection has been so high as to threaten the viability of a project, the national government has demonstrated a willingness to back down or compromise. While such decisions might make short-term economic sense, they have served to increase many people's distrust of the government. Whether local authorities would do in better in protecting the environment should decision-making power be devolved to them is debatable—experience elsewhere makes one doubtful.

Despite the current turmoil and questioning of Papua New Guinea's reliance on mining revenue, there is no doubt that mining will remain an important feature of political and economic life in the country. This is, in part, related to the depressed conditions in agriculture, which are likely to continue for some time to come. Moreover, even though the Bougainville mine is closed and the exploration boom may be over, a number of large existing mines are still operating or soon to commence production and several major mining and oil ventures are going ahead. The closure of the Bougainville mine resulted in a drop in gold production nationally from 32.6 tons in 1988 to around nineteen tons in 1989. However, with Misima capable of producing 7.2 tons per year when in full production, Lihir twenty-four tons, and Porgera twenty-five tons, even without Panguna or new developments, Papua New Guinea's gold production is likely to rise to over one hundred tons per year by 1995.[152]

There are additional international factors which may contribute to the development of additional mining projects in Papua New Guinea over the next few years. A recent report by the Economist Intelligence Unit has suggested in the near future that mining investment is likely to be diverted from developed countries where environmental regulations are on the rise to those countries where such regulation is more lax.[153] Indonesia and Chile are cited as ideal examples of countries which offer relatively lenient environmental controls and a degree of political stability, but even Papua New Guinea might be attractive, if it is willing to forego the same environmental standards as developed countries, which is likely under existing conditions as well as under a more decentralized structure. Such optimistic prospects do not, however, mean that mining will at last be able to solve the country's overall developmental problems. Increased revenue alone has not proven to be the answer in the past and is unlikely to be in the future. The danger is that politicians may be tempted by the "pot at the end of the rainbow" which they perceive almost within their grasp once again to avoid making difficult decisions and implementing important reforms—despite the lessons to be learned from the Bougainville crisis.

Notes

1. Judith A. Bennett, *Wealth of the Solomons* (Honolulu: University of Hawaii Press, 1987), pp. 84-5. On shell money connections between the Solomon Islands and Papua New Guinea in recent times (especially with Bougainville), see John Connell, "The Bougainville Connection: Changes in the Economic Context of Shell Money Production in Malaita," *Oceania*, Vol. 48, No. 2, 1977, pp. 81-101.

2. R.W.Robson, *The Pacific Islands Year Book* (Sydney: Pacific Publications, 1944), p. 282. For additional background information on mining in Papua New Guinea in the late nineteenth and early twentieth centuries see: Allan M. Healy, *A History of the Development of the Bulolo Region, New Guinea* (Canberra: Australian National University, 1967); and H.N. Nelson, *Black, White and Gold: Gold Mining in Papua New Guinea, 1878-1930* (Canberra: Australian National University Press, 1976).

3. On the Kukukuku, see John K. McCarthy, *Patrol Into Yesterday* (Melbourne: F.W. Cheshire, 1963), pp. 90-126.

4. For biographical data on Levien see Ion Idriess, *Gold Dust and Ashes* (Sydney: Angus, 1933).

5. As for the other prominent pioneers, the Big Six squandered their fortunes back in Australia, while Shark-Eye Park retired to Canada as a millionaire.

6. Quoted in R.W.Robson, *Year Book*, p. 242.

7. Description of the Edie Creek camp is taken from, Edmond Demaitre, *New Guinea Gold* (London: Geoffrey Bles, 1936).

8. Demaitre, *New Guinea Gold* , p. 70.

9. McCarthy, *Patrol into Yesterday*, p. 85.

10. McCarthy, *Patrol into Yesterday*, p. 86.

11. Richard Curtain, "The Migrant Labour System and Class Formation in Papua New Guinea," in *South Pacific Forum*, Vol. 1, No. 2, 1984, p. 133.

Also see, Colin Newbury, "Labour Migration in the Imperial Phase: An Essay in Interpretation," *Journal of Imperial and Commonwealth History*, Vol. 3, No. 2, 1975, pp. 234-56; and Colin Newbury, "Colour Bar and Labour Conflict on the New Guinea Goldfields, 1935-1945," *Australian Journal of Politics and History*, Vol. 21, No. 3, 1975, pp. 25-38.

12.James Sinclair, *Wings of Gold: How the Aeroplane Developed New Guinea* (Sydney: Pacific Publicaitons, 1978).

13. The discussion of Burns Philp and Carpenter comes from Kenneth Buckley and K. Klugman, *The Australian Presence in the Pacific: Burns, Philp 1914-1948* (Sydney: George Allen & Unwin, 1983).

14. H.E.Stephensen, ed., *Bougainville: The Establishment of a Copper Mine* (St.Kilda: Construction, Mining, Engineering Publications, n.d.); contains reprints of "The N.H. Fisher Report 1936" (pp. 362-71), and "The J.E. Thompson Report 1962" (pp. 374-79) on gold mining on Bougainville. The Thompson report provides official gold production figures for Bougainville (p. 375): 1935-41 production was 1,789 ounces, worth £19,497; no production 1949-55; and for 1949-55, production was 491 ounces, worth £5,013.

15. On development of the mine, see H.E. Stephensen, *Bougainville*; Bougainville Copper Pty. Ltd., *Bougainville Copper: An Introduction*, n.d.; Richard Bedford and Alexander Mamak, *Compensation for Development: The Bougainville Case* (Christchurch: Department of Geography, University of Canterbury, 1977); Raymond F. Mikesall, *Foreign Investment in Copper Mining* (Baltimore: Johns Hopkins University Press, 1975); C. O'Faircheallaigh, *Mining and Development* (London: Croom Helm, 1984); M.L. Treadgold, *The Regional Economy of Bougainville* (Canberra: Development Studies Centre, Australian National University, 1978); Bougainville Copper Ltd., *Annual Report*, published yearly; S. Zorn, "Bougainville: Managing the Copper Industry," in *New Guinea and Australia, the Pacific and Southeast Asia*, Vol. 7, No. 4, 1973, pp. 23-40.

16. John Momis and Eugene Ogan, "Bougainville '71: Not Discovered by CRA," in *New Zealand and Australia, the Pacific and Southeast Asia*, Vol. 6, No. 2, 1972, pp. 32-40.

17. Bedford and Mamak, *Compensation for Development*, pp. 10-11. On the indigenous people of the area, see Douglas Oliver, *Bougainville: A Personal History* (Melbourne: Melbourne University Press, 1973); Eugene Ogan, *Business and Cargo: Socio-economic Change among the Nasioi of Bougainville* (Canberra: New Guinea Research Bulletin, Australian National University, 1972); Donald D. Mitchell II, "Frozen Assets in Nagovisi," in *Oceania*, Vol. 53, No.1, 1982, pp. 55-66. Also see, T.K. Moulik, *Bougainville in Transition* (Canberra, Development Studies Centre, Australian National University, 1977).

18. Bougainville Mining Ltd., *Prospectus*, 1971.

19. "Bougainville Mining Ltd., 1973, Half Year Report," in Stephensen, *Bougainville*, pp. 384-85.

20. "Bougainville Mining Ltd., 1973, Half Year Report," in Stephensen, *Bougainville*, pp. 384-85.

110   *Papua New Guinea*

21. See Philip Daniel and Rod Simms, *Foreign Investment in Papua New Guinea: Policies and Prospects* (Canberra: National Centre for Development Studies, Australian National University, 1986), pp. 51-57.
22. See Bedford and Mamak, *Compensation for Development.*
23. Diana Conyers, *The Provincial Government Debate* (Boroko: Institute of Applied Social and Economic Research, 1976); Ralph Premdas, "Ethnonationalism, Copper and Secession on Bougainville," in *Canadian Review of Studies in Nationalism*, Vol. 4, No. 2, 1977, pp. 247-65; Leo Hannett, "The Case for Bougainville Secession," in *Meanjin Quarterly*, Vol. 34, No. 3, 1975; N. Sharp, "The Republic of the North Solomons," in *Arena*, No. 40, 1975, pp. 119-27; Alexander Mamak and Richard Bedford, *Bougainville Nationalism* (Christchurch: Department of Geography, University of Canterbury, 1974).
24. Douglas Oliver, "The Winds of Change," in Stephensen, *Bougainville,* p. 95.
25. R.L. Kay, "Mine Operations at Bougainville," in Stephensen, *Bougainville*, p. 81.
26. Lamar F. Hutchinson and Trevor A. Pfeiffer, "Project Management," in Stephensen, *Bougainville*, p. 105.
27. Kenneth Good and Peter Fitzpatrick, "The Formation of the Working Class," in Azeem Amarshi, et al., *Development and Dependency: The Political Economy of Papua New Guinea* (Melbourne: Oxford University Press, 1979), p. 142.
28. Ralph Premdas, "Political Science in the South Pacific: A Survey of the Literature and an Agenda of What Needs to be Done," in *Journal of Pacific Studies*, Vol. 9, 1983, p. 186.
29. C. O'Faircheallaigh, "Review of Papua New Guinea's Mineral Policy 1964-82: Some Preliminary Findings," in D. Gupta and S. Polume, eds., *Economic Policy Issues and Options in Papua New Guinea* (Canberra: Development Studies Centre, Australian National University, 1984), p. 64.
30. Rio Tinto Zinc Ltd., *Annual Report 1979.*
31. "Bougainville Growth will Beat Price Fall," in *Times of Papua New Guinea*, 26 April 1984, p. 27.
32. In 1981, Prime Minister Julius Chan referred to Ok Tedi as "the pot of gold" that was to be the country's salvation.
33. For information on the initial establishment of the Ok Tedi mine, see Richard Jackson, *Ok Tedi: The Pot of Gold* (Boroko: University of Papua New Guinea, 1982); William S. Pintz, *Ok Tedi: Evolution of a Third World Mining Project* (London: Mining Journal Books, 1984); "Ok Tedi Gold—A Copper Bottomed Investment," in *Asia Banking,* March 1985, p. 16; "Kennecott's Midas Touch," in *Asia Banking,* March 1985, pp. 19-20, and 23; and "The Ok Tedi Crock of Gold," in *Islands Business,* June 1983, pp. 14-16.
34. For information on the ethnography of the people of the region, see F. Barth, *Ritual and Knowledge among the Baktaman of New Guinea* (New Haven: Yale University Press, 1975); Dan Jorgensen, "Life on the Fringe: History and Society in Telefolmin," in *The Plight of Peripheral People in Papua New Guinea: Volume I: The Inland Situation* (Cambridge, MA: Cultural Survival, 1981), pp. 59-79; Dan Jorgenson, Taro and Arrows (Ph.D. Thesis, University

of British Columbia, 1981); and P. Quinlivan, "Afek of Telefolmin," in *Oceania*, Vol. 25, 1954, pp. 17-22.

35. Jackson, *Ok Tedi*, p. 69.

36. See Daniel and Dims, *Foreign Investment*, pp. 61, and 66-67.

37. For further details on the negotiations see Pintz, *Ok Tedi*, pgs. 72-78, and 96-97.

38. *Asia Banking*, March 1985, p. 16.

39. "Doubt Over Next Stage," in *Times of Papua New Guinea*, 21 June 1984, pp. 1-2.

40. "$288m for Ok Tedi," in *Islands Business*, May 1986, pp. 6-7.

41. "Double Talk for Ok Tedi," in *Times of Papua New Guinea*, 21 June 1984, p. 1; "New Cyanide Spill at Ok Tedi Mine," in *Times of Papua New Guinea*, 2 June 1985, p. 3; "Cyanide Spill May Stay a Mystery," in *Times of Papua New Guinea*, 28 July 1985, p. 7.

42. "MP to Seek Court Order Closing Ok Tedi Mine," in *Financial Times*, 10 October 1989, p. 36; and "Fury Over Waste Dumping," in *Financial Times*, 13 October 1989, p. 32.

43. R. Jackson and T.S. Ilave, *The Ok Tedi Monitoring Project: Report No. 1* (Boroko: Institute of Applied Social and Economic Research, 1983).

44. "Ok Tedi: Questions that Still Need Answers," in *Times of Papua New Guinea*, 14 June 1984, pp. 8-9.

45. The IASER report is summarized in R. Jackson, "A Progress Report on the Monitoring of Ok Tedi and Some Policy Questions Relating to Monitoring in Papua New Guinea," in Gupta and Polume, *Economic Policy*, pp. 76-80.

46. See Raymond Goodman, Charles Lepani, and David Morawetz, *The Economy of Papua New Guinea* (Canberra: Development Studies Center, Australian National University, 1985); C.G. Goldthorpe, *Plantation Agriculture in Papua New Guinea* (Port Moresby: Institute of National Affairs, 1985); and Michael Chossudovsky, "Income Differentiation in Papua New Guinea," in *South Pacific Forum*, Vol. 4, No. 1, 1987, pp. 1-26.

47. See sources in note.25. Also see, "Gold Rush Hits Islands of South Pacific," in *Asian Wall Street Journal*, 3-4 January 1986; and Robert Keith-Reid, "Scrambling for Pacific Gold," in *Islands Business*, December 1985, pp. 10-13.

48. *Post Courier* (Port Moresby), 3 August 1987, p. 11.

49. "Threat to the Mines," in *Times of Papua New Guinea*, 2 June 1985, p. 3.

50. New Guinea Goldfields, *Wau Mine Upgrading Environmental Plan* (Natural Research Systems Pty. Ltd., 1985).

51. "Record First-half Result at Renison," in *Financial Times*, 10 February 1989, p. 24; Renison's New Guinea Goldfields recorded an A$1.75 million loss during the last half of 1988, while overall Renison recorded a healthy profit. Also see "Mine Closing," in *Islands Business*, October 1989, p. 48.

52. "PNG Govt. Share," in *Islands Business*, December 1985, p. 7.

53. *Fiji Sun*, 29 January 1987, p. 14.

54. *Post-Courier*, 27 July 1987, p. 8.

55. *Sydney Morning Herald*, 6 October 1987, p. 27.

56. *Fiji Sun*, 5 February 1987.

57. "MIM Floats World's 'Biggest Gold Mine'," in *The Australian*, 6 October 1987, p. 12.

58. Porgera Joint Venture, *Porgera Project Environmental Plan* (Natural Research Systems Pty. Ltd., 1988); and *Sydney Morning Herald*, 30 October 1987, p. 23.

59. Chris Sherwell, "Papua New Guinea's Porgera Gold Estimate Increased 26%," in *Financial Times*, 11 April 1989, p. 36.

60. *Financial Times*, 10 February 1989, p. 24; and *Islands Business*, November 1989, p. 51.

61. Chris Sherwell, "MIM Revives Stalled Issue of Highlands Gold Mine," in *Financial Times*, 3 November 1989, p. 20.

62. *Financial Times*, 1 February 1990, p. 26.

63. Colluvial ore refers to ore found in rubble and silt exposed by an earlier landslip or earthquake.

64. See Rowan Callick, "Going for Gold," in *Islands Business*, October 1988, pp. 6-11; and S.K. Witcher, "Stone Age Characters Thrive from Asian Klondike," in *Asian Wall Street Journal*, 9-10 December 1988, pp. 1 and 6.

65. Permission was given after completion of the environmental impact study; *Mt. Kare Colluvial Gold Project Environmental Plan* (Melbourne: Mt. Kare Mining Pty. Ltd., 1988).

66. Rowan Callick, "Going for Gold," p.11.

67. *Financial Times*, 15 December 1988, p. 32.

68. Glenn Burge, "Lihir Prospect May Hold 14m Ounces of Gold," in *Sydney Morning Herald*, 30 July 1987, p. 27.

69. *Post-Courier*, 30 July 1987, p. 9; and *Post-Courier*, 3 August 1987, p. 1.

70. "Lihir Gold Deposit May Be the Largest Outside South Africa," in *Financial Times*, 8 February 1989, p. 38; and see "Niugini Seeks to Raise A$70m-A$100m," in *Financial Times*, 7 March 1989, p. 27.

71. *Financial Times*, 29 March, 1989, p. 31; and "Texas in PNG," in *Pacific Islands Monthly*, April/May 1989, p. 35; Battle Mountain was spun off from Pennzoil in 1985.

72. Kenneth Gooding, "Battle Mountain's Crock of Gold," in *Financial Times*, 2 January 1990, p. 18.

73. Institute of Applied Social and Economic Research, *Social Impact Study of the Misima Gold Mine* (Port Moresby: Department of Minerals and Energy, 1986).

74. "Chan's Gold Move Probed," in *Fiji Sun*, 11 October 1986, p. 8; "Chan Digs into Gold for Coming Elections," in *Fiji Sun*, 12 October 1986, p. 6; "Sir Julius Faces Attack Over Family, Gold Shares," in *Fiji Sun*, 14 October 1986, p. 8; and "Moresby Bank Lending Prompts Call for Probe," in *Fiji Sun*, 18 October 1986, p. 9.

75. "Gold Report Digs Up Names," *Islands Business*, May 1987, pp. 11-12.

76. Natural Research Systems, *Misima Project Environmental Plan* (Port Moresby: Placer PNG Pty. Ltd., 1987).

77. Glenn Burge, "Placer's Raising to Develop Misima," in *Sydney Morning Herald*, 16 July 1987, p. 21.; and "Placer Cleared for $270m Gold Project in PNG," in *Sydney Morning Herald*, 23 June 1987, p. 27.

78. "PNG Govt Obstacle for Placer Project," in *The Australian*, 8 October 1987, p. 16; and "Placer Finds PNG Snag," in *Australian Financial Review*, 29 October 1987, p. 52.

79. "Placer Settles its Misima Financing," in *Australian Financial Review*, 6 November 1987, p. 20.

80. "PNG Approves $286m Placer Island Gold Mine," in *Sydney Morning Herald*, 18 December 1987.

81. "Lessons for the Region from the Mine at Misima," in *Islands Business*, January 1990, pp. 51-52. The article is based on a report by the South Pacific Regional Environmental Programme on the effects of mining at Misima.

82. "PNG Gold Finds Hailed by City Res," in *The Australian*, 6 July 1987, p. 17.

83. "Talks Continue on PNG Gold Projects," *Financial Times*, 15 December 1988, p. 32.

84. Travis Q. Linay, "The Mineral Industry of Other Pacific Islands," in *Minerals Yearbook*, Vol. 3 (Washington, DC: United States Department of the Interior, 1987), p. 1163.

85. *The Australian*, 11 December 1987, p. 16.

86. *Australian Financial Review*, 7 August 1987, pp. 1-2.

87. Chris Sherwell, "Exploiting the Boom," in *Financial Times*, 3 April 1989, p. 16.

88. *Post-Courier*, 29 July 1987, p. 31.

89. Chris Sherwell, "Gold in Those Hills," in *Financial Times*, 3 April 1989, p. 16.

90. Coverage in the media of events on Bougainville has been extensive. Among the more important initial surveys of the situation are: David Robie, "Bougainville: One Year Later," in *Pacific Islands Monthly*, November 1989, pp. 10-18; and Bill Standish, "Bougainville: Undermining the State in Papua New Guinea," in *Pacific Research*, November 1989, pp. 3-5, and 10;

91. *Pacific Islands Monthly*, January 1988, p. 26.

92. *Pacific Islands Monthly*, April 1988, p. 28.

93. Carrie Albon, "Francis Ona: The Man Behind the Legend," in *Islands Business*, May 1989, pp. 27-30.

94. *Pacific Islands Monthly*, January 1988, p. 28.

95. See David Robie, "Bougainville."

96. See Wally Hiambohn, "Landowners Resort to Sabotage in Panguna," in *Pacific Islands Monthly*, January 1989, pp. 16-19.

97. *Pacific Islands Monthly*, February 1989, p. 41.

98. *Times of Papua New Guinea*, 16-22 February 1989, p. 4.

99. Frank Senge, "Sabotage, Killings Grow as Bougainville Crisis Deepens," in *Pacific Islands Monthly*, April/May 1989, pp. 12, 14. Disturbances began on 17 March, when a lone gunman armed with a semi-automatic rifle sprayed the laborers' house on Arova Plantation with bullets, killing two

highlanders and wounding another three. The act was reported to have been motivated by retribution for the killing a week earlier of a woman, and was not related to the Ona case. The following week, riots and mass demonstrations occurred in the towns of Toniva, Kieta, and Arawa. In addition, Arova International Airport was burnt down, the runway dynamited and two aircraft burnt. The police armory at Buin was also raided and burnt and district office at Torokina burnt.

100. *Provincial Select Committee Report on the Panguna Crisis* (Arawa: North Solomons Provincial Government, 1989).

101. Peter Larmour, "Ethnicity and Decentralisation in Melanesia: A Review of the 1980s," in *Pacific Viewpoint,* in press.

102. *Times of Papua New Guinea,* 4-10 May 1989; *Pacific Islands Monthly,* June 1989, p. 35; *Asian Wall Street Journal,* 25 May 1989, p. 8; and "Turning Purple in Bougainville," in *The Economist,* 13 May 1989, p. 30.

103. *Pacific Islands Monthly,* October 1989, p. 23.

104. *Times of Papua New Guinea,* 1-7 June, 1989, p. 1.

105. *Pacific Islands Monthly,* July 1989, p. 17. Those instructed to draw up the plans were Paul Bengo, Morea Vele, Web Kanawi, and Henry ToRobert.

106. Richard Dinnen, "Bougainville Nightmare," in *Pacific Islands Monthly,* July 1989, p. 18.

107. "New Worries for Bougainville," in *Pacific Islands Monthly,* July 1989, pp.34-35.

108. Carrie Albon, "The Colonel Goes After Ona," in *Islands Business,* August 1990, p. 24.

109. "Troubled Times Ahead," in *Pacific Islands Monthly,* September 1989, pp. 31-33.

110. See Rowan Callick, "Learning from Bougainville," in *Islands Business,* October 1989, pp. 21, 23-25, and 27-28.

111. *Times of Papua New Guinea,* 7-13 September 1989, p. 4.

112. *Post-Courier,* 14 September 1989. Kauona had been a lieutenant in the PNG Defence Force before deserting in 1988 to join Ona and the militants. One other important figure among the militants was Damien Damen, who lead a cargo cult (the "50 toea people") supportive of an independent Bougainville (see Carrie Albon, "Church Intervention Fails: Could Secession Succeed?," in *Islands Business,* July 1989, p. 27).

113. On the events of early September, see Carrie Albon, "Back to the Battle," in *Islands Business,* October 1989, pp. 12-13, and 16-18; and *Pacific Islands Monthly,* October 1989, p. 11.

114. Frank Senge, "Back to Square One," in *Pacific Islands Monthly,* August 1989, pp. 10-11

115. Carrie Albon, "New Colonel in Charge of Bougainville," in *Islands Business,* November 1989, pp. 18-20.

116. Albon, "New Colonel," p. 19.

117. *Pacific Islands Monthly,* December 1989, pp. 34 and 36.

118. *Pacific Islands Monthly,* December 1989, pp. 34 and 36.

119. *Pacific Islands Monthly,* January 1990, p. 29.

120. *Pacific Islands Monthly,* January 1990, p. 29.

121 *Pacific Islands Monthly*, January 1990, p. 32.

122. Kenneth Gooding, "Bougainville Copper Mine to be Moth-balled," in *Financial Times*, 3 January 1990, p. 22; Frank Senge, "Counting the Losses in a State of War," in *Pacific Islands Monthly*, February 1990,. pp. 12-13. BCL also found itself embroiled in a court case in Australia when the four insurance companies with whom it held policies covering the mine denied liability for the losses incurred as a result of the security problems. The insurance companies were taken to court in Melbourne and asked to pay A$500 million. The matter was settled out of court for A$102.5 million at the end of February (*Financial Times*, 1 March 1990, p. 19).

123. This included U.S.$80 million from the International Monetary Fund and U.S.$50 million from the World Bank in the form of a structural adjustment loan (Chris Sherwell, "Papua New Guinea Calls for Financial Assistance," in *Financial Times*, 16 January 1990, p. 4). An agreement was reached with the International Monetary Fund for a three-year K82 million standby facility in late February (Chris Sherwell, "Papua New Guinea in Defence of Integrity," in *Financial Times*, 20 February 1990. p. 4). The International Monetary Fund asked for no extra adjustments beyond those already announced by the government in January.

124. Sherwell, "Papua New Guinea in Defence of Integrity."

125. Chris Sherwell, "Killings Force CRA Group to Withdraw fro Bougainville," in *Financial Times*, 8 February 1990, p. 14; and "Operation Evacuation," in *Pacific Islands Monthly*, March 1990, p. 18

126. Robin Bromby, "The Bougainville Horror," in *Pacific Islands Monthly*, February 1990, pp. 23-25; and Rowan Callick, "The Agony of Bougainville," in *Islands Business*, February 1990, pp. 12-15, and 17-18.

127. Robin Bromby, "Then there is Light: The Hope after Bougainville," in *Pacific Islands Monthly*, March 1990, pp. 23-25.

128. Robin Bromby, "The Bougainville Horror," p. 24.

129. *Financial Times*, 19 January 1990, p. 4.

130. Frank Senge, "Round One for the Militants," in *Pacific Islands Monthly*, April 1990, p. 16; and "Bougainville Left to Rebels as PNG Troops Pull Out," in *Financial Times*, 14 March 1990, p. 4. Also see Rowan Callick, "The War Port Moresby Lost," in *Islands Business*, March 1990, pp. 18-22.

131. One of the incidents involved allegations that security forces had looted the Panguna mine before leaving (*Fiji Times*, 27 February 1990, p. 8).

132. On the attempted coup, see Rowan Callick, "Bougainville: Revolutionary Army Takes Charge, in *Islands Business*, April 1990, pp. 21-22; Frank Senge, "Namaliu vs Tohian: What Really Happened?," in *Pacific Islands Monthly*, April 1990, pp. 16-17; "PNG Coup Bid Fails," in *Fiji Times*, 16 March 1990, p. 1; and "Papua Coup Fails," in *Financial Times*, 16 March 1990, p. 4.

133. Frank Serge, "Bougainville: The Crisis Deepens," in *Pacific Islands Monthly*, June 1990, p. 17; also see *Financial Times*, 9 May 1990, p. 4.

134. *Financial Times*, 18 May 1990, p. 6; *Financial Post*, 18 May 1990, p. 2; and *Far Eastern Economic Review*, 31 May 1990, p. 14.

135. Frank Serge, "The Crisis Deepens," p.18.

116 *Papua New Guinea*

136. Sean Dorney, "Talk of Peace," in *Islands Business,* September 1990, pp. 54-58; also see *Financial Times,* 7 September 1990, p. 4..

137. Mary-Louise O'Callaghan, "Bougainville Blockage", in *Far Eastern Economic Review,* 25 October 1990, p. 13.

138. The coffee industry was particularly hard hit by low prices and disease (see "Coffee Anyone?" in *Islands Business,* October 1990, p. 22. In addition, companies owning cocoa and coconut plantations had been hurt by low prices and, in some instances, by the loss of control of plantations on Bougainville (see "Crop Crisis Worsens as PNG Restricts Funding," in *Pacific Islands Monthly,* October 1990, pp. 27,30. One result of the downturn in plantation agriculture was the loss of employment by a few thousand workers.

139. The Consultative Group for Papua New Guinea is comprised of the World Bank, International Monetary Fund, Asian Development Bank, Australia, Japan, New Zealand, the European Community, and the United States.

140. *Financial Times,* 19 May 1990, p. 90, p. 2.

141. see *Pacific Islands Monthly,* August 1990, p.17.

142. "Making Investment Safer," in *Pacific Islands Monthly,* October 1990, p. 32.

143. *Financial Times,* 14 August 1990, p. 19. CRA also suffered. CRA's earnings for the first half of 1990 were down twenty-seven per cent (to A$269.5 million) because of falling aluminium prices and problems on Bougainville. In particular, its copper-gold operations reported an A$16.9 million loss, down from an A$26.3 million profit for previous half (*Financial Times,* 5 September 1990, p. 23).

144. *Financial Times,* 3 May 1990, p. 22; and *Pacific Islands Monthly,* July 1990, p. 32. During 1989, the Ok Tedi mine produced 135,308 tons of copper (up from 52,677 in 1988) and 510,367 ounces of gold (up from 381,365 in 1988), with total revenue rising nearly thirty-nine per cent to K460.4 million.

145. "Good-news Pogera Beats the Odds," in *Pacific Islands Monthly,* October 1990, pp. 31-32.

146. *Financial Post,* 18 May 1990, p. 18. Papua New Guinea accounts for a quarter of Placer Dome's gold output. Also see John Schreiner, "Placer $1B War Chest Seeks Target: CEO Wants to Buy More Properties," in *Financial Post,* 8 October 1990, p. 14.

147. Barbara Durr, "Placer Dome Puts a Shine on its Activities," in *Financial Times,* 23 October 1990, p. 25.

148. "Lihir Delay," *Pacific Islands Monthly,* June 1990, p. 26.

149. *Financial Times,* 22 August 1990, p. 24.

150. Kenneth Gooding, "Low Gold Prices Hold Back $1bn Lihir Island Project," in *Financial Times,* 31 October 1990, p.29

151. Mary-Louise O'Callaghan, "Trouble in Pipeline: Oil Controversy Further Erodes Confidence in PNG," in *Far Eastern Economic Review,* 14 June 1990, pp. 55-56; also see *Financial Times,* 24 July 1990, p. 34. Those behind Monticello Enterprises include the head of the PNG Banking Corporation,

two former finance secretaries, and an outspoken lawyer on landrights issues.

152. The Gold Institute (*World Mine Production of Gold, 1989-1993,* Washington, DC: Gold Institute, 1990) estimates that Papua New Guinea's gold production will rise from 1,083 million ounces in 1989 to 1.79 million in 1993.

153. See Kenneth Gooding, "Greening Cost of Mining will Outweigh Political Risks," in *Financial Times,* 19 April 1990, p.38.

4

The Solomon Islands

Despite repeated efforts to discover large mineral deposits, the Solomon Islands so far has failed to live up to its name, and nothing has been found comparable to the copper and gold deposits just across the border in Papua New Guinea.[1] The Spanish explorer Alvaro de Mendaña visited the archipelago in 1568 and provided it with its name, based on his belief that there were rich gold mines somewhere in the islands—the fabled mines of King Solomon. Mendaña spent six months unsuccessfully looking for gold before returning to Peru, where he sought support to lead another expedition to the islands. A second expedition under his command sailed in 1595, this time with the intent of establishing a colony. The attempt to establish a settlement on the island of Ndendi, in the Santa Cruz Group, failed and only a few stragglers survived. Thereafter, the islands received few other European visitors for the next two centuries, and the search for King Solomon's mines had to wait until the 1930s.

Gold was found in the hills behind Berande on Guadalcanal in 1932, with the field becoming known as Gold Ridge.[2] The extent of the gold deposits were uncertain. The terrain was extremely difficult and mining initially was limited to small shafts and simple sluice methods. No doubt envious of developments in New Guinea at the time, the administration of this poor, copra-producing colony passed a new mining law in 1937, in an effort to attract sufficient investment to increase gold production. About a month after the act was passed, Australian interests floated shares in Solomon Islands Gold Sluicing Ltd. in Melbourne, with the intention of initiating large-scale sluicing. The issue received little interest, however, and, by the end of the year, the company's plans had to be scaled downwards considerably.

Solomon Islands gold shares went through a brief boom on the Melbourne exchange in late 1939, but the bubble burst within a matter of weeks after an engineering report became public that recommended abandoning the field. Optimism returned in early 1941, when representatives of the Theodore group of Australia, which was associated with Emperor Gold Mining in Fiji, announced that they intended to look into the possibility of developing the Gold Ridge field. Later in the year, the group decided to initiate a five year program of further exploration and development, but the war intervened before any additional steps could be taken. Mining at Gold Ridge did not stop entirely during the war, and a few Australian miners continued to work deposits despite the Japanese occupation, but significant mining and exploration was not to resume in the colony until the 1950s.

The gold mining activities of Europeans on Guadalcanal created resentment among the local Melanesian population after payable gold was found in 1937. This resentment led to support for the Chair to Rule movement which was spreading through the colony seeking improved political and economic conditions from the British administration. In April 1939, one local headman from Aola, Guadalcanal, presented the colonial administration with a petition urging political reform. In his petition the headman noted: "about 3 1/2 years ago they have been digging the gold; but we don't know that it helps other people or our own island in the work of Priests or Deacons or teachers or Plantations or Government or Hospitals or any other different works."[3] The petition was ignored and, a short time later, the authorities arrested some of its leaders. The movement went underground after this, to reemerge towards the end of the war as Maasina Rule, centered on the island of Malaita.

British authorities drew up plans for the postwar reconstruction of the Solomon Islands in 1943 that called for major political and economic reforms. Among other things, the plans called for diversification of the economy and assessment of the potential for exploitation of mineral, fish, and timber resources. These proposals were given further expression in a 1945 ten-year plan prepared for the colony by the high commission for the Western Pacific. The period immediately following the end of the war was taken up primarily with reconstruction of the colonial infrastructure and agricultural sector of the economy. The reconstruction phase ended in 1955, when a system was instituted of five-year plans and direct British grants-in-aid to supplement local government earnings.

The mining sector received some attention in the early 1950s, and in 1952 the colonial government announced liberal terms for gold mining enterprises, as part of its effort to attract foreign investment.[4] The budget under the colony's first *Development Plan* (1955-1960) also included additional funds for mineral surveys. These initiatives resulted in further exploration on Guadalcanal, culminating in the announcement of important finds at Gold Ridge early in 1955.[5] The following year, Australian-based Clutha Development Company initiated an exploration program at Gold Ridge, but further work ceased when Clutha decided that its samples did not justify large-scale mining.[6] Small-scale alluvial mining continued, producing perhaps a few hundred ounces of gold a year, but this was not what the colonial authorities had in mind for the colony's mining industry.

During the late 1950s, government surveyors and foreign mining interests began to search for other metals and minerals elsewhere in the archipelago. The British Phosphate Commissioners discovered an estimated ten tons of phosphatic rock on Bellona in 1956. In the 1960s and early 1970s, several potential commercial mineral deposits were found on other islands: nickel on Santa Isabel and San Jorge; bauxite on Kolombangara, Vaghela, and Rennell; chromite on San Jorge; and copper on Guadalcanal, Florida, Rennell, and Santa Isabel. Of these various deposits, only those on Vaghela, Rennell, and Bellona were sufficiently attractive to foreign mining companies to warrant immediate further investigation. In the meantime, alluvial gold mining continued at Gold Ridge (yielding 400-700 ounces of gold a year by the early 1970s), which surveys indicated had gold deposits of around 10,000 ounces.

The Solomon Islands gradually moved towards independence during the 1970s. A new constitution was adopted in 1970, creating a single Governing Council with a majority of elected members. The functioning of the council centered on several committees, including one for natural resources, which were given the responsibility for initiating legislation. Constitutional reform in 1974 led to the replacement of the Governing Council with an almost completely elected Legislative Council with a chief minister who had the right to select his own cabinet. Solomon Mamaloni was appointed chief minister. Next, in early 1976, the Solomon Islands became internally self-governing and then, in July 1978, it became independent.

Political reforms were accompanied by economic policies, starting with the country's *Development Plan* for the years 1971-1973, aimed at reducing external dependence and achieving greater self-reliance. Specifically, the intention was to generate revenue from large resource-based projects in order to replace British aid. Accordingly, the government signed three preliminary agreements in 1972: (1) with Taiyo Ltd. of Japan to undertake tuna fishing, (2) with the Commonwealth Development Corporation to develop an oil palm industry on Guadalcanal, and (3) with Mitsui Mining & Smelting of

Japan to work the bauxite deposits on Rennell Island. The agreement with Taiyo formed a joint venture with the government known as Solomon Taiyo Ltd. The palm oil project also was a joint venture, between the Commonwealth Development Corporation and the government (with a small share going to local landowners). In addition to these initiatives, the government sought to promote import substitution through a large rice growing scheme on Guadalcanal, carried out as a joint venture between the government and C. Brewer & Co. Ltd. of Hawaii. In addition, the government encouraged development of the commercial forest industry, which was dominated by Levers Pacific Timbers (founded in 1968).

While most of these initiatives met with at least modest success, mining alone proved a failure. The focus of hope was the isolated raised coral atoll of Rennell.[7] At the time, the atoll was inhabited by about 1,300 ethnic Polynesians, a distinct minority community comprising about four per cent of the national population.[8] The Polynesians generally felt themselves superior to the Melanesian majority and were suspicious of outside authorities. The Rennellese had minimal relations with the outside world and possessed virtually nothing of a cash economy when mineral exploration began.

The primary deposits of bauxite are scattered throughout Rennell's dry western lagoon, which is also the only large site suitable for agriculture, with smaller quantities found on the eastern portion of the atoll.[9] Government geologists conducted initial testing of the deposits in 1967-68. Prospecting rights were then awarded by the government to Mitsui Mining & Smelting Company in early 1969. Next, government officials held meetings with the Rennellese to discuss the proposed mining project and compensation rates. The officials secured an agreement to allow further exploration with the provision that only Rennellese were to be employed by Mitsui. Mitsui set about completing work on an airstrip, building a rough road, and establishing a campsite. A feasibility study at the time estimated that there was twenty-eight million tons of recoverable bauxite on the island.

A problem with the project developed when the Rennellese expressed their dissatisfaction with existing compensation rates for damage to coconut palms. The islanders took their case to the High Court, where they won a favorable settlement in mid-1970. In September of the same year, the government, optimistic that mining would commence soon, began negotiations with the Rennellese. The islanders rejected the initial offer and a second offer was only accepted after protracted negotiations. For the Rennellese the issue was twofold: ensuring adequate economic benefits and deciding whether, in fact, they wished to allow a project that would have such a profound impact on their way of life. The agreement established compensation rates for land, crops, and certain trees. Each individual was to receive an allowance of SI$400 and members of the community would be entitled to five per cent of any royalties received by the government. Finally, in addition to having the land returned to them after the cessation of mining, the Rennellese were offered government land elsewhere in the country with a house. During 1970, a group of Rennellese toured various possible resettlement sites and decided on two possible locations. The total coast of the agreement was estimated to be around SI$1 million.

In early 1971, the government set about to acquire 24,000 hectares in western Rennell for a trial mine. Arguments arose over compensation for trees, as the Rennellese quickly set about after the initial agreement planting various trees in hopes of receiving compensation, and over determination of ownership. With disputes continuing, by mid-1972, the government had paid out some SI$65,000 for 130 hectares of mining and road land. Additional income was generated by employment of about seventy islanders in construction. Having spent almost SI$1 million, in August 1972, Mitsui withdrew its staff from the island and suspended further work. The decision was made on the basis of technical problems that emerged during the trial mine phase and because of depressed world prices for bauxite. The amount of cash provided to the Rennellese by the project had resulted in the construction of houses and water tanks, the opening of village stores, and the importation of large quantities of consumer goods. Some money was banked, but the cash was withdrawn as employment ceased and gradually other commercial activity died out.

Mining talks resumed in 1974, this time also involving Conzinc Riotinto of Australia (CRA), which was looking into bauxite deposits on Wagina, in the Western Solomons. After unsuccessful talks with the two companies individually, the government suggested that CRA and Mitsui consider a joint project to build an alumina plant in the Solomon Islands to process ore from their respective sites. The companies agreed to the proposal, reluctantly, and a feasibility report was prepared. The report was presented in April 1977, and suggested construction of the plant on Rennell. The estimated cost of the plant was SI$200 million. In subsequent negotiations, the companies expressed their belief that such a level of expenditure was not feasible given current market conditions. CRA allowed its prospecting licence to expire and pulled out of the Solomon Islands altogether, while Mitsui retained an office in Honiara and held on to its licence and conducted a few more tests on Rennell.

Against the backdrop of these negotiations, the government held talks on Rennell concerning final compensation settlements for the work that had been carried out. A settlement was finally reached in April 1975, for a total of SI$2 million. The government and Rennellese also engaged in discussions relating to the negotiations with CRA and Mitsui. The Rennellese became increasingly frustrated and continued to express their desire for Mitsui to develop a mine, but by the end of the 1970s it was clear to most of them that the likelihood of this happening was not very good.

The *Development Plan* for 1980-1984 provided an opportunity to assess the overall economic development of the Solomon Islands during the years leading up to independence. In terms of gross domestic product, the economy performed relatively well; at constant 1978 prices growing from SI$54.9 million in 1973 to SI$75.5 million in 1978, for an average annual increase over the four years of 6.6 per cent. This figure is somewhat less satisfying when the average annual population growth rate of 3.4 per cent is taken into account.[10] Exports played a large role in this increase, rising from around SI$9 million in 1970 to over SI$29 million in 1978, and allowing the country to maintain a relatively healthy trade balance. The export sector had also become much more diversified. Exports in 1965 were valued at SI$4.8 million, with copra accounting for SI$4.5 million (93%) of this amount. By 1973, the value of exports had risen to SI$8.8 million, with copra falling to second place (SI$2.8 million) behind timber (SI$3.7 million), and with fish (SI$1.5 million) in third place. Although copra exports, after reaching this low point, grew significantly during the remainder of the decade, so too did exports of timber and fish (with palm oil starting to play an important role in 1976), and by 1978 they were roughly equal in value. Severe fluctuations in the value of these commodities in 1974 and 1975, led the government to pursue a policy of even greater diversification.

In addition to the problem of market fluctuations, the wealth that had been generated remained poorly distributed regionally and across sectors of the economically active population. While monetary incomes rose from SI$21.2 million in 1973 to SI$34.8 million in 1978, the additional money was highly concentrated in the small commercial and salaried sectors located mainly on Guadalcanal. Rural households, which comprised ninety per cent of the population, accounted for only ten per cent of monetary income. The authors of the *Development Plan* estimated that the average annual cash income for all rural households in 1974, a boom year for cash crops, was only just over SI$50 per head (with fourteen per cent of the households having no cash income), a situation they referred to as "a disturbing picture."[11]

More cautious in its assessment of the potential for developing a mining industry, the government continued to see mining as possibly providing help in overcoming these crucial developmental problems. Thus, the 1980-1984 *Development Plan* stated in regard to mining: "Recognizing the difficulties in exploiting these resources, including the problem of securing prospecting and mining rights from local landowners, the government expressed hope that future mining development would help to provide foreign exchange earnings and generate employment."[12]

Optimism for mining's future in the 1980s was generated by the gold boom that swept across Melanesia in the wake of higher gold prices and new mining technology. In 1979, around A$200,000 worth of gold was exported. As the price of gold increased, a growing number of prospectors were attracted and the value of gold exports rose to A$600,000 in 1980. It then dropped to A$416,000 in 1981, as the price of gold began to decline. Most of the gold was produced by Solomon Islanders panning along the Chovohio River in the Gold Ridge area. Between 200 and 300 miners paid a SI$10 government license fee to pan for gold, which they sold to about a dozen licensed gold buyers (whose license fee was SI$500). Although the gold buyers paid the miners only a fraction of the value of the gold, prospectors earned on average about SI$2,000 a year. The government received additional revenue from a fifteen per cent tax on gold that was exported. This tax gave rise to smuggling, a problem which became increasingly serious during the 1980s and that led to the arrest of several expatriates.

The government did not wish to discourage local prospectors, but to generate higher levels of revenue from mining it realized that larger-scale mining operations were necessary. In 1971-72, government geologists surveyed Gold Ridge and concluded that, although there were no large deposits of gold, there was potential for open-cut mining to exploit low-grade ore. Such mining was thought capable of yielding up to 10,000 ounces of gold per year. CRA Exploration, which was also involved in examining the possibilities for bauxite mining at this time, looked into the Gold Ridge deposits but concluded that current world prices for gold did not justify developing a mine. When the price of gold rose in 1980-81, however, attention was once again drawn to Gold Ridge, and, in August 1982, the government invited tenders from international mining companies to prospect the area. Three tenders were received and, in early 1983, the government awarded a three year licence to Amoco Minerals Solomons Ltd. (a subsidiary of Amoco in Australia).[13] Elsewhere in the archipelago, British aid supported geological mapping in the Western Solomons. The results attracted some foreign interest, and Newmont took out a small licence to examine gold deposits on New Georgia in March 1983. By 1984, gold exports had risen in value to SI$700,000—an improvement, but not a substantial one, and there was considerable evidence that gold smuggling was on the rise.

The mining sector's potential assumed even more importance in the mid-1980s, as the Solomon Islands experienced severe economic problems. In 1984, the country began to experience a widening adverse trade balance as the value of exports declined and imports rose. The situation became even more serious in 1986, when the country suffered widespread damage from Cyclone Namu. One indicator of the deteriorating economic situation was the foreign debt, which rose from SI$79 million in 1984 to SI$280 million in 1988, at the same time that the gross domestic product was in decline. Moreover, the number of jobs in the country stagnated at around 24,000, while the population continued to grow rapidly.

Amoco began some work at Gold Ridge in the middle of 1983, and discovered that the site held up to three million recoverable ounces of gold. While holding onto its licence through its subsidiary Cyprus Minerals Australia, Amoco held back on any significant investment to develop the site. In early 1987, Arimco NL agreed to spend SI$3.5 million over three years for further exploration and development of the Gold Ridge site in exchange for a fifty pe rcent interest. This proposal was approved by the government in the middle of the year and a joint venture was formed under the name of Arimco (Solomon Islands) Ltd.

Another licence was granted to Mavua Gold Development, owned by Zanex Ltd. of Australia (a subsidiary of Houston Resources Ltd.), to work river gravel along the Chovohio River in conjunction with local landowners. Mavua Gold installed and recovery plant and began operations, until the plant was destroyed by Cyclone Namu in 1986. A secondhand plant was then installed with a production capacity of 17,000 ounces of gold per year. Among the other foreign companies to take out or apply for licences by the end of 1985 were Negri River Corporation, Dominion Mining, Canada Northwest, Kira Ona Gold, Aurex Alluvials Ltd., and Austpac Resources.

In virtually all cases, however, actual exploration and investment remained minimal in the face of what the companies saw as undue problems in dealing with the government and in settling agreements with local landowners, and Mavua Gold's operation remained the country's only large-scale gold mine. After considering the installation of additional recovery plants to boost production to 50,000 ounces per year, toward the end of 1987, Zanex expressed its frustration and accused the government of pursuing tax policies that were "not conducive for profitable mining."[14] The government, for its part, did not want to be seen by the population as serving the interests of foreign capital at the expense of the local population and, in general, was a long way from establishing uniform procedures for handling land-related issues. And many local landowners were wary of foreign mining interests. The government and regional business media continued to be upbeat on the possibilities for gold mining in the Solomon Islands,[15] but mining companies themselves had become increasingly ambivalent and mineral exploration declined throughout the Solomon Islands.

The Solomon Islands had another change of government in 1989, as Solomon Mamaloni became Prime Minister once again. The Prime Minister stated that his government was anxious to get the economy moving (in fact, the gross domestic product had risen by eight per cent in 1988), largely through concessions to the private sector. The 1990-1994 *Development Plan*, announced during the latter part of 1989, focused on agriculture (and to a lesser extent timber) and the government proclaimed its aim to transform the country's agricultural sector into "a modern and commercial enterprise within 10 years."[16] Mining did not feature prominently in the government's plans and, of some SI$100 million in possible foreign investments announced by the government in July 1989, mining accounted for only SI$1.9 million.[17]

As new legislation more favorable to mining interests remained mired in debate and negotiation in 1989, relatively little exploratory work was carried out by mining companies. Shortly after the 1989 election, Magnum Resources Ltd. of Australia, which held prospecting licences in the Solomon Islands, reported that it had carried out no work in the country during the first quarter of the year while it waited to see how the new government would treat the mining industry and specifically the extent to which its new policies would "assist exploration and overcome currently onerous (and often unresolvable) access problems."[18] Among the companies still active in the country, Regent Mining (involved in a joint-venture with Newmont Australia) completed access negotiations with landowners on one prospect, but, on the whole, by the end of the year the mining sector remained in the doldrums with most outstanding issues still unresolved.[19]

Largely in response to outside factors (discoveries in Papua New Guinea, sharp price rises for gold, and the like) and government encouragement, the Solomon Islands has witnessed periodic bouts of activity and optimism in the mining sector. These periods have been of relatively short duration, and after the latest round of gold fever interest once again has waned. Known ore deposits are small and the problems of getting a mining operation underway in the country are considerable. It now looks that if the Isles of Solomon are to produce any fabulous wealth it will have to be from some other source than mining—and for this, perhaps, the country should consider itself blessed.

Notes

1. For background on the Solomon Islands see: Judith Bennett, *Wealth of the Solomons* (Honolulu: University of Hawaii Press, 1987); and Peter Larmour and Sue Tarua, eds., *Solomon Islands Politics* (Suva: Institute of Pacific Studies, University of the South Pacific, 1983).

2. Further details concerning attempts to develop the Gold Ridge site are to be found in brief articles scattered throughout *Pacific Islands Monthly* from April 1932 until the latter part of 1941. Also see, John C. Grover, "A Concise History of the Search for Gold in the Solomons," in *Transactions of the British Solomon Islands Society*, Vol. 2, 1955, pp. 1-11; and John C. Grover, "The History of Exploratory and Mining Ventures in the Solomons," in *Geological Survey of the British Solomon Islands Memoir*, Vol. 1, 1955, pp. 10-15.

3. Quoted in Bennett, *Solomons*, p. 262. On the Chair and Rule and Maasina Rule movements, see Hugh Laracy, ed., *Pacific Protest* (Suva: Institute of Pacific Studies, University of the South Pacific, 1983).

4. "Miners Invited In: B.S.I. Wants a Gold Industry," in *Pacific Islands Monthly*, July 1952, p. 130.

5. "Important Gold Discovery Could Change Solomons' Economic Outlook," in *Pacific Islands Monthly*, September 1955, p. 11.

6. "Clutha on the Job in Guadalcanal," in *Pacific Islands Monthly*, October 1956, p. 22; and "Gold Ridge: Clutha will not Proceed," in *Pacific Islands Monthly*, October 1956, p. 22.

7. The atolls are about two hundred kilometers southwest of the larger island of San Cristobal and are themselves over twenty kilometers apart. Rennell atoll is eighty kilometers in length and sixteen kilometers wide, while Bellona is only 11.5 kilometers long and three kilometers wide.

8. The Rennell islanders only became Christians in 1939. Prior to the war the island was visited by anthropologist H.I.Hogbin (see, "A Note on Rennell Island," in *Oceania*, Vol. 2, No. 2, 1931, pp. 174-178). After the war more extensive research was carried out by Danish anthropologists,

including Kaj Birket-Smith (see, *An Ethnographical Sketch of Rennell Island,* Copenhagen: Munksgaard, 1956) and Torben Monberg (see, *The Religion of Bellona Island,* Copenhagen: National Museum of Denmark, 1966).

9. Information on the Mitsui bauxite mining project on Rennell is provided in Torben Monberg, *Mobile in the Trade Wind: The Reaction of the People on Bellona Island towards a Mining Project* (Copenhagen: The National Museum of Denmark, 1976); David Ruthven, "Rennell Bauxite," in Peter Larmour, ed., *Land in Solomon Islands* (Suva: Institute of Pacific Studies, University of the South Pacific, 1979), pp. 94-104; and Judith Bennett, *Solomons,* pp. 333-34. Also see: "Bauxite, Copper Interest in Rennell," in *Pacific Islands Monthly,* July 1969, p. 122; Judy Tudor, "The Boom at Last?," in *Pacific Islands Monthly,* July 1971, p. 51; Toshiro Ueda, "The Solomons Has a New Image for a Younger Generation," in *Pacific Islands Monthly,* June 1976, pp. 46-7; "Mitsui Abandons Rennell Bauxite," in *Pacific Islands Monthly,* August 1977, p. 64; and "Mitsui Still Interested in Solomons Bauxite," in *Pacific Islands Monthly,* September 1977, p. 60.

10. Although the Solomon Islands is relatively underpopulated, rapid population growth over the past few decades has been a major economic problem. During the 1980s, the situation became even more serious as the country's population grew by forty-five per cent between 1977 and 1986 (to reach a total of 286,000).

11. *Solomon Islands National Development Plan 1980-1984,* Vol. 1 (Honoraria, 1980), p. 22.

12. *Development Plan 1980-1984,* p. 91.

13. Material on mining in the early 1980s is based primarily on personal interviews; also see Robert Keith-Reid, "Solomons Mines Search," in *Islands Business,* June 1983, p. 18. Amoco is a subsidiary of Standard Oil Company of the United States.

14. John Connell, "Mining the Rim of Fire," in *Pacific Islands Monthly,* March 1988, p. 23.

15. See *Pacific Islands Monthly,* November 1987, p. 38. The optimistic article points to SI$2 million proposed by foreign interests for exploration and estimates that exploration fees in the immediate future will be greater than the country's foreign aid receipts.

16. *Pacific Islands Monthly,* September 1989, p. 34; also see *Solomon Islands National Development Plan 1990-1994* (Honiara, 1989).

17. *Pacific Islands Monthly,* August 1989, p.32.

18. *Pacific Islands Monthly,* June 1989, p. 35.

19. What some might consider a naively upbeat view about mining in the Solomon Islands was expressed in an American-sponsored mining survey published by the East-West Center in late 1989. Allen Clark, the author of the report and head of the center's minerals policy program, is reported to have characterized the Solomon Islands as one of the most "exciting" prospects in the region, despite the lack of firm information on the county (cited in *Fiji Times,* 15 November 1989, p.9).

5

New Caledonia

New Caledonia, consisting of one large island and several nearby smaller islands, was annexed by France in 1853 and has remained a French colony ever since.[1] The main island of New Caledonia, "La Grande Terre," contains very large deposits of nickel and chrome, as well as significant deposits of iron, manganese, and cobalt (and smaller amounts of other minerals). Mining was not, however, of much relevance in the early years of the colony. Initially, Europeans were attracted to New Caledonia by its sandalwood, and during the latter half of the nineteenth century it served primarily as a penal colony. New Caledonia's economy during the nineteenth century was dependent on French government expenditure, and to a lesser extent on pastoralism and farming. Agricultural development was not overly successful and the ending of convict labor in 1897 resulted in an economic crisis for the colony. The governor at the time hoped to build a viable colonial economy on the basis of coffee production and attracting French settlers, but coffee production remained limited and few additional colonists were enticed to come to New Caledonia.

The number of Europeans in New Caledonia was relatively limited until the 1870s, when the number of convicts increased sharply. The growing European presence placed considerable pressure on the Melanesian population and there were a number of violent clashes, culminating in a major outbreak of fighting in 1878. The bulk of Melanesian land was alienated during the latter half of the nineteenth century and disease and other factors contributed to a sharp decline in the indigenous population, until, by the early twentieth century, Melanesians represented only a little over half of the colony's population.

The history of mining in New Caledonia began in 1860, when a few prospectors began exploring river banks for gold. Gold mining

began in 1863, with activities culminating in the development of the
Fern Hill mine, in the far northeastern corner of the main island, by
four Australian prospectors in 1869. Optimistically referred to by
some as "l'Eldorado calédonien," the Fern Hill mine was acquired by
interests associated with Australian John Higginson.[2] Between 1871
and 1878 the mine produced 213 kilograms of gold, worth 650,000
francs. In 1878-79, hydraulic methods were introduced to mine gold
at Galarino (near Fern Hill) and St. Louis (in the south). The initial
interest in gold had only just begun to fade when a new mining rush
began in 1873, as the result of the discovery of rich copper veins at
Balade (also near Fern Hill) by a group of prospectors in 1872. La
Balade mine was also acquired by John Higginson. Between 1873 and
1902 the mine produced 50,000 tons of copper concentrate and 1,000
tons of matte copper.

As the quantities found of gold and copper proved to be relatively
small, the booms soon faded. In their place, nickel and chrome soon
emerged as major sources of mineral wealth. The origins of nickel
mining in New Caledonia are associated with the activities of Jules
Garnier, a geologist, and John Higginson, who became known as the
"Roi du Nickel" in New Caledonia. Jules Garnier was sent to New
Caledonia in 1863 by l'Ecole des Mines de Saint-Etienne to conduct
a geological survey of the colony. He returned to France in 1867, an
enthusiastic proponent of the potential for mining in New Caledonia.
Following the discovery of significant nickel deposits in 1873, a
nickel rush occurred between 1874 and 1877. This time, the rush
provided the basis for the establishment of a durable mining industry.
In 1880, Higginson obtained financial backing from the Banque
Rothchild to found the Société le Nickel (SLN), which quickly became
the largest mining enterprise in New Caledonia. Chromite mining
began in 1880, and proved to be a consistently profitable undertaking.
The Le Tiebaghi mine, owned largely by English interests, was found
to be one of the richest chromite mines in the world.

The 1880s was a volatile period for the nickel industry in New
Caledonia. Mining activities increased during the early part of the
decade, and a couple of nickel plants were built, including one by
SLN in 1883. By 1885, the SLN plant was the only one remaining in
the colony and overproduction caused several mines to close. SLN
found itself in financial difficulty and it was taken over by the
Banque Rothchild (representing German, French, and Belgian
investors) in 1890. The takeover resulted in an infusion of capital
which allowed SLN to open a second nickel plant. But increased
production of nickel in Canada, following the discovery of large

deposits in 1892, led to a weakening of the nickel market for SLN, which soon found itself in financial trouble again.

Increased world demand for nickel after 1898 helped to reverse the nickel industry's fortunes in New Caledonia just as the colony was facing an economic crisis brought on by the ending of convict labor. Finding few other areas of economic growth, mining began to assume a much more important place in the colonial economy. Some 600,000 tons of nickel was mined in New Caledonia between 1873 and 1900. As the industry continued to grow, between 1900 and 1923, New Caledonian nickel production amounted to over three million tons. Significantly, however, by the latter part of the nineteenth century, French interests in the New Caledonian mining industry had largely been replaced by British, Australian, and, to a lesser extent, German and Belgian interests.

The New Caledonian nickel industry encountered problems in the international market during the early twentieth century largely because of the monopolistic conditions that prevailed at the time. The nickel mining company Inco was founded in 1902 by J.P. Morgan of the United States.[3] Through Inco, Morgan was able to gain almost complete control of the Canadian nickel industry. By 1913, Inco accounted for fifty-five per cent of the world's nickel production, Mond Nickel (which later was taken over by Inco) another eleven per cent, and SLN the remaining thirty-three per cent. Thus, almost all of the world's nickel supply was controlled by Morgan and his associates, on the one hand, and by the Rothchild bank and its European associates, on the other hand. Rather than benefitting from its large share of world production, SLN found itself squeezed between Morgan and European interests. The North American market was closed to SLN by Morgan and most of SLN's nickel had to be exported to Europe, where a group of arms manufacturers and steel companies worked together to force SLN to agree to sell its nickel at a relatively low price.

Although it was the largest, SLN was not the only nickel mining company in the colony. The most important of the other nickel mining companies was Société Calédonienne Minier, which was founded in 1902. In addition, Société Hauts Fourneaux, a subsidiary of Maison Ballande (which already had extensive shipping and commercial interests in the colony), built a second nickel plant in 1910. Prior to this, much of New Caledonia's ore was exported in unprocessed form. The addition of another local furnace allowed for the significant reduction of production. The opening of the new Doniambo smelter also served to mark the beginning of Noumea's industrialization. One side effect of this was the emergence of an urban proletariat: the number of industrial workers in Noumea being 200 in 1910 (170 Europeans and 27 Melanesians) and rising to 320 by the First World War.[4]

New Caledonia produced an average of about 50,000 tons of chromite a year between 1900 and 1912, representing around twenty-five per cent of the world's supply. After 1912, although New Caledonian production levels remained fairly constant, its share of world production declined as new sources of chromite were discovered elsewhere. The Tiebaghi mine was the largest chromite mine in the colony. There were also a few smaller mines in the south. Société le Chrome initially was the largest chromite mining company in New Caledonia. It was bought by Société le Tiebaghi, primarily representing English capital, in 1910, which thereafter dominated production in the colony. The other major company engaged in chromite mining was Société Chimique du Chrome, which was owned mainly by English and Australian interests. The principal buyers of New Caledonian chromite were located in Germany and the United States.

While nickel and chromite dominated mining during the first half of the twentieth century, other minerals were mined in small quantities. Small deposits of copper and gold continued to be mined. Cobalt started to be mined on a regular basis in 1883 and continued to be mined until around the time of the First World War. Cobalt production averaged around 3,000 tons a year, and experienced a brief boom between 1900 and 1905, when annual production reached 5,000 tons. Cobalt mining went into decline and then ceased altogether following the discovery of large deposits in Canada and the Belgian Congo. South of the main island, some phosphate was mined on Walpole Island until the Second World War. A little oil was produced near Koumac. In addition, there was a little mining of manganese and antimony and there were attempts to mine mercury, lead, and zinc. Since nickel smelting depended on coal, attempts were made to find local sources. Large quantities of coal were discovered at Dumbea and Moindu, but the quality was too poor for the Doniambo furnaces and the industry continued to rely heavily on coal imports from Australia.

Finding workers for the mines became a serious problem with the end of convict labor. The Melanesian population resisted mine work and, in any event, was not considered to be well suited for it by Europeans. Instead, the Melanesians were pushed onto reserves, where they provided a pool of cheap labor for European farmers and ranchers. SLN had begun recruiting Chinese indentured laborers in

1884, but their number was never very great, and, by 1887, there were only 111 Chinese laborers in the colony. A few workers also were recruited from Indonesia (mainly from Java) in 1891, with the assistance of Dutch colonial authorities. Again, there were not very many of them, around 300 in total by 1903.

Société le Nickel started recruiting Japanese workers in 1892, and they came to represent the largest body of indentured workers in the mining industry prior to the First World War.[5] Between 1892 and 1919, there were 6,880 Japanese workers brought to New Caledonia. Starting in 1900, Vietnamese also were recruited. After an agreement in 1911 allowed Japanese workers to bring their families and take up residence, quite a few left mining for farming and commerce. They were sufficiently successful that before long Japanese immigrants were seen as a threat by members of the local European settler community. Lobbying efforts by European small business interests convinced the colonial authorities to stop further Japanese immigration and recruitment of Japanese workers was halted in 1919. Thereafter, the mining industry recruited most of its workers from Indonesia and Vietnam.

While nickel and chromite mining did help the New Caledonian economy avert disaster during the early years of the twentieth century, its overall benefit to the colony was limited. Taxes, royalties, and duties, in keeping with practices of the day, were fairly low and most employment went either to poorly paid indentured workers or to a small number of, often temporary, expatriate Europeans. Moreover, although New Caledonia was a French colony, the mining industry was largely in non-French hands and was oriented, for the most part, to countries other than France.

New Caledonia was not attacked by Germany during the First World War, but it suffered from labor and commodity shortages as a result of the disruption of shipping caused by the war. Overall, however, despite hardships suffered by the population of New Caledonia as a whole, the mining companies did very well during the war since the demand for nickel and chrome rose sharply. The British cut off mineral exports to Germany, but New Caledonia had little difficulty in finding other buyers for its minerals at prices far higher than those prevailing before the war. Thus, chromite prices increased from U.S.$14.75 a ton in 1914 to U.S.$47.99 a ton in 1918. Such price rises resulted in a sharp increase in the value of New Caledonia's exports, from 15.4 million francs in 1914 to forty-three million francs in 1920.

During the brief depression that followed the First World War, Inco forced the price of nickel down in an effort to drive a new competitor, Banco, out of business. The plan worked and Banco was forced into liquidation. At the same time, both SLN and Société Calédonienne Minière suffered as a result of the low prices. When Inco allowed the nickel price to rise after 1924, the two companies once again were able to record annual profits. The price of chromite declined after the war, largely because of a drop in demand, causing financial troubles for chromite miners in New Caledonia. One result of this was that SLN was able to take over the assets of Société le Chrome, giving it a commanding position over this portion of the colony's mining industry as well.

Nickel production in New Caledonia during the interwar years (mainly coming from mines at Thio, Bourail, and Kone) averaged around 150,000 tons of ore per year. In 1920, nickel and chromite accounted for forty-seven per cent of New Caledonia's exports by value. Other important exports included copra (sixteen per cent) and cotton (seven per cent), as well as meat, coffee, and hides. The value of the colony's exports grew to 98.8 million francs by 1928, on the eve of the depression, with mining assuming an increasingly important place in the colonial economy. At the same time that the value of exports was rising, the value of imports also went up—to 159.9 million francs in 1928. Overall, while mining helped to generate a degree of buoyancy in the colonial economy after the war, it failed to produce a particularly healthy economy. New Caledonia remained dependent on the French government for many of its expenses and, the relative success of the mining sector contributed to the neglect of agriculture and other areas of the economy. More investment capital was coming into the colony than ever before, but virtually all of it was going into mining, and capital for agriculture became even more difficult to acquire. Agriculture came to be left almost entirely to the Melanesians, while the European settler population, by and large, preferred to live off of the revenue from mining or the French government. Despite this trend toward the dominance of mining during the interwar years, however, New Caledonia still had the most diversified economy in the South Pacific.

The depression of the early 1930s caused a severe crisis in the mining sector as demand and prices dropped sharply. As a result, the value of New Caledonian exports dropped by more than half between 1928 and 1932 (exports were valued at 43.1 million francs in 1932). As the depression ended, the nickel and chrome markets improved during the latter half of the 1930s because of increased demand, especially by Germany and Japan. As a result of the growth of the market, Inco allowed SLN to increase its world share of nickel exports from ten per cent to seventeen per cent. The additional sales were exclusively to Europe. New Caledonian exports recovered to 54.9 million francs by 1936 and then increased rapidly to 146.4 million francs in 1938 (imports in 1938 were 158.5 million francs).

The depression had severely weakened SLN's main competitors in New Caledonia and, a short time later, it was able to buy both Société Calédonienne Minière and Société Hauts Fourneaux. At the same time, the New Caledonian mining industry was attracting the attention of Japan and Germany as they sought to build up their military power. The Krupps of Germany acquired a large number of shares in SLN and German interests were purchasing nickel from SLN and the smaller miners largely to supply arms factories.[6] To some extent, Japanese interests were in competition with SLN, as Japanese capital financed development of a new nickel mine at Kaoua in 1939 and sought to employ technology that would allow them to bypass SLN's smelters. Japanese capital was also dominant in Société le Fer, which operated an iron mine at Goro. The company used Japanese workers and exported the iron ore to Japan.[7] Japanese and Germans involvement in the mining industry, including their two markets, came to an end following the outbreak of the Second World War; nickel exports to Japan being halted in 1941.

Labor for the mines during the 1920s and 1930s was provided mainly by indentured workers from Java and Vietnam. Over 3,000 Asian workers were recruited in 1921. Their number increased substantially during the 1920s, and, by 1929, there were more than 14,000 indentured workers in New Caledonia (over half of whom were Javanese)—their total number being larger than the European population in the colony. The Javanese were the most popular workers with the mining companies since they were considered to be docile and adaptable.[8] In contrast, the Vietnamese had a reputation as trouble-makers. Although they lacked unions, in 1927, Vietnamese workers went on strike at the Moindou mine and at SLN's smelter in Noumea.[9] The cause of indentured mineworkers was taken up by Florindo Paladini, a member of the French Communist Party, who engaged in political activities in the colony on behalf of poor Europeans, indentured workers, and the Melanesians throughout the interwar years. The number of indentured workers in the mines declined with the onset of the depression and increased toward the end of the 1930s as the mining industry recovered. By 1939, there were 3,900 indentured workers in the colony.

After the fall of France in June 1940, elements within New Caledonia's settler population considered establishing an autonomous conservative French state to serve their own interests. When De Gaulle announced his Free French government later in the year, however, the settlers pledged their support. The Americans and Australians considered New Caledonia to be of considerable strategic importance because of its location (especially its proximity to Australia) and its mineral resources. The outbreak of hostilities in the Pacific led to considerable disagreement between the French colonial administration and the Americans and Australians over responsibility for the defence of New Caledonia. The issue was decided in favor of the Americans, and about 15,000 American troops landed in New Caledonia in March 1942. New Caledonia became the general headquarters for American forces in the southwest Pacific, and over 200,000 Allied troops passed through the island during the war. The United States military came to dominate life on the island and the American military administration decided policy in most spheres.

The immediate impact of the war on the colony was to seriously disrupt the New Caledonian economy. Nickel production in New Caledonia peaked in 1940 at 478,000 tons of ore, but then wartime conditions disrupted markets and led to an acute shortage of labor and finance, and production declined precipitously. The arrival of American forces, however, led to an abrupt change, producing an unprecedented economic boom.[10] Among those who profited most from the war during the American occupation were the mining companies. Export duties were suspended and prices for nickel and chromite soared. An excess profits tax was imposed on the mining companies, but this did little to dampen profit levels. The only dark spot on the horizon, as far as the mining sector was concerned, was a decision by the United States (which consumed some three-quarters of the world's nickel), concerned over the Japanese threat to New Caledonia and in response to increased prices and demand, to begin a crash program to develop additional sources closer to home and to find means of reducing the amount of nickel required for nickel plating.[11]

Wartime prosperity led to an increased government budget and to major improvements in the colony's infrastructure. The infusion of American capital and the service sector boom was transitory, however, and the war did little to alter the colony's dependency on mining and outside government support. Agriculture remained neglected and glaring regional disparities were left largely intact.

On the political front, the war also saw the founding of a communist party in New Caledonia, called Progress Social.[12] Progress Social joined with the more moderate Comité Calédonien party to call for economic reforms, including an income tax, breaking up the large cattle ranches, and nationalization of the mining industry.

Melanesians, who had been brought in greater numbers into wage employment, were one audience for these ideas, but an even more ready one was to be found among the Asian workers.

Unlike most other residents in New Caledonia, Asian mineworkers benefitted little from wartime economic conditions. With the onset of the war, the 3,471 workers in the colony could not be repatriated, and, as their contracts expired, they were anxious to find employment away from the mines, where they could earn much more. The Progress Social party assisted Asian mineworkers in petitioning the American military command, in early 1944, to take steps to improve their situation. The petition received no reply and the military command, which considered continued output of the mines vital to the war effort, forced the Asians to continue working in the mines. This policy, effectively one of forced labor, led to industrial unrest and, eventually, to a strike in April 1945. The strike aroused fear among the European settlers of a communist-inspired revolution and the French administration stepped in an jailed the leaders and forced the other strikers back to work.

Mining and Postwar Political Change

The war had upset the colonial social order and the immediate postwar period was an unsettled one for New Caledonia. Immediately after the war, conservatives, moderate liberals, and radicals among the settler population vied for influence in the midst of political reforms that included a gradual incorporation of Melanesians into the political process. Such reforms were implemented by the colonial authorities as part of France's effort to improve its human rights image in the international community and, in part, to defuse pressure for more radical change.

To promote what they considered the correct political evolution of the colony, and specifically to limit the influence of radical political ideas among the Melanesians, Catholic and Protestant missionaries established organizations to promote moderate Melanesian leadership and the colonial authorities established the Service of Native Affairs with the aim of "reviving the Melanesians' taste for tribal life, so that they could fulfil their manifest destiny as a peasantry."[13] According to this view, Pacific islanders were not supposed to become members of the proletariat, but to remain quasi-traditional villagers under the control of their chiefs and the church. These efforts were only partially successful and the results were not always those anticipated by liberal reformers.

Many conservative settlers were opposed to any concessions to the Melanesians, but they were divided on other political issues and soon lost control of territorial politics to more moderate forces. In 1951, a liberal reformist party emerged, the Union Caledonienne (UC), under the leadership of Maurice Lenormand. The UC dominated the Territorial Assembly throughout the 1950s and 1960s, although its position gradually weakened during the 1960s, and the UC finally lost its majority in the Assembly by the end of the decade. The UC was opposed to independence, but favored democratic reforms and increased autonomy for New Caledonia. The UC also saw itself as pro-Melanesian in a rather paternalistic fashion.

The political left called for the nationalization of the nickel industry in the 1945 territorial electoral campaign, citing the fact that SLN's profits in 1938-39 had been three times the entire revenue of the colony and the company's practice of repatriating almost all of its profits. The electoral victory of conservatives associated with the Comité Calédonien, who advocated policies favoring the status quo where SLN's corporate interests were concerned, blocked this threat. The UC's attitude towards the mining industry was much more critical than that of the conservatives, but it stopped far short of the demands made by the more radical parties and, in practice, the UC did little to threaten SLN's virtual autonomy.

The New Caledonian nickel industry faced financial difficulties immediately after the war and SLN recorded losses in 1947 and 1949. These problems were, in part, a result of having to pay increased wages following labor agitation, largely by Vietnamese workers, and because of the high price of Australian coal. To improve its financial position, SLN lobbied the colonial government for a reduction in duties and, when this failed, it sought to reduce costs through mechanization. Demand and the price of nickel increased sharply in 1952, after the outbreak of the Korean War. It took time, however, for SLN to increase its production in order to benefit from the favorable market conditions. The nickel market remained relatively healthy for the next ten years. As a result, profits rose, and so did the number of employees, from around 1,500 to over 3,000.

The nickel industry entered a recession in 1962. As a result, nickel production declined to a low of 15,000 tons and SLN laid off 800 workers and approached the government for further financial concessions. A request for a tax exemption on nickel exports, in particular, led to a political crisis. The French-appointed governor supported the exemption, but the UC majority in the Territorial Assembly was opposed. When a bomb exploded in the Assembly building a few days later, the Assembly was dissolved and later the

UC's Lenormand had his civic rights suspended for five years. The SLN was granted export concessions and was allowed to import machinery more cheaply for the purpose of reducing labor costs. As a result of this assistance, although SLN recorded a loss in 1962, the following year it recorded a profit once again and found itself in a much better position to increase profitability in the years ahead.

Events surrounding and following the Second World War had resulted in French interests gaining dominance over the colony's mining industry, and in the decades after the war New Caledonia's nickel not only supplied France with the bulk of its own import needs for the metal but also provided the country with an important source of foreign exchange earnings. During the 1960s, French authorities made constant reference to just how important they considered New Caledonia's nickel industry to be for France. They made it clear that it was a primary reason for France retaining control of the territory and emphasized that nickel mining in New Caledonia should, first and foremost, serve the interests of France over those associated with other countries. Such statements were accompanied by greater direct involvement in the mining industry by the French government. Thus, in a 1965 speech, President de Gaulle of France stated that the French state should retain control over the nickel industry "in order to preserve French independence in the world economic system."[14]

The election of Pompidou to the presidency in 1969 was of considerable importance to the New Caledonian nickel industry. Pompidou was closely associated with the Rothschild bank, and through the bank to SLN. Having such friends in high places helped SLN maintain its prominent position in the colony, but government interest in the industry also resulted in increasing control of the industry as a whole by French authorities. Government regulation of the industry was formalized in January 1969, with enactment of the *lois Billotte*, which gave the French Ministry of Industry power to authorize mining and to set mineral export quotas for New Caledonia.

While the nickel industry underwent its ups and downs during the postwar period, the chromite industry, after an initial upturn, virtually collapsed. Immediately after the war, Société le Tiebaghi had invested in further mechanization to increase production and reduce labor costs. Most of the chromite mining companies merged in 1949 to form the Société Calédonienne du Chrome. Chromite mining also experienced a boom in 1952 as a result of the Korean War. The following year, however, it went in to a recession. This, combined with technical problems and a loss of some important markets, placed the chromite industry in New Caledonia on a seemingly irreversible downward trajectory. Chromite exports fell from a record 122,000 tons in 1953 to 22,000 tons in 1961. The Tebaghi mine reduced its workforce from three hundred to thirty before shutting the mine down altogether in 1962. An attempt to reopen the mine in 1967 ended in failure.

The mining industry's mechanization efforts after the Second World War were motivated largley by a shortage of labor as the number of indentured workers declined. Once the war was over, Vietnamese mineworkers sought to be repatriated, despite industry efforts to retain them. The last indentured Vietnamese mineworkers left in 1962. About one thousand Vietnamese remained in the colony, mostly living in Noumea and showing little interest in mine-work. The number of Indonesian workers also declined until only a few hundred remained. As the demand for labor increased during the 1950s, the mining industry turned to the local Melanesian population, to the alarm of some European colonists, who feared a radicalization of the Melanesians. The first Melanesians (thirty Loyalty Islanders) had been recruited to work at the Tiebaghi mine in 1938. This "experiment" proved successful and gradually more Melanesians were employed in the mines. Their numbers grew and working conditions changed after the war, when indentured and forced labor for Melanesians was abolished. There were 540 Melanesians employed in the mines in 1952, and, by 1965, Melanesians comprised approximately thirty-five per cent of the colony's two thousand mineworkers.

New Caledonia's Melanesian community did not supply sufficient labor to replace the Asian workforce and the mines turned to the Polynesian communities from France's other colonies in the South Pacific: Wallis and Futuna and French Polynesia. At first, the number of Wallis and Futuna Islanders in New Caledonia was quite small, but adverse economic conditions on Wallis and Futuna in 1958 led six thousand islanders to migrate to New Caledonia over a two year period. They took up residence mainly in and around Noumea, where they formed relatively closed communities. For the most part, the Wallis and Futuna Islanders found employment in the construction and mining industries. Migrants from French Polynesia came mainly from the Australis and Iles Sous le Vent (especially Makatea and Raiatea).[15] In the late 1950s, they were attracted primarily by employment on public works projects. After 1962, many came to work in the nickel mines. For this latter group, the migration route commonly led from the phosphate mines on Makatea (see chapter 6), to the Forari phosphate mine in the New Hebrides (see note 9, chapter 1), and then to New Caledonia.[16] Employment opportunities created by the nuclear testing program back in French Polynesia caused many of these workers to return home, but some remained in New Caledonia.

Wages and conditions of employment for mineworkers gradually improved during the decades following the Second World War. Organized mineworkers staged several strikes after the war and were able to negotiate some gains. One major strike by Vietnamese workers in 1953 at the Tiegbaghi mine lasted three months and served to stir up fears of communism among conservative settlers when the Vietnamese carried banners with photos of Ho Chi Minh. The union movement remained divided until 1956, when a relatively unified movement grew out of a major strike against Maison Ballande. Around this same time, in 1955 and 1956, there were strikes in the mining industry as well. The industry saw further strikes following the difficulties of 1962, in 1964, 1966, and 1967. The degree of solidarity exhibited among European, Melanesian, Vietnamese, and Javanese mineworkers in taking industrial action was of concern to the mine-owners.[17] In particular, the Melanesians had not proven to be as docile and tradition-bound as had been anticipated, but had joined unions and taken part in strikes alongside non-Melanesian workers. The only workers not exhibiting such solidarity were the Polynesians.

The Syndicate des Ouvriers et Employés de Nouvelle-Calédonie (SOENC) was formed in 1965, and quickly established itself among SLN's workers. The union movement grew further in 1968, with the founding of the Union des Syndicate des Ouvriers et Employés de Nouvelle-Calédonie (USOENC) to serve as an umbrella for most of the unions around the colony. Although not directly associated with a local political party, these unions were very active politically and saw political action as an important part of seeking to enhance the rights and conditions of workers. Through their activities at the workplace and their influence within the colony as a whole, organized labor achieved substantial gains in wages and conditions during the 1960s.

The Nickel Boom and the Independence Struggle

The New Caledonian economy experienced a nickel-based boom between 1969 and 1972, that had profound implications throughout the colony.[18] Even before the boom began, nickel accounted for about ninety-eight per cent of the value of New Caledonia's exports. Moreover, mining, smelting and related operations provided about sixty per cent of the colony's employment. Almost everything else could be accounted for by the colonial administration. The boom led to substantial growth in almost all sectors of the economy. Nickel production had grown slowly from its 1962 low point. Now it rose to 120,000 tons in 1970 (peaking at 150,000 tons the following year), at which point the French high commissioner predicted, optimistically, that production would reach 200,000 tons by 1976. New Caledonia's gross domestic product rose by forty-six per cent from 1969 to 1970. Much of the profit from mining went to SLN and other mining interests, but there was still a good deal of money left over to flow into the local economy. Government revenue went up substantially from 2,556 million CFP in 1968 to 9,637 million in 1972. In its wake, the boom brought a high rate of inflation and trade deficits as imports of machinery and consumer goods outstripped revenue from mining. Moreover, new investment outside of the mining industry was mainly in the service sector and little was done to diversify the economy in productive areas.

The mining boom brought a challenge to SLN's monopoly. Much to the alarm of French authorities, international mining companies such as Inco, Amax, Patino, and Kaiser had expressed interest in New Caledonia in the late 1960s. This prompted one French senator to argue that "the interest of New Caledonia is best preserved by the French state, which alone can act as a referee to prevent the take-over of mining activities by foreign groups."[19] Between 1967 and 1969, local members of the Territorial Assembly had argued in favor of allowing these foreign firms into New Caledonia to increase investment in the colony and promote rationalization of the industry. In anticipation of a liberalization of the industry, these companies undertook preliminary surveys of possible mining and plant sites. Inco spent a large amount of money prospecting in the Goro area in the southern part of the main island through a joint venture, in which Inco held a forty per cent share, with a French consortium. Meanwhile, Patino sought to develop a nickel project in the north in conjunction with SLN. The French government responded to this "threat" by cancelling Inco's contracts and reducing Patino's participation in the proposed northern project to ten per cent. Both companies lost millions of dollars and found themselves effectively blocked from further participation in the New Caledonian mining industry.

Prominent members of the settler commercial class, seeking to dilute SLN's economic dominance as a means of promoting economic development for the colony, were closely associated with the entry into New Caledonia of these foreign mining interests. Politics and economic have always been closely interrelated in New Caledonia, and many of the colony's leading political figures are also among its commercial elite. Many of these individuals profited by the nickel boom, especially those with direct interests in nickel mining. Three figures who stand out in this regard are Jacques Lafleur, Edouard Pentecost, and Roger Laroque. Among other things, Lafleur and Pentecost are New Caledonia's most important *petits mineurs*, or small miners, who sell most of their ore to SLN, while Laroque is commercial director of Ballande.

Laroque has been a leading conservative politician since he was first elected mayor of Noumea in 1953. He became leader of the Union Democratique (UD), which was formed in 1968 and soon emerged as one of the most important rightest parties in the colony. The UD opposed autonomy and favored doing away with Melanesian reserves in order to integrate them more fully into the economic life of the colony. It also urged the French government to promote economic development of New Caledonia through large industrial projects. Ballande, of which Laroque is commercial director, and the associated SMT held the largest number of mining concessions in the colony after SLN.

Jacques Lafleur owns one of the largest personal fortunes in New Caledonia, with interests in land, cattle, commercial enterprises, and mining. A leading figure in rightest politics, he and Laroque split in 1970 and Lafleur formed the Entente Democratique et Sociale (EDS), which beceme the colony's other main rightwing party. Lafleur's mining interests are through COFREMMI, which holds a number of mining concessions. Edouard Pentecost is a wealthy self-made businessman of mixed ancestry, who made much of his fortune through mining. He ran unsuccessfully as a conservative candidate a couple times in the 1960s and was associated with the rightest Union de la Nouvelle Republique. He played a leading role in establishing the Génération Sociale et Libérale, an important pro-Giscardian movement in New Caledonia, in 1975. He owns a large number of mining concessions through SMMNC. It is also worth noting that prominent UC figure, Maurice Lenormand holds a couple of mining concessions as well through Calédomines.

The nickel boom contributed to a rise in migration from overseas. The labor force grew by fifteen per cent between 1967 and 1972, with new migrants accounting for most of the new workers. New Caledonia's population had roughly doubled between 1887 and 1969. Between 1969 and 1976 it increased by 33.5 per cent. As late as 1956, the indigenous Melanesians had constituted a majority in the colony (fifty-one per cent), but migration from elsewhere in the Pacific and by French colonists from Algeria and Vietnam during the late 1950s and early 1960s had resulted in them becoming a minority. By 1969, the indigenous Melanesians represented forty-seven per cent of the population. With the onset of the mining boom, the proportion of Melanesians declined even further, to just under forty-two per cent by 1976 (when the total population of the colony reached 133,233). While the Melanesian population grew by seventeen per cent between 1969 and 1976 as a result of natural increase, the populations of the colony's other communities, bouyed by migration, grew by much larger percentages (see table 5.1): the European population grew by thirty-seven per cent, the Wallis and Futuna Islander population by 53.9 per cent, and the French Polynesian population by 89.6 per cent. In 1976, Europeans accounted for 38.1 per cent of the population, Wallis and Futuna Islanders 7.2 per cent, and French Polynesians 4.7 per cent (Vietnamese and Indonesians accounted for 5.2 per cent).

The arrival of these new migrants had an important social and political impact because of their overall conservatism and lack of sympathy for the Melanesians. The Wallis and Futuna Islanders by the early 1970s had begun to mix more freely with other communities in the colony, but their views differed from the indigenous Melanesians on many issues, such as support for unions and independence. When they began to participate in politics in the early 1970s, they backed the more conservative, pro-French parties. The French Polynesians held similar conservative views and shared with many Polynesians a sense of superiority in relation to the darker skinned Melanesians. Tahitian workers in the building industry did, however, stage a strike in 1971.

Such demographic changes contributed to important alterations in the colony's politics by increasing the number of pro-French migrant settlers while, at the same time, making the Melanesians feel even more alienated and threatened. Rightist parties such as the EDS and UD, their support swollen by the new migrants, challenged the UC from one side, as new radical groups emerged to threaten the UC's traditional base of support within the Melanesian community. Within the UC itself, the party was being pulled in opposite directions by conservative settlers urging moderate policies and Melanesians pushing for a more radical stand. At the end of 1970, a group of Melanesians led by Yann Celene Uregei broke with the UC to form the Union Multiraciale de Nouvelle Caledonie (UMNC).

The UMNC had the support of young Melanesian radicals, led by Nidoish Naisseline, who in 1969 had begun activities to oppose the colonial regime. Naisseline and those associated with him formed the Reveil Canaque (Kanak Awakening) in June 1970, and later the

TABLE 5.1 Migration To and From New Caledonia, 1969-1976

Year	Net Migration
1969	+2,897
1970	+5,716
1971	+4,361
1972	+488
1973	-1,229
1974	-283
1975	-907
1976	-921

Source: Service de la Statistique, *Annuaires Statistiques,* 1976-78 (Noumea).

Foulards Rouges (Red Scarves) as their political front. Although staunchly opposed to French colonialism and anxious to promote a cultural revival within the Melanesian community, the Foulards Rouges advocated inter-communal cooperation in solidarity against what were viewed as common class enemies.

The declining political status of the UC became clear in the municipal elections that followed the formation of the UMNC, in which the UC lost a number of seats. Lenormand, once again leader of the UC, sought to retain support among Melanesians and poorer members of the European community by siding with organized labor in a number of disputes, including some at SLN and advocating autonomy (but not independence) for New Caledonia. Lenormand attempt to undermine Melanesian support for the UMNC by offering assistance to Naisseline, and he collected money from SLN workers to support Naisseline's travel. The failure to call for independence was based, in part, on a fear that francophone New Caledonia would be swamped by the surrounding anglophone countries as well as by political and economic considerations. This overture to the left was only marginally successful and resulted in a group of the UC's European councillors leaving the party to form the Mouvement Libéral Calédonien, primarily to oppose the idea of autonomy. This split cost the UC its majority in the Territorial Assembly, and was followed by the subsequent rise of political forces the left and right.

The nickel boom came to an abrupt end in 1972, with a downturn in the world market in the face of oversupply and declining demand. Production fell sharply and the colony's Gross domestic product declined by six per cent between 1972 and 1973. The sudden end of the boom left New Caledonia in a critical position. Government expenditure had risen sharply, wages were much higher, the

population had grown, people's aspiration had gone up, and all of a
sudden there was substantially less money to go around. While all
sectors of the community suffered, the impact of the crisis was far
from uniform. Among those who were able to withstand the effects
of the crisis better than many was the organized workforce in the
mining industry itself. Thus, while employment in the mining
industry in general declined by six per cent from 1972 to 1975, SLN
still employed around 4,500 workers in 1977—a number estimated
by its management to be at least five hundred more than was
needed.[20] Large business interests were also able to insulate
themselves to some extent by lobbying successfully for tax reforms
and other government assistance. Others were not so lucky and
unemployment and bankruptcies became widespread.

In searching for a reason for the severity of the crisis, virtually
everyone in the colony blamed the French government. But the
reasons for blaming France varied, as did the proposed solutions.
The rightest parties felt that France had not done enough to encourage
foreign investment and a liberalization of trade other aspects of the
economy and now called on France to help the settler commercial
interests that they represented. In particular, they wanted the
government to intervene and help with the budget deficit. Those
favoring autonomy blamed the crisis on poor planning, which they
felt could be alleviated through devolution of power and by taking
such steps as establishing a price stabilization fund, limiting the
repatriation of profits by the mining companies to France, and
promoting a much more diversified economy. Pro-independence
Melanesians linked the crisis to colonialism and saw a solution in the
granting of independence, nationalization of the mines and
diversification of the economy.

The French government's response was mainly in the form of
budgetary assistance and financial support for the nickel industry.
SLN was perceived by many Europeans in the colony to be the chief
beneficiary of these actions, while small businesses were left to
suffer the consequences of the economic downturn. Many of these
settlers felt that even the Melanesians were being treated more
favorably by the French government than they were. Some
Melanesians did benefit from the favors done by the government for
SLN, but benefits were insufficient to alter the growing support
within the Melanesian community for independence.

After the initial shock of 1972, the international nickel market
deteriorated even further in the mid-1970s. The additional downturn
began in 1975 and, as demand continued to decline and stocks piled
up, by 1977, the nickel market was the worst that it had been in

TABLE 5.2 Nickel Production, New Caledonia, 1976-1986

Year	Quantity*
1976	119.7
1977	116.8
1978	65.2
1979	80.5
1980	86.6
1981	78.2
1982	60.1
1983	46.2
1984	58.3
1985	72.3
1986	64.1

*Metric tons (metal content).
Sources: World Bureau of Metal Statistics, *World Metal Statistics Yearbook 1986;* British Geological Survey, *World Mineral Statistics, 1982-86.*

decades. New Caledonian nickel exports dropped by twenty-five per cent in 1977, and Japan (which purchased half of New Caledonia's nickel) demanded that the price be lowered by twenty per cent. SLN responded by cutting back production sharply in 1978, and production has not risen significantly since then. The situation was not particularly bright for SLN, but nor was it one of despair. SLN was still able to make money most years, even though its labor costs were higher than those in many developed countries and the market remained depressed. Moreover, SLN's parent company, IMETAL, had only thirty per cent of its capital tied up in SLN and could afford a few bad years. Likewise, the so-called "small miners" like Lafleur and Pentecost no longer made the profits that they had at the beginning of the decade, but the earnings of most of them were still substantial.

Nor was the world nickel market so bad that expansion of production in New Caledonia was out of the question. The northern nickel project which had begun during the late 1960s, had been derailed by the French government on largely nationalistic grounds, but there was still considerable interest in the project. The problem was that most of the interest, as before, was expressed by non-French companies—Amax, in particular.[21] In fact, Amax's possible involvement was seen as sufficiently threatening for the French government to secure a fifty-one per cent stake in the project in 1976, in an effort to keep the foreign company out of New Caledonia.

Having taken this step, however, the government failed to find other sources of investment for the project. Even when two major French companies, Creusot-Loire and Pechiney, announced their interest in the project, they made it clear that they did not consider it viable without Amax's participation. Continued intransigeance on the part of the French government not only led Amax to lose patience but it also upset Europeans in the colony who saw the northern project as important for the economic well-being of New Caledonia.

The French government had acquired a fifty per cent interest in SLN in 1974 through Société Nationale Elf-Aquitaine (SNEA). The other half remained with IMETAL, which was largely in the hands of the Banque Rothchild and the Banque de l'Indochine et de Suez (which held a monopoly on credit in the colony). SLN expressed a willingness to expand its operations in New Caledonia, provided that the government agreed to certain concessions. In 1976, SLN offered to increase its investment in mining and processing substantially in exchange for tax stabilization benefits. Local political parties favoring autonomy or independence were opposed to what they perceived as another "handout" to SLN, but the conservative parties (who held a majority in the Territorial Assembly) favored the idea. An agreement was reached whereby the government would grant SLN twenty years of tax stabilization in return for an investment by SLN of CFP20,000 million over five years.

In 1976, nickel accounted for 97.2 per cent of the value of New Caledonia's exports, and most of this nickel still was exported by SLN. Non-French mining interests effectively remained barred from the colony. New Caledonia's gross domestic product had regained ground in 1974 and 1975, but had declined again in 1976 and 1977. Building and services remained depressed during this period. The only bright spot was tourism, which began to be actively promote by the French government, and which some saw as a possible avenue to reduce dependence on nickel exports. Tourist arrivals had been fairly stagnant in the late 1960s and early 1970s, at around 8,000 visitors a year. Starting in 1973, however, the industry began something of a boom itself, as the number of arrivals rose to 18,000. The largest number of new tourists came from Australia, with Japan and New Zealand accounting for most of the remainder. Economic benefits to the colony of the tourist boom, however, were limited. Profits tended to be repatriated and growth of the industry increased demand for imports. The remaining sector of the economy, agriculture, continued to be neglected. The workforce in agriculture declined steadily from the 1960s onward: from thirty-five per cent of the total in 1963, to twenty-five per cent in 1976, and to twenty-two per cent in 1982. The level of food imports remained high and agricultural exports were negligible. Coffee production, for example, increased from a mere 531 tons in 1975 to 650 tons in 1980.

The problems with the nickel industry after 1972 were not solely responsible for the evolution of politics in New Caledonia during the remainder of the 1970s and 1980s, but the industry's influence on the colony's politics was considerable and provided an important backdrop for all that transpired. Essentially, what happened after the 1972 crisis was that the middle ground in New Caledonian politics disappeared as the Melanesian community moved further to the left and the extreme right within the European community gained support from other Europeans.

Between 1971 and 1973, the Foulardes Rouges worked with the Uregei's UMNC, but, in 1973, the Foulardes Rouges broke with the UMNC to join forces with a more radical newly formed European group, the Union des Jeunesses Caledoniennes (Union of Caledonian Youth). During 1974, members of these and other radical groups were involved in several violent confrontations with the police and in general there was a radicalization of the Melanesian community, as frustration grew over perceived French intransigeance on questions of reform. This shift led the UMNC to become increasingly militant, until, in September 1975, Uregei issued a call for New Caledonian independence in the Territorial Assembly. He was supported in his demand by eleven other Melanesian councillors. In the months that followed, there were more confrontations and political positions on both sides hardened.

The more radical Melanesian groups were distrustful of existing parties like the UC and UMNC, and in May 1976 they launched their own united front for independence, the Palika. The Palika was fervently communal and anti-capitalist and made it clear that if it came to power, SLN would go. The nickel industry featured prominently in Palika's 1977 manifesto. Listed among Palika's primary aims in the manifesto were: "to oppose the system of repression established by the French, and the exploitative nickel industry; the return of all land stolen by settlers, missionaries, the SLN and the French government, for the benefit of the Kanak people on a communal basis; and the nationalization of industries."[22]

Despite the attacks on SLN by Palika, French authorities and local rightists suspected the SLN of supporting the Palika. These suspicions were aroused by SLN's policy of pursuing accommodation with all political factions in pursuit of long-term self-interest. This accommodationist approach upset rightwing politicians in particular, who saw this as one more instance where their interests and those of SLN's did not necessarily coincide.

Independence was the central issue in the 1977 Territorial Assembly elections, which were contested by a record eleven parties and 457 candidates (out of a total population of only 137,000). The rightists remained divided into a number of parties, with Lafleur's EDS, now under the Reassemblement pour la Caledonie (RPC) banner, being dominant. The RPC won twelve of the Assembly's thirty-five seats (more than any other single party). The UC once again found itself losing ground to parties on its left and right. It had come out in favor of independence, which had cost it most of its European support. But the UC was able to retain nine seats, making it still the largest party of the center-left. Among those running for the UC was Jean-Marie Tjibaou, who was to emerge as the leader of the independence movement in the 1980s. The remaining fourteen seats were divided among nine other parties. Among the more radical pro-independence parties, the Palika, which had decided to participate in the election, won two seats.

The 1977 election confirmed the increasing split between Melanesians and Europeans, and political parties found themselves having to identify with one community or the other. Although only thirty per cent of the electorate voted for parties favoring independence, eighty per cent of the Melanesians voted pro-independence. The communal divide also manifest itself geographically, with rightwing parties drawing most of their support from Noumea and the adjacent towns and the pro-independence parties receiving their support in the eastern rural areas, where most of the Melanesians lived.

The growing communal division also made itself felt in the union movement. After the 1977 election a growing split emerged within USOENC between those, largely Melanesians, wishing it to take a more radical stance in favor of independence and those, mainly Europeans, desiring to adopt more moderate policies. These differences led to the formation of the Kanak and Exploited Workers Union (USTKE) in 1981, which accused the USOENC of serving the interests of European workers rather than those of Melanesians. Within a couple of years the USTKE had grown almost as large as the USOENC and assumed a prominent role in pro-independence politics.[23]

In 1979 Giscard d'Estang's government sought to contain the growing support for independence among the Melanesian population in New Caledonia by tightening political control of the colony.

Included in its reforms was elimination of small parties receiving less than 7.5 per cent of the vote and gerrymandering of electoral boundaries to ensure that pro-French parties would retain their majority in the Assembly. In the 1979 Territorial Assembly elections that followed, the pro-independence group won fourteen seats to fifteen seats for the rightwing Reassemblement pour la Calédonie dans la Republique (RPCR) and seven seats for the more moderate Fédération pour une Nouvelle Société Calédonienne (FNSC). The reforms served to unify the right to some extent, but they also created a more unified independence movement under the banner of the Independence Front (which held nine seats). When this political initiative did not prove adequate, the French government announced a financial program to assist in the economic recovery of the colony. The development plan, under State Secretary for Overseas Departments and Territories Paul Dijoud, included undertakings aimed specifically at Melanesians, including employment training and educational reforms—again, with the intent to undermine support for independence.

The French presidential campaign assumed considerable importance in New Caledonia since the two main contenders advocated quite different policies towards the colonies: the conservatives offering more of the same, while the socialists, having been lobbied by the pro-independence parties from New Caledonia, had come out in favor of decolonization. Support for decolonization by the Socialist Party had increased in the wake of the rise of rightwing extremist elements in New Caledonia. Such extremists formed the Mouvement pour l'Ordre et la Paix and were linked to the murder of a Melanesian youth in January 1980. The victory of Socialist Party candidate François Mitterand in 1981 created optimism among the pro-independence forces, but led many Europeans in the colony to move even further to the right.

The murder of UC secretary general Pierre Declercq by rightwing extremists in September 1981 resulted in a further radicalization of the pro-independence parties and prompted the Socialist government to immediate action on New Caledonia. In December 1981, the Socialists announced that they intended to bring about major reforms in such areas as land and the role of Melanesians in government without delay as part of a process of decolonization. The following month, steps were taken to begin economic and social reforms, which were to be followed later by political reforms. At the same time, the more moderate settler party, the FNSC, agreed to work with the Independence Front in the Territorial Assembly, although it did not as yet come out in support of independence. A no-confidence motion in June ended the RPCR's control of the Assembly, which now passed to the center-left coalition of the Independence Front and FNSC, with the Independence Front holding a majority of seats on the Government Council. The stage seemed to be set for a gradual transfer of power and eventual decolonization.

Nickel production declined during these early years of the 1980s (falling by one-half between 1980 and 1984), with little prospect of improvement in the market. In light of market conditions and the political uncertainty, SLN was not inclined to invest in expansion of its operation. In fact, it closed its mine at Poro and a new center at Népoui. The hours of minework also was reduced. In 1983, the Socialist government assumed control of SLN. The Banque Rothchild had been nationalized in 1982, and the following year the government took over completely: with a seventy per cent share held by ERAP, fifteen per cent by IMETAL, and fifteen per cent by SNEA. The company had recorded a substantial loss in 1982 and, in 1983, the government arranged for a loan of around A$100 million. The following year, reforms allowed SLN only to pay taxes only on its profits. The takeover and financial efforts to salvage the industry, in a sense, represented further steps in the trend that had been noticeable for a number of years towards greater direct government involvement in the industry. In addition, the Socialist's initiative could be seen as helping to set the stage for an eventual transfer of at least partial ownership of the company to a Melanesian government in New Caledonia. It was also a move that met with considerable disfavor by "small" mining interests in the colony, such as Jacques Lafleur.

After the surge of activity in early 1982, progress with reform slowed and tensions within New Caledonia escalated as the Melanesians became impatient and the European settlers resorted to more extreme measures. The situation was not helped by the fact that, despite sympathy for the Melanesians in Paris, in New Caledonia, the European-dominated administration sided openly with anti-independence extremists. And the support of the Socialists was not proving as great as the pro-independence Melanesians had hoped. The situation turned particularly violent in January 1983, when two gendarmes died during a shootout as they tried to dislodge a group of Melanesians who had squatted at a sawmill to protest its pollution of nearby waterways.

Progress again seemed to have been made in July 1983, when the French government brought twenty Melanesian leaders to Paris for talks. They agreed to a moderate plan of autonomy as a prior step to independence. It was soon apparent, however, that little had been accomplished. The Melanesian independence movement changed its name to Front de Libération National Kanak et Socialist (FLNKS), which included the UC, Palika, UPM, LKS (which broke away from the Palika and eventually left the FLNKS as well), and the USTKE trade union. A growing number of those within the FLNKS were becoming frustrated with what they perceived as a lack of progress in implementing reforms and the continued harassment of Melanesian activists in New Caledonia. Divisions within the movement occurred in relation to the November 1984 Territorial Assembly election. The majority of political leaders within the FLNKS, which was now led by Jean-Marie Tjibaou of the UC, decided to boycott the election, while the LKS (Libération Kanak Socialiste, led by Naisseline) decided to contest the elections and broke with the FLNKS.

The 1984 boycott proved to be a turning point in New Caledonian politics, ushering in a period of political violence unseen in the colony since the early part of the century.[24] Violence erupted, as Melanesians around the colony, led by Eloi Machoro, erected barricades, occupied polling booths, and destroyed ballots. As a result of the boycott, Lafleur's RPCR won thirty-four of forty-two seats. The FNSC, now called the ULO, had supported the notion of self-government and, in so doing, had lost most of its European support. Having won seven seats in the last election, this time it won only one seat. Even further to the right than the RPCR, the newly formed Front National, with links to Jean-Marie Le Pen's Front National in France, won a seat. The only real opposition to the right remaining in the Assembly was the LKS, which won six seats.

The boycott had coincided with a strike by two thousand workers at SLN. The strike was over conditions of employment, but the union had sought to improve its bargaining position by holding the strike at the same time as the election and its members staged their own disruptions in the Noumea area.

To counter the FLNKS claim to represent the Melanesian population, the RPCR put forward a cabinet of five Melanesians and five Europeans, with a Melanesian, Dick Ukeiwe, as its head. Jacques Lafluer was satisfied to run the operation from the background. After the swearing in ceremony, Lafleur pledged that the RPCR would restore investment confidence in the colony and pointed to the Japanese in particular as a possible source of new investment. For the FLNKS, the Territorial Assembly had ceased to be a legitimate political body. Instead, the pro-independence forces declared their own provisional government, led by Jean-Marie Tjibaou.

The months immediately following the election were marked by considerable violence. The worst incidences included an ambush of unarmed Melanesian activists, in which nine were killed (including two of Tjibaou's brothers) by armed settlers, and, then, the killing of Eloi Machoro and an associate by gendarmes. A state of emergency was declared by the French government and the number of security forces in the colony was increased to six thousand. In an effort to defuse the situation, President Mitterrand flew to New Caledonia for a twelve hour visit and succeeded in convincing Tjibaou to adopt a more moderate position.

The nickel industry suffered considerably from the violence. The mining town of Thio became a stronghold of Melanesian militants, who succeeded in closing the SLN mine near the town. Many of the Europeans in Thio supported extreme rightwing organizations. Its mayor, Roger Galliot, was linked with various armed groups and with the Front National. When Melanesian militants occupied the town for three weeks after the election, most of the community's Europeans left. During his visit in January, Mitterrand promised that the Thio mine would be reopened soon, but moves to reopen the mine prompted rightwing extremists (anxious to prompt further French military intervention) to set fires and use explosives against the facility, causing A\$3 million worth of damage and delaying its opening. Further violence occurred at Thio when rightwing settlers organized a "picnic," in response to a call by Lafleur for his supporters to defy the government curfew, and clashed with Melanesians in the town. The value of lost production between November 1984 and February 1985 was estimated to be around A\$15 million. Tourism also was hit by the political violence, and the number of tourist arrivals was drastically reduced.

In January 1985, High Commissioner Edgard Pisani had proposed holding a referendum in July on declaring independence in January 1986. The FLNKS was not happy with the terms of the referendum, especially provision to allow recent migrants to vote. Provoked by European extremists, the FLNKS announced that it would declare independence in January 1986 regardless of the of the outcome of the referendum. The French government sought to control European extremists (Pisani ordered the expulsion of some of the more notable ones) and began new negotiations with the FLNKS. The curfew was lifted in June and a new high commissioner arrived. The next month, the government unveiled a new plan which called for the creation of four regional governments and devolution of power to these regions. Each region was to have its own elected assembly and the regions were to elect members to a national assembly. The plan was rejected by the Territorial Assembly. The FLNKS also rejected it at first, but then decided to go along. The FLNKS felt that such a decentralized system would give them a chance to improve conditions for

Melanesians in the rural areas, while leaving the bigger question of independence until later.

Elections for the new assemblies were held at the end of September 1985. This time, the only violence were a few explosions beforehand, probably the work of rightwing extremists. The FLNKS won control of the three rural regions and the RPCR won control of the Noumea region. Because of the way representatives were apportioned, the RPCR was able to win twenty-nine of the forty-six seats in the national assembly.

The FLNKS had been highly critical of SLN on a number of issues during the disturbances. One issue concerned the lack of employment for Melanesians and the treatment of those Melanesians who were employed. Out of a total of 2,300 SLN employees, only three hundred were Melanesian. By the end of 1985, relations between SLN and the Melanesian community had begun to improve as SLN took steps to promote better employment opportunities for Melanesians. The number of Melanesians employed at the Thio mine itself rose to ninety-five out of a total workforce of 243 by the latter part of 1986, and one Melanesian was promoted to foreman and another sent to France by the company to train for a managerial position.[25]

Just as a peaceful settlement favoring the Melanesian community seemed possible, the change of government in France and the resumption of power by the conservatives, returned the colony to a situation like that prevailing under the former conservative government. The new minister for overseas territories, Bernard Pons, visited New Caledonia in April 1986, and announced plans to nullify the authority of the regional assemblies. This political about-face was accompanied by increased militarization of New Caledonia. This time, not only did the number of security forces rise (to 9,500 by early 1988), but the military adopted a policy of "nomadization," which entailed establishing small outposts throughout the Melanesian countryside. Such actions prompted Melanesian leader Jean-Marie Tjibaou to comment that New Caledonia "looks like an occupied country."[26] The third part of the new government's program for New Caledonia was an A$80 million package to "reconstruct" the colony's economy. Part of this amount was to be targeted for the predominantly Melanesian areas.

Tjibaou, one of the moderates within the FLNKS, announced his willingness to go along with the new situation, hoping to consolidate the FLNKS position within the three regions and believing that confrontations at this point would not bring better results. But escalating violence placed increasing pressure on the moderates to take a more militant stand. In September, troops shot a Melanesian youth, the following month those responsible for the 1984 massacre were released to a heroes' welcome, and then, in November, the RPCR held a rally in Thio in an effort to provoke the FLNKS into violence. In the confrontation that ensued, twelve people were injured and one European youth died. French authorities arrested only the FLNKS supporters involved and blamed the FLNKS for the incident.

The next blow to the FLNKS came when High Commissioner Pons announced that the regional boundaries were to be redrawn. The new boundaries gerrymandered the colony in such a way as to leave the Melanesians with two regions in the poorest part of the territory, while the Europeans were to be given two regions that included most of New Caledonia's mineral, agricultural, and pastoral resources, in addition to Noumea.

The French government went ahead with a referendum on independence in September 1987, knowing that the Melanesian community would stage a boycott. As expected, only a small percentage of Melanesians voted and the other communities, who did vote, voted against independence. During the referendum campaign and in the period that followed, however, it became clear that Lafleur's influence was waning as more and more European settlers were coming to see the RPCR as representing the interests of the rich only. Some of this disaffection found its way into support for the FLNKS, but much more of it went to the Front National.

The success of the FLNKS boycott of the election masked growing divisions within the independence forces. Militants within the FLNKS and outside of it were growing restless of accommodation to the French. Following an April 1988 meeting of the FLNKS to discuss the boycott of the upcoming Territorial Assembly elections, a group of militants occupied the site of a planned hospital. The hospital was part of the French government's development package for the Melanesian regions and the militants hoped to rally opposition to this form of perceived bribery. Gendarmes removed the militants without too much trouble, but the weeks that followed proved to be some of the most violent to date. The worst event began when a group of Melanesian militants took several gendarmes hostage on the island of Ouvea. The siege that ensued ended with the deaths of nineteen Melanesians and four gendarmes.

The escalation of violence in April and May 1988 has been blamed by some on the Chirac government as it sought to present a tough image to the French electorate during the campaign that taking place at the time.[27] After Chirac's defeat, the new prime minister, Michel Rocard, sent a mission to New Caledonia to investigate the Ouvea massacre. The new government was greeted with considerable relief by moderates within the FLNKS, and, under Rocard's auspices, Tjibaou and Lafleur met in Paris in June—the first time that they had talked in five years. The Paris meeting resulted in the Matignon Agreement. This accord called for the creation of three largely autonomous provinces after twelve months, followed by a nine year transition period, and a referendum on independence in 1998. The new boundaries still placed much of the wealth of the colony in territory that would be under European control, including Thio, but they were an improvement over the previous plan. Tjibaou also negotiated the release of some two hundred Melanesian political prisoners and financial assistance amounting to FF300 million for economic development of the Melanesian regions to begin what he referred to as "the green revolution."

Back in New Caledonia, Tjibaou and Lafleur were faced with the task of selling the Matignon Agreement to their respective constituencies. Both faced criticisms; Tjibaou from militants such as those associated with the USTKE, and Lafleur from the likes of the Front National. The agreement was approved by referendum in November 1988, but the voter turnout was low and the results indicated that problems remained in convincing those on the extreme in both communities. Fifty-seven per cent of the voters in New Caledonia approved the agreement. The support was largely Melanesian, but included a fair number of Europeans. A larger number of Europeans, however, either did not vote or voted against it. The extent to which extremists in both communities were opposed to any compromise was made all too clear on 4 May 1989, when two militant Melanesian activists assassinated Jean-Marie Tjibaou and another prominent FLNKS leader, Yeiwéné Yeiwéné, on Ouvea.

François Burke was named to replace Tjibaou as temporary leader of the FLNKS over another contender for the post from the Palika about two weeks after the assassination. While some observers initially felt that the assassination might draw the independence movement together,[28] complaints from the smaller parties within the FLNKS of UC dominance and a UC decision to run candidates against those of other pro-independence parties in municipal elections in 1989, indicated that divisions remained and could easily grow. Since May 1989, the level of violence in New Caledonia has subsided, but the relative peace that exists remains fragile and could easily be upset by developments within or outside of New Caledonia.

A significant development in April 1990 was the announcement of an agreement between Jacques Lafleur and Melanesian interests to sell them his eighty-five per cent share of the nickel mining company Société Miniére du Sud Pacifique to Melanesian interests in the northern province of the colony.[29] Commenting on the agreement, Lafleur stated: "I am in favour of the Melanesians being drawn into the economy."[30] The deal entailed selling the colony's largest privately owned nickel mine to the northern regional councils dominated by the FLNKS for FFr1.8 billion (£195 million)—about one-third of its estimated value. Previously, the only Melanesian with a capital stake in the nickel industry had been civil servant Frank Wahuzua, owner of a small nickel operation known as Melanesian Nickel.

During the latter part of the 1980s, the New Caledonian nickel industry has had to confront a relatively poor international market and political instability at home. Despite the political disturbances of 1985, nickel production reached 72,300 tons in that year, largely as a result of momentum that it had been gaining previously. The following year, however, SLN decided to cut its output and total production declined to 64,100 tons, in part, because of continued political uncertainty, but also because of the weak international market.[31] The international situation did not improve in 1987, and SLN closed down one of its three electric furnaces at the Doniambo smelter for maintenance for four months, leading to reduction of total New Caledonian output for the year to only 37,800 tons. In an effort to reduce costs even further, SLN also cut back its workforce by 250 to 2,050 in 1987.

Since 1988, annual nickel production has averaged 45,000 tons (roughly seven per cent of world supply). Most of SLN's nickel is sold to Japanese stainless steel makers, and relatively high rates of production have served to keep demand and prices from falling further. However, even with greater political stability, market conditions and the still uncertain long-term political prospect for New Caledonia have precluded a major growth in the colony's nickel industry. Also, in June 1990 SLN suffered a strike at its Doniambo plant, resulting in lost production of over 3,000 tons. World nickel prices rose by eighteen per cent at the start of the strike, but settled again as the strike was resolved.[32]

This does not mean that New Caledonia does not have considerable potential for future expansion at some point. Nickel reserves are still relatively large and additional exploration could enhance their size further. There are also possibilities for other minerals. The chromite industry was revitalized when Cromical S.A. resumed working at the Tieghbaghi Mine.[33] Chromite reserves in 1987, however, were estimated to be adequate only for another three years of operation. The future of chromite mining received a boost in 1987, however, when Australian Pacific Ltd. conducted shallow offshore drilling at its Baie des Pirgues and two adjacent prospects, identifying substantial alluvial deposits of chromite.[34] There are also possibilities of mining other minerals. After some initial interest in copper and gold in the nineteenth century, the growth of nickel and chromite mining caused these and other minerals largely to be ignored. Nevertheless, the colony is known to possess potentially significant reserves of antimony, copper, gold, iron ore, lead-zinc, manganese, and phosphate.[35]

Any discussion of the future of New Caledonian mining should also pay attention to environmental questions—even though such considerations have not been of much importance in France or New Caledonia to date. Following a 1982 survey of the environmental impact of mining in New Caledonia, geographers Eric Bird, Jean-Paul Dubois, and Jacques Iltis noted: "Compared with other mining areas elsewhere in the world, the impact of opencast hilltop mining in New Caledonia has been exceptionally severe and extensive."[36] They also point to the very poor regeneration of vegetation where mining has ceased, and indicate that, despite recent efforts to improve the situation, "the movement of mining waste into rivers, and eventually to the sea, is bound to continue for many decades after mining comes to an end."[37] Environmental problems caused by mining in New Caledonia undoubtedly will become even more serious in the years to come—what is still unclear is the extent to which they will assume more importance in colonial politics.

Although far from the only consideration, the future prospects for mineral wealth undoubtedly play a role in continued French interest in New Caledonia. While most developed countries no longer see outright colonial control as a means of ensuring access to needed mineral wealth, some vestige of this earlier aspect of political economy seems to remain in the case of France. The future prospect for mining also is important to the extent to which it encourages the non-Melanesian settlers to remain in New Caledonia and another mineral boom would, undoubtedly, have serious consequences for current political compromise. Finally, whereas in the past only tourism has rivalled mining in economic importance, the economic initiatives focusing on the predominantly Melanesian regions of New Caledonia have at least the potential of creating a more balanced economy. Such initiatives are an immediate response to Melanesian agitation and violence which, more broadly, are in part a reflection of the failure of mining to provide adequately for the people of New Caledonia.

Notes

1. For background material on New Caledonia see: Michael C. Howard and Simione Durutalo, *The Political Economy of the South Pacific to 1945* (Townsville: Centre for Southeast Asian Studies, James Cook University, 1987), pp. 60-4, and 120-31; Virginia Thompson and Richard Adloff, *The French Pacific Islands* (Berkeley: University of California Press, 1971); Myriam Dornoy, *Politics in New Caledonia* (Sydney: University of Sydney Press, 1984); Alan W. Ward, *Land and Politics in New Caledonia* (Canberra: Department of Political and Social Change, Research School of Pacific Studies, Australian National University, 1982); Donna Winslow, "Labour Relations in New Caledonia to 1945," in *South Pacific Forum*, Vol. 3, No. 1 1986, pp. 97-112; Donna Winslow, Changement Social et Identité Ethnique en Nouvelle-Calédonie (Ph.D. Thesis, University of Montreal, 1988); Helen Fraser, *New Caledonia: Anti-Colonialism in a Pacific Territory* (Canberra: Peace Research Centre, Australian National University, 1988); John Connell, *Sovereignty and Survival* (Sydney: Department of Geography, University of Sydney, 1989); John Connell, *New Caledonia or Kanaky? The Political History of a French Colony* (Canberra: National Centre for Development Studies, Australian National University, 1987); and C.F. Bird, Jean-Paul Dubois, and Jacques A. Iltis, The Impacts of Opencast Mining on the Rivers and Coasts of New Caledonia (Tokyo: United Nations University, 1985).

2. John Higginson (1839-1904) first came to New Caledonia in 1859, and engaged in trading, shipping. agriculture, and mining. He became a naturalized French citizen in 1876, and established important business interests in New Caledonia and the New Hebrides. See P. O'Reilly, *Calédoniens: Répertoire Bio-bibliographique de la Nouvelle-Calédonie* (Paris: Société des Océanistes, 1953); A. Auvray, *Les Nouvelles-Hébrides: Mémoire de John Higginson* (Paris: Coutances, 1926); and Howard and Durutalo, *The Political Economy of the South Pacific to 1945*, pp. 69-70.

3. See Michael Tanzer, *The Race for Resources* (London: Heinemann, 1980).

4. Connell, *New Caledonia or Kanaky?*, p. 109; and B. Brou, *Espoirs et Réalities: La Nouvelle-Calédonie de 1925 à 1944* (Noumea: Société d'Etudes Historiques de la Nouvelle-Calédonie, 1975), p. 229.

5. See M. Kobayashi, "Les Japonais en Nouvelle-Calédonie," in *Bulletin de la Société d'Etudes Historiques de la Nouvelle-Calédonie*, Vol. 43, 1980, pp. 57-72.

6. Wilfred G. Burchett *Pacific Treasure Islands: Voyage through New Caledonia, its Land and Wealth, the Story of its People and Past*. (Melbourne: Cheshire, 1941), p. 52.

7. Connell, *New Caledonia or Kanaky?*, p. 108.

8. Winslow, "Labour Relations," p. 104.

9. The first recorded strike by mineworkers occurred in 1892, when poor working conditions led Japanese workers to strike at the Thio mine. The government intervened and sent ten strike leaders to prison.

10. See Thompson and Adloff, *The French Pacific Islands*, p. 275.

11. Alfred E. Eckes, Jr., *The United States and the Global Struggle for Minerals* (Austin: University of Texas Press, 1979), pp. 111-12.

12. Thompson and Adloff, *The French Pacific Islands*, p. 277.

13. Thompson and Adloff, *The French Pacific Islands*, p. 289.

14. The speech was made on 27 April 1965, and is quoted from Myriam Dornoy, *Politics in New Caledonia*, p. 145.

15. J. Fages, *Les Tahitiens de Nouvelle-Calédonie* (Papeete: ORSTOM, 1975), p. 27.

16. Dornoy, *Politics in New Caledonia*, p. 75.

17. Thompson and Adloff, *The French Pacific Islands*, pp. 459-60; see also Dornoy, *Politics in New Caledonia*, pp. 225-26.

18. On the economic swings of the 1960s and 1970s, see Dornoy, *Politics in New Caledonia*; Connell, *New Caledonia or Kanaky?*; B. Brou, "Un Siècle de Crisis et de 'Booms': Les Hauts et les bas de l'Economie Calédonie," in *Bulletin de la Société d'Etudes Historiques de la Nouvelle-Calédonie*, Vol. 40, 1979, pp. 33-49; as well as J.H. Bradbury, "International Movements and Crises in Resource Oriented Companies: The Case of INCO in the Nickel Sector," in *Economic Geography*, Vol. 61, 1985. pp. 129-43.

19. Senator Louvel, from Calvados, speaking on 13 December 1968, quoted in Dornoy, *Politics in New Caledonia*, p. 146.

20. Dornoy, *Politics in New Caledonia*, p. 227.

21. Additional background information on Amax is available in Michael C. Howard, *The Impact of the International Mining Industry on Native Peoples* (Sydney: Transnational Corporations Research Project, University of Sydney, 1988), chapter 5.

22. *Manifeste du Parti de Libération Kanak*, 1977 (mimeograph).

23. The USTKE has been quite active among employees of such companies as Ballande, but has not been a significant force in SLN. For example, a May Day demonstration march in 1990 organized by the USTKE involved some 3,000 people from such companies as Ballande, UTA, and Club Med.

24. For accounts of the 18 November 1984 election, see the December 1984 issues of *Islands Business* and *Pacific Islands Monthly*.

25. Helen Fraser, "Dien Bien Thio: Calm Returns," in *Pacific Islands Monthly*, October 1986, p. 23.

26. *Islands Business*, March 1987, p. 25.

27. *Islands Business*, May 1988, p. 5.

28. Such as Helen Fraser.

29. The agreement is reprinted and discussed in *Les Nouvelles Caledoniennes*, 18 April 1990, pp. 2-4.

30. Quoted in "Pacific Nickel Mine Sold to Melanesians," in *Financial Times*, 18 April 1990, p. 4; and "Kanaks Clinch Nickel Deal," in *Fiji Times*, 19 April 1990, p. 5. Also see, *Far Eastern Economic Review*, 3 May 1990, p. 12.

31. "SLN Reduces Output," in *Pacific Islands Monthly*, October 1986, p. 6.

32. See *Financial Times*, 21 June 1990, p. 26; 17 July 1990, p. 30; 20 July 1990, p. 28; and 24 July 1990, p. 34.

33. Chromite production in New Caledonia by gross weight in recent years has been as follows: 91,380 tons in 1983, 84,152 tons in 1984, 149,476 tons in 1985, 163,325 tons in 1986, and 152,756 tons in 1987: source, United States Department of the Interior, *Minerals Yearbook, Vol. 3: International*, 1987.

34. 230 million tons of ore at a grade of 3.5 per cent.

35. Three million tons of iron ore were mined a Baie de Prony between 1956 and 1968. Sixty thousand tons of manganese was mined near Bourail, Poya, and Ouaco from 1918 to 1922 and from 1949 to 1953 (source: Bird, Dubois, and Iltis, *The Impact of Opencast Mining*, p. 18).

36. Bird, Dubois, and Iltis, *The Impact of Opencast Mining*, p. 49.

37. Bird, Dubois, and Iltis, *The Impact of Opencast Mining*, pp. 49-50.

6

The Phosphate Islands

The growth of modern agriculture in the nineteenth century led to considerable demand for fertilizer. Guano deposits on a number of Pacific islands were exploited during the middle of the century, but many of these were soon depleted. The guano trade was superseded by phosphate mining and Pacific island phosphate came to play a vital role in the development of agriculture in Australia, New Zealand, Japan, and elsewhere. From around 1900 onwards, increasing amounts of phosphate were taken from four islands in the Pacific: Nauru, Banaba (also known as Ocean Island), Makatea, and Angaur.[1]

The London-based firm of John T. Arundel became one of the leading guano traders in the region in the 1870s. In addition, there were several smaller American, British, and Australian firms involved in the business. Work was carried out by indentured laborers recruited from a number of different islands. John Arundel joined with another firm, Henderson & MacFarlane, in 1897 to form the Pacific Islands Company. Arthur Gordon (Lord Stanmore), who had served as governor in Fiji during the 1870s, became chairman of the company, which had interests in copra and phosphate. William Lever bought a large amount of stock in the company in 1902, thereby adding to its capital and influence in high places. At the same time, the company sold its plantation holdings to William Lever's company Lever Brothers for £25,000 in order to concentrate solely on phosphate. With this reorganization, the company's name was changed to Pacific Phosphate Company.

The phosphate industry in the region before the First World War was dominated by German interests on Angaur (which was a German possession) and elsewhere by the Pacific Phosphate Company. Increased phosphate production brought with it greater demand for labor. It also entailed more difficult questions about land ownership and mining rights. Most of the guano had been collected on isolated, uninhabited islands frequented by large numbers of birds. Phosphate mining now, however, took place on inhabited islands where the phosphate companies had to come to terms with the inhabitants.

Nauru

The Germans assumed control of the tiny (twenty-four square kilometers) island of Nauru in 1888 with relatively little enthusiasm. It was an isolated, war-torn, and small island that produced only limited amounts of copra. The newly appointed administrator was able to curb warfare between the clans by implementing a system of indirect rule in which clan chiefs were made responsible for the behavior of the members of their clans. By the latter part of the 1890s, the German firm of Jaluit Gessellschaft was responsible for most of the administration and economy of the island. The island administrator was a company employee and the company was granted a monopoly on Nauruan trade. But little was actually done by Jaluit to develop the island. In particular, it failed to maintain regular shipping with the island. Thus, at one point Nauru was visited by only a single ship over an eight month period. This hindered the development of the copra trade which was the island's sole export.

Pacific Islands Company employee Albert Ellis discovered phosphate deposits on Nauru and on Banaba in 1900.[2] The Pacific Islands Company then made overtures to Jaluit to allow it to mine Nauru's phosphate. After the Pacific Islands Company was reconstituted to become the Pacific Phosphate Company in 1902, the new company continued the negotiations. The German government gave its consent for Jaluit to transfer its right to export phosphate from Nauru to the Pacific Phosphate Company in 1905. The next year, the two companies signed an agreement. In return for allowing the Pacific Phosphate Company to mine and export phosphate, Jaluit was given shares in the company, royalties on the phosphate (guaranteed to amount to £50,000 between 1906 and 1915), and was allowed to retain its monopoly over all other commerce.

Phosphate mining began on Nauru in 1907. Although at first the staff was both German and British, before long the British had assumed almost complete control of the industry. During the latter half of 1907, 11,630 tons of phosphate were shipped. Between 1908 and 1913, a total of 630,000 tons, worth £945,000, was exported. About half of the phosphate went to Australia and most of the remainder to Japan. Royalties to the Nauruan landowners were set at 1.5 pence per ton and some compensation was agreed to. The total amount paid to the Nauruans between 1907 and 1913 was £1,320. In light of the profits being made, the amount was quite small. But given the times, the Nauruans were probably lucky to have received anything.

One hundred Nauruans were contracted to work as miners in 1906, but none of them renewed their contracts, although a few did continue to work for the company as boatmen. Instead, a pattern was established of relying on indentured laborers from off the island. Most of the laborers were recruited from southern China (via Hong Kong) and the Caroline Islands. The Caroline Islanders worked mainly in shipping while the Chinese were employed mostly in mining. Workers were recruited on three year contracts. Poor health inspection procedures led to a dysentry epidemic in 1907, in which a number of laborers and about 150 Nauruans died. Relations between the Nauruans and the Chinese were poor, while those between Nauruans and Caroline Islanders were much more cordial (leading to some intermarriage).

The colonial administration relied on phosphate royalties for revenue, sparing the Nauruans from head taxes and the like. For the most part, the German administration left the Nauruans alone since they were perceived to have become largely irrelevant to the economy of the colony. Education was left to missionaries. The presence of tradestores and widespread use of money encouraged Nauruans to find ways to earn small amounts of cash. In addition to selling copra, some of them began selling fish and garden products to those working at the mine. So many changes and the presence of such a large number of new people on the island contributed to a worsening of health conditions among the Nauruans, who suffered in increasing numbers from tuberculosis, leprosy, various infant diseases, and problems associated with poor nutrition. The Nauruan population, which earlier had been decimated by warfare, declined even further, from 1,550 in 1905 to 1,310 in 1913.

Great Britain declared war on Germany in September 1914. Australia immediately sent a warship to seize Nauru, while the Japanese took possession of the phosphate-producing island of Angaur to the north.[3] Shipments of phosphate from Nauru resumed almost immediately after the establishment of Australian rule. From 1914 until mid-1920, around 500,000 tons of phosphate were shipped. Pacific Phosphate Company's capital stood at £1.2 million in 1915. German interests in the company were sold at auction in July 1917 to the British firm Elder, Dempster & Company for £600,000. Royalty rates of 1.5 pence for Nauruans and six pence per ton for the administration that had prevailed under German rule continued.

Immediately after the war, there was a struggle between Britain and Australia for control of Nauru. A compromise was reached and, in July 1919, the Nauru Island Agreement was signed by Britain, Australia, and New Zealand (it was ratified the following year). The primary concern of all parties involved was getting the phosphate as cheaply as possible. According to the agreement: (1) administration of the island initially was to be assigned to Australia under an appointed administrator; (2) a board of commissioners was established, comprised of one member from each country, which held title to the deposits and set the price of phosphate; (3) compensation was to be paid to the Pacific Phosphate Company (£3.5 million at first and an additional £531,500 later); and (4) phosphate exports were to be distributed at the rate of forty-two per cent to Britain, forty-two per cent to Australia, and sixteen per cent to New Zealand (Britain did not actually take such a large share, primarily because of the shipping costs involved).

The Nauruans themselves, essentially, were left out of the Nauru Island Agreement. Their rights were established under a League of Nations mandate that confirmed Australian seizuranty. Nauru was made a "C" mandate, which was the lowest possible status, giving minimal rights to the native inhabitants. In effect, this meant that the three countries were free to do as they liked with the phosphate.

As the extent to which "the ideals and effectiveness of the mandate system could be subverted by rapacious powers" became more apparent, there were calls for reform of the Nauruan mandate from several quarters.[4] Of particular concern was the fact that no provision had been made for governmental oversight of the administrator. The agreement was modified in 1923, and at least one of the participating governments was required to take responsibility for the actions of the administrator. While the situation remained far from ideal, this was an improvement and Nauru's mandate status at least meant that the islanders, or others on their behalf, could appeal to the Permanent Mandates Commission if it was felt that Nauruans were being improperly treated. In practice this did not mean a lot, but it did serve as something of a check.

The Nauruan chiefs supported Australian rule and the majority of islanders voted in favor of continued Australian administration in 1918. As with the Germans before them, the Australians adopted a paternalistic attitude towards the Nauruans. The district chiefs were allowed to deal with minor offences and to elect a head chief. An

Advisory Council was created in 1925. It included two European members nominated by the administrator and two Nauruans who were elected. The council was reconstituted in 1927 as a wholly Nauruan Council of Chiefs. As with such councils in other colonies, this new council had no actual power and served primarily in an advisory capacity.

Very little of traditional Nauruan life remained by the early 1920s. In addition, the islanders continued to suffer from diseases. An influenza epidemic in 1920 resulted in the death of 230 Nauruans. Leprosy had become a serious problem in the 1920s, but it was brought under control in the early 1930s. By the 1930s, tuberculosis had become the main killer.

The British Phosphate Commissioners (BPC) retained most of the Pacific Phosphate Company's staff when it took over mining on the island. BPC operations expanded greatly in 1922, with exports reaching 182,100 tons (valued at £823,045 or £450 a ton) that year. Royalties to the Nauruans on this amounted to £2,227, of which £759 was paid into a trust fund. Demand for Nauruan phosphate increased sharply during the interwar years with the expansion of agriculture in Australia and New Zealand. Following considerable investment in infrastructure, exports rose to 318,185 tons in 1927, worth £780,070. Construction of a cantilever was completed in 1930, allowing for further increases in phosphate exports. After a brief pause brought on by the depression, exports in 1934 rose to 500,000 tons. The volume of exports peaked in 1940 at one million tons—representing one-eighth of world phosphate production. Significantly, as the volume of phosphate exported rose, the unit price went down. Between 1922 and 1941, the BPC were able to reduce the price from A£4.52 a ton to A£0.70 a ton. Australia received about seventy per cent of the phosphate annually, with the remainder going to New Zealand. The division of phosphate exports between the two countries was the subject of continuous argument, with the commissioner of each country seeking to get as much as possible.

When the Australians took over the island in 1914, there were about one thousand workers employed in the phosphate industry. About half of these were Caroline Islanders and the other half were from China. When the Japanese assumed control of the islands to the north, however, further recruitment of Caroline Islanders stopped. In response, in 1921, one hundred and twenty workers were brought from Papua New Guinea on a trial basis. Many of them died of diseases, in part because of the poor diet on Nauru, and those who survived were repatriated in 1924. Workers thereafter were recruited exclusively from China, through Hong Kong. The Australian administration sought to establish standards for employment with the Chinese and Native Labour Ordinance of 1922, which provided for a nine hour day and a six-day work week, with overtime on Sundays and holidays. Wages ranged from £1 20s to £1 16s a month for laborers and £8 10s to £5 a month for mechanics. The Chinese workers repatriated an average of around three-quarters of their wages. They were not allowed to become permanent residents, an issue of particular concern to the Nauruans, who feared complete alienation on their small island. The number of Chinese indentured workers reached 1,000 in 1928, declined to 696 in 1932, and then increased to over 1,500 by the late 1930s.

The three ethnic communities on the island remained largely isolated from one another. The European community was a small, residentially and occupationally discrete group that had little to do with the Nauruans or the Chinese. The Chinese were confined to their compounds in the evenings, with most of the rest of their time spent at work. The Nauruans were hostile to the Chinese and generally avoided them. Most Nauruans were confined to their own districts at night (although they were allowed out for a few more hours than the Chinese). Exemptions from curfew regulations were provided to a small number of Nauruans who lived a European style of life.

Nauruan acculturation and improved education led to demands for greater compensation from mining in 1924. A new agreement was reached in 1927: landowners (land was individually owned) were to receive a lump sum of £40 per acre and royalties of six pence a ton (four pence paid directly and two pence paid into a trust) and a further one and one-half pence per ton was to go into a trust for all Nauruans. In addition, provision was made to review the agreement every five years. By and large, it appeared as if the Nauruans were quite happy with the new arrangement and, in 1927, total payments to Nauruans amounted to £4,053.

The individual nature of Nauruan landownership and the structure of the new agreement meant that most of the money went to those owning land which was being mined (they received about two-thirds of the money paid in 1927). When the agreement was next reviewed, the landowners' royalty rate was increased to six and three-eighths pence per ton and, in 1938, the amount went to eight pence a ton. Although much of the money paid to individuals was dispersed among relatives or spent communally, wealth differences were emerging and, to some extent, this was reflected in different standards of living. Little of this wealth, however, was invested in such a way as to ensure non-royalty incomes in the future and those whose land was mined early later were to find themselves much worse off than those whose land was mined later, when royalty rates had increased substantially.

About half of government revenue came from the six pence a ton royalty paid to it by the BPC. This amounted to £4,488 in 1923 and had risen to £25,066 by 1933. The remainder of the government's revenue came from duties and a head tax (which the new administration had seen fit to levy on the Nauruans, in keeping with colonial practice elsewhere). About one-quarter to one-third of the budget was spent on Nauruans. The general trust for Nauruans received around £4,000 to £5,000 a year during the 1930s. Most of this money was spent on education, which was seen by the administration, in part, as a means of keeping Nauruan youths occupied.

Following the Japanese attack on Pearl Harbor in December 1941, European residents were taken off Nauru in February 1942. The Nauruans, along with Chinese and some Korean laborers, were left on the island. The Japanese landed on Nauru in August 1942, anxious to exploit the island's phosphate. The Allies considered landing on Nauru and Tarawa in August 1943, but instead invaded the island of Makin. A landing was made on Tarawa later, but the Allied command decided to leave the Japanese garrison on Nauru until the end of the war. During this time the island remained almost completely cut off from the outside world. Initially the Japanese had been able to export some phosphate, but very little was shipped during the latter half of the war.

The Japanese occupation of Nauru became increasingly harsh as the war progressed. The Chinese and Korean laborers suffered extreme hardships and many died of starvation. At first the Japanese treated the Nauruans in much the same paternalistic manner as had previous colonial rulers. The situation changed during 1943, as the war turned against the Japanese. Nauruans were conscripted into labor battalions in March 1943, and then, as importing supplies to the island became difficult, the Japanese decided to deport the Nauruans. In June 1943, six hundred Nauruans under Head Chief Detudomo were sent to an atoll in Truk. The forty-nine inmates of the leprosarium were killed a short time later. By the time the war was over, around 460 Nauruans had died.

The Japanese on Nauru surrendered to an Australian warship in September 1945. The mining infrastructure had been severely damaged during the war and repair work began almost immediately, but export of phosphate did not resume until 1947. The Nauruans were returned home from Truk in January 1946. Recruitment of Chinese laborers resumed shortly after the end of the war. By 1948, there were 1,400 Chinese and 125 European BPC employees on the island. A survey of phosphate reserves indicated that 459 acres had been worked out over the previous four decades and that a further 3,055 acres remained to be mined.

Viviani argues that the upheaval caused by the war forced the Nauruans "for the first time to look outward as a people."[5] In addition, the temporary cessation of mining and resultant loss of royalties encouraged them to seek employment as a means of greater security. The administration, for its part, showed more interest in employing Nauruans as a means of reducing costs. By 1948, all of the 364 potentially employable Nauruan males were working: 209 for the administration, 116 for the BPC, and 39 for the Nauru co-operative.

The price of phosphate had risen considerably as a result of wartime shortages. At the urging of the chiefs, in May 1947, the BPC agreed to a greater rate of compensation. This entailed £45 per year for the lease of land being mined and an increase in royalties from eight pence to one shilling one pence. This included an increase of two pence in the rate paid directly to landowners (which now became six pence), a doubling of payments to the community trust (to three pence), and the creation of a long term investment trust into which two pence was paid (the landowners' trust remained at two pence).

Nauru was made a Trust Territory of the United Nations after the war. Australia was given the trusteeship and, while the United Nations was limited in what it could force Australia to do on behalf of the Nauruans, the Trusteeship Council was able to exert more pressure than the League of Nations. Thus, at the urging of the United Nations and the Nauruan chiefs, Australia agreed to establish a Local Government Council in 1951, for which elections were held in December 1951. The council's limited powers proved to be a source of frustration to the Nauruan chiefs, but they felt that some progress had been made. Pressure on the Australian administration also led to improved educational standards and the placing of Nauruans in more responsible posts.

Head Chief Detudomo died in 1953. He was succeeded by a thirty-two year old school teacher, Hammer de Roburt, the grandson of a high chief and descendant of a nineteenth century beachcomber. Nauruan administrative employees went on strike over pay and conditions the same year. The strike lasted three months, a union was formed (the Nauruan Workers' Organization), and, in the end, the strikers achieved most of their goals.

A United Nations mission to Nauru in 1953 recommended consideration of eventual resettlement of the Nauruans because of the gradual destruction of the island by mining. While many older

Nauruans were against this, De Roburt supported the notion, favoring a move to Australia. Given the "White Australia" policy prevailing at the time, not surprisingly, the Australian administration resisted, claiming that resettlement would not be in the best interest of the Nauruans, since it would threaten their communal identity and they would not fit in well in Australia.

Also, in part because of United Nations pressure, royalty rates were increased in 1950, with an additional three pence per ton being paid into the long term trust. Such increases, however, did not alter the fact that in relative terms the amount paid to Nauruans remained low. In the fiscal year 1950-51, a total of £55, 268 was paid in royalties and, of this amount, only £16,288 was in cash. In contrast, 1951 phosphate exports amounted to 950,744 tons, worth A£1,378,578. The price of a ton of phosphate was A£1.45, more than twice the 1941 price. Over the next few years royalties paid to the landowners were increased by another three pence a ton.

Demand for phosphate remained high after the Second World War. Annual production on Nauru in the 1950s averaged around 1.2 million tons and in the early 1960s it reached 1.6 million tons. The value of phosphate also rose. The price per ton reached A£2.08 in 1958 and then proceeded to climb even higher until, in 1966, it was A£2.82. The total annual value of phosphate exports during the latter part of the 1950s went as high as A£2.8 million and it rose to A£4.7 million in the early 1960s. Higher production and rising phosphate prices created greater tension between the Nauruans and the BPC. It was not only the royalty rate that upset Nauruans, however, but also the treatment they were afforded by the Australians.

Completion of work restoring the infrastructure and greater mechanization led to less demand for mineworkers. Between 1951 and 1952, the number of mineworkers was reduced from 1,411 to 1,167. Moreover, fewer of the workers recruited came from China (or Hong Kong). The number of Chinese workers was reduced to 747 in 1952, with the remaining 420 workers coming from the Gilbert and Ellice Islands. Recruitment of the latter came about largely as a result of pressure from the British, who were anxious to find employment for the inhabitants of the colony.

Nauruan attitudes towards other groups living on the island reflected their insecurities in the face of a growing feeling of becoming aliens in their own land and gained them the reputation as the "Scots of the Pacific": "somewhat dour in their relationships with Europeans, tending to be themselves only when they were among their own people."[6] Relations between Nauruans and Chinese remained strained after the war. And, unlike the Caroline Islanders earlier, who had been well received by the Nauruans, the Gilbert and Ellice Islanders were not so warmly welcomed. Because of the need for skilled workers as a result of mechanization, the term of indenture contracts for the Gilbert and Ellice Islanders was lengthened from one to three years and the workers were allowed to bring their families. Special care was taken to ensure that the Chinese did not become permanent residents. This helped to allay Nauruan fears to some extent, but they remained concerned about their fellow Pacific islanders. The Nauruans disliked the Gilbertese and Ellice Islanders because they were indentured laborers (giving the Nauruans a sense of superiority), because they worried that these islanders might want to stay, and because of the preferential treatment that they perceived them receiving from the Australians, largely because of the political disputes that had come to sour relations between Nauruans and Australians.

By the late 1950s, the Nauruan chiefs had begun to favor an end to the BPC's paternalism in return for a greater share of the profits. The BPC agreed to a further increase in the royalty rate in 1961, but both the BPC and the Australian administration were increasingly hostile to the growing assertiveness of the Nauruans and pressure from the United Nations. In the course of arguing, the Nauruans pointed out that Nauruan phosphate was being sold at less than half the rate of comparable phosphate from Makatea. In 1964 the Nauruans asked for the phosphate deposits to be transferred legally to the Nauruan people. They called in consultants (Kenneth Walker and John Melville) to assist in preparing submissions. In the submissions, it was pointed out that, while the world price of phosphate was £6 4s, the rate paid for Nauruan phosphate was only £2 10s. The response of the BPC was to increase the royalty rate in 1965 and again in 1966.

The issue of resettlement was discussed again during the early 1960s. The estimated life of the phosphate reserves was less then thirty years by 1960, and Hammer de Roburt and other Nauruans were increasingly concerned about the future of the Nauruan people once mining ceased. This time some progress was made and an island off the Queensland coast was decided on for resettlement in 1963. The following year, however, an inability to agree on the political status of the resettled Nauruans led to the collapse of the talks. Discussions now turned to the prospects for rehabilitating the island. The BPC argued that rehabilitation was not feasible and the Australians and even the United Nations tended to agree.

Such dim prospects for Nauru's future did not keep the Nauruans or the United Nations from pushing for Nauruan independence once there seemed no possibility of resettlement. The United Nations

called on Australia to establish a legislative council and to grant
Nauru independence after the council had been in existence for two
years. The Australians were slow to act on this, but finally agreed to
establish a council in 1965. In the debate over the issue in the
Australian Parliament, Labor Party parliamentarians had argued for
steps to be taken to safeguard the interests of indentured workers on
the island, but no such safeguards were incorporated into the bill
that eventually was passed. Since none of the parties actually involved
in the negotiations had much interest in this issue (least of all the
Nauruans), it did not figure in subsequent negotiations either.

These political initiatives were accompanied by discussions in
1965 over the future of the phosphate industry on the island. The
participating governments in the BPC proposed a partnership, in
which Nauru would have a fifty per cent interest. The Nauru
representatives responded with a counter-proposal of complete
Nauruan ownership, with the BPC serving as a managing agent.
After prolonged negotiations, the Nauru Phosphate Agreement was
signed in June 1967. According to the agreement, Nauru would
assume control of the industry and, in return, it would guarantee an
exclusive supply of phosphate to Australia and New Zealand at an
annual rate of two million tons a year (Britain stopped buying Nauru
phosphate in 1966, when the price increased following renegotiation
of the royalties). The price was set at U.S.$11.00 per ton (U.S.$1.00
per ton under the current international price) for the first three
years. Thereafter, the price was to be adjusted according to changes
in the international market. The Nauruans also agreed to purchase
the BPC's assets on the island for A$20 million.

Independent Nauru

Nauru became independent in January 1968, with Hammer de
Roburt as its president. The Nauruans had achieved what no other
small group of native peoples had been able to accomplish: they had
gained control of a large mining complex on their territory as a
completely independent nation-state. Moreover, it was a well-
established industry with a relatively dependable market. Within
the perimeters of the international phosphate market, and the size of
their reserves, it was largely up to the Nauruans to decide how to
proceed. Their population at the time was approximately three
thousand, with another three thousand Pacific islanders, Chinese,
Europeans, and others living on the island, mostly employed in the
mining industry. By Third World standards, the Nauruans were a

relatively well educated people and the mining industry gave them
a per capita income of over U.S.$1,600 a year.

Among the issues debated around the time of independence was
how to distribute the profits from mining. At the heart of the debate
was the question of how much was to go to individual landowners
and how much to the Nauruan people as a whole. It is an issue, as we
shall see, that has continued to be of importance to the present—and
one that has plagued the Banabans, another group of phosphate
islanders with a tradition of individual land ownership. De Roburt
emerged as a champion of national over private interests. Despite
this, and the existence of redistributive mechanisms, wealth
differences among the islanders did become progressively more
marked.

New royalty rates were established in 1969. The total royalty was
to be A$4.50 per ton. This amounted, in 1969, to approximately A$9
million, which was equal to A$3,000 on a per capita basis.[7] The
division of royalties, however, was not on a per capita basis. Out of
the A$4.50, the landowners received A$1.40: A$0.60 was paid into
the Nauruan Landowners Cash Royalty Fund, and A$0.80 was placed
in trust in the Nauruan Landowners Royalty Trust Fund. With
phosphate production of 2,241,450 tons in the fiscal year 1967-68,
this meant a direct cash payment to those whose land was being
mined of roughly A$1.3 million and payment into the trust for all
landowners of about A$1.8 million. Divided among, say, four hundred
landowners, this would mean a cash payment of A$3,250 each. The
remainder of the A$4.50 included payments into the following: the
Long Term Investment Fund A$1.70, the Nauru Housing Fund A$0.20,
the Nauru Rehabilitation Fund A$0.60, and the Nauru Local
Government Council's Nauru Royalty Fund A$0.10.

The other important issue at the time had to do with the status of
non-Nauruans living on the island. The Nauruans decided to restrict
citizenship to Nauruans and to others with some Nauruan ancestry
under certain circumstances. In this way, the Chinese and virtually
all other non-Pacific islanders were, effectively, excluded from
becoming permanent residents or citizens.

The Nauru Phosphate Corporation (NPC) was incorporated in
June 1969. It assumed full control of the BPC's assets on Nauru in
July 1970. It was not a particularly auspicious time for the industry.
The international price of phosphate had dropped steadily from
U.S.$14.00 a ton in 1965 to U.S.$11.00 in 1970. There was an oversupply
of phosphate worldwide and a recession in Australian agriculture in
1970-71, which further depressed Nauru's market. Phosphate
production on Nauru declined to 2,059,905 tons in 1970-71 (of which

1,218,300 tons went to Australia and the remainder to New Zealand and Japan).

Despite these problems, actual revenue from mining increased. Thus, NPC's revenue went from A$4 million in 1969-70 to A$6.3 million in 1970-71. Since this accounted for eighty-five per cent of the Nauru government's budget, it meant that government expenditure was able to increase at a significant rate. The government was able to provide more services for the Nauruans in terms of housing, health care, and communication. Air Nauru began operation in late 1969, with an eight passenger Falcon fan-jet.[8] Also, while a large portion of imports (total imports amounted to A$4.2 million in 1967-68, in comparison with A$15 million worth of exports) were accounted for by goods intended for the mining industry (such as machinery and building material), a good deal was also spent on materials for housing, transportation, and food for the Nauruan population. It is worth noting that alcohol was not yet an important item: in 1965-66 imports of provisions amounted to A$1.2 million, of which alcohol accounted for only A$46,844, and much of this was for the expatriate mining staff.

The international price of phosphate began to recover slowly in the early 1970s. By 1973, it was up to U.S.$13.75 a ton. Then came the oil crisis and with it the price of phosphate shot up dramatically: to over U.S.$54 in 1974 and above U.S.$67 the next year. In terms of quantity, however, the market had not improved for Nauru. Many of its phosphate buyers had stockpiles because of declining demand by farmers. Nauru's production peaked at 2.4 million tons in 1973-74, and then began to decline: 1.9 million tons in 1974-75, 1.5 million tons in 1975-76, and 0.9 million tons in 1976-77 (the low point). At the same time, the price of phosphate began to drop, although to nothing like previous levels: to about U.S.$36 in 1976, and declining to a low of U.S.$29 in 1978.

Then, with the minerals boom of the late 1970s, the situation reversed itself and the price of phosphate began to rise once again: to a peak of U.S.$49.50 in 1981. In response to growing demand, Nauru's phosphate production rose as well: 1.5 million tons in 1977-78, 2.2 million tons in 1978-79, and 2.0 million tons in 1979-80. The NPC also began to export quantities of upgraded calcinated rock, in an effort to improve the industry's profitability: from 8,500 tons in 1977-78, to a high of 55,435 tons in 1980-81. As the boom turned to recession, prices and production dropped: the price declining to around U.S.$37 in 1983 and production dropping to 1.5 million tons in 1980-81 and to 1.7 million tons in 1981-82.

By this time, concern over the future of Nauru's mining industry was becoming more pronounced. In mid-1981, it was estimated that some twenty-four million tons of ore remained to be mined. At production of two million tons a year, this meant that only twelve more years remained. Even at a lower extraction rate of 1.7 million tons, mining would only continue for fourteen more years (or to 1995)—an estimate that, fortunately, proved to be a little on the conservative side.

The two factors, price fluctuations and depletion of reserves, came to dominate the political economy of the republic. The phosphate boom of the early 1970s provided Nauru with considerably more money and significantly transformed life on the island. Sudden wealth quickly proved to be a mixed blessing. To get some idea of the difference that the initial price surge made to Nauru's finances, taking 1969-70 production of 2.2 million tons at the 1970 average international price of U.S.$11 a ton, the total value of Nauru's production is about U.S.$24.2 million. In comparison, 1973-74 production of 2.4 million tons at U.S.$54.50 per ton yields U.S.$130.8 million—more than a five-fold increase.

Despite subsequent declines in the price of phosphate and in the level of production from its levels of the early 1970s, Nauru's earnings from phosphate mining have remained substantially higher than at any time in the island's past. Total phosphate earnings in 1983-84, after the second boom had ended, were still around A$120 million. Such high earnings were reflected in government budgets. Thus, government revenue in 1970-71 was A$7.6 million, in 1975-76 it had risen to A$34.8 million, and, by 1981-82, it had reached A$91.3 million. Taking the early 1980s population of around five thousand Nauruans as a constant, this translates into the following amounts on a per capita basis: A$1,520, A$6,960, and A$18,260—a substantial increase over a ten year period, even if inflation is taken into account. The amount paid to landowners and the various trust funds increased as well. The current royalty rate for the trust funds is A$9.75 per ton, divided as follows: A$1.75 to the Long Term Investment Fund, A$0.50 to the Nauru Housing Fund, A$3.25 to the Nauru Rehabilitation Fund, and A$4.75 to the Nauruan Landowners Royalty Trust Fund. In the early 1980s, the total was around A$17 million per year.

The impact of so much money on the Nauruans was dramatic. As John Connell remarks: "Internally, Nauru is in many respects, a comprehensive welfare state."[9] Basically, all the essentials came to be provided for and most services, such a telephones and air travel, were to be had for the taking (a situation that has caused considerable consternation for the country's auditors). A great deal of what has been paid out to individuals continues to be spent on conspicuous consumption: automobiles, video sets, stereos, and, especially, food. It is this last item that has come to cause a particularly serious problem for Nauru.

Health statistics, like almost all figures for Nauru, are either confidential or questionable, but it is possible to piece together a general picture. The daily caloric intake has been estimated at an average of six thousand per person. Moreover, much of what is consumed is high in salt and sugar content and low in nutritional value—"junk-food." To take just one item, the empty containers of which ring the island, Nauruans consume some eight million cans of beer a year (all imported from Australia). Whereas increased wealth initially led to an improvement in health standards, the impact soon turned to disaster. The average life expectancy is probably around forty-five years. As one commentator has noted, impressionistically: "The Nauruans have always had a tendency to stoutness, but their wealth has given them the freedom to gorge themselves without limit, and they are now the most grossly overweight people in the world. As a result, diabetes is a plague."[10] A study by the Diabetes Institute in Melbourne released in 1988, based on health studies of Nauruans since the 1970s, indicated that at least one-quarter of the Nauruan population suffered from diabetes.[11] If neglected, diabetes can lead to complications like respiratory diseases, heart ailment, kidney diseases, blindness, gangrene, stillbirths, and congenital abnormalities. Thus, it is not surprising that the report also noted that Nauruans were prone to gout, high blood pressure, and cancer, and had a high incidence of blindness and amputated limbs. The second biggest killer on the island is also related to phosphate wealth—road deaths, mostly as a result of drinking.

The government launched a program of medical checkups in 1983, at which time it was discovered that a number of individuals were too ill to come to the hospital without assistance. The De Roburt government responded with a half-hearted program to try to come to terms with the problem, including a campaign to increase public awareness and stocking special diabetic foods in the co-op store. To date, these efforts have had only limited results.

Increased phosphate earnings, because of individual ownership, have also served to create even greater inequality of wealth. One important factor in this regard is when one's land is mined. Another is the relative size of phosphate reserves on one's land. Thus, the characterization common around the Pacific that all Nauruans are wealthy is something of a distortion. While all adult Nauruans receive a guaranteed minimum income (around A\$4,500 per year in the early 1980s), beyond this there are substantial differences in individual and family wealth.

Knowing that the phosphate reserves will not last forever, Hammer de Roburt and his close associates (including long-time adviser Kenneth Walker) set about in the 1970s to invest overseas, with the aim of creating a situation that would allow the people of Nauru to sustain their current standard of living after the end of phosphate mining. At the heart of this strategy are the investments of the Nauru Phosphate Royalty Trust. A general breakdown of its assets for the financial years 1980-81 and 1981-82 are provided in table 6.1. According to the 1968 ordinance establishing the trust, it may invest money in: (1) securities of or guaranteed by the Commonwealth or States of Australia, (2) other securities approved by the cabinet, (3) fixed deposits approved by the cabinet, and (4) "in such other manner as approved by Cabinet." In general, investment decisions have been made by a small group of individuals with no public discussion of priorities or practices. As John Connell comments: "Nauru has no development plan and possible strategies for the development of Nauru are rarely discussed in parliament, or outside it, but are essentially formulated by the President, Hon. Hammer de Roburt, and the Nauruan Cabinet."[12] To this list one must add Kenneth Walker's contribution.

Turning first to stocks, bonds, and cash deposits, most investments have been in Australia.[13] In 1981-82, the trust held Australian ordinary shares with a market value of A$84.4 million (acquired at a cost of A$74.5 million). Investments in the United States for 1981-82 included cash and deposits worth U.S.$2.9 million, fixed interest deposits worth U.S.$9.8 million, and shares with a market value of U.S.$18.6 million (total value U.S.$31.3 million). During the 1981-82 financial year, the cabinet decided to diversify and invest in Asia. Investment managers were appointed in Tokyo and Hong Kong in May 1982. A total of A$10 million was invested in Japan and A$5 million in Hong Kong. By the end of the financial year, these investments were valued at A$9.3 million and A$4.9 million respectively.

This is not the place for a detailed analysis of stock investments by the Nauru Phosphate Trust, but, overall, its stock portfolio had an uneven record in the 1970s and 1980s.[14] Thus, Nauru's shares fared badly during the recession of the early 1980s, its cost to market value ratio declining from 1.65 in 1980-81 to 1.13 in 1981-82. Taking mining stocks for example, many of these were purchased during the boom period in Australian mining shares in the late 1970s, and the value of such shares declined as the boom came to an end in the early 1980s.

Thus, the initial cost of the mining shares was A$10.6 million. By the end of the 1981-82 financial year, their market value was A$8.9 million. While this loss was far from being a financial disaster, it does highlight one important reason for Nauru's desire to diversify its overseas investment and points to the extent to which Nauru's economic fortunes have been tied to overseas economic fluctuations beyond simply the price of phosphate.

Another important source of Nauru's overseas investments is real estate. By far its largest real estate investment is Nauru House, a fifty-two story office building located in the center of Melbourne. Its initial cost was A$40.6 million and, by 1981-82, as a result of continued growth in Melbourne's real estate market, it was estimated to be worth A$90 million. Market value aside, there have been problems generating income from the building. For a number of years there were difficulties with a low occupancy rate and rental arrears in the building. In 1980, only fifty-nine per cent of its potential area had been leased. Steps were taken to improve this situation and the occupancy rate reached eighty-seven per cent by mid-1981. By the middle of the following year, this had been increased to almost ninety-eight per cent. The amount of rent owed by Australian and other non-Nauruan interests in the building was reduced from A$62,578 at the end of the 1980-81 financial year to A$2,481 by the end of the following financial year. The trend was different, however, for the Republic of Nauru and other related bodies, who comprised the main lease-holders. Their arrears went from A$363,885 in 1980-81 to A$513,103 the next year. By the late 1980s, the rental situation had improved considerably and Nauru House was generating a return of about A$12 million a year. In mid-1989, however, another problem appeared when pieces of concrete began falling off the building as a result of structural problems relating to corrosion of the steel enforcement beams.[15]

Consideration was given to purchasing additional property in Australia in the early 1980s. A shopping center in New South Wales was investigated, but it was decided not to proceed after the Australian Investment Review Board ruled that the investment would be taxable. Despite the fact that it now appeared as if future investments by the trust in Australian real estate would be taxable, the trust went ahead the following year and purchased three additional properties in Melbourne: Nylex House for A$8.8 million, the Glensborough Private Hotel for A$650,000, and property adjacent to Nauru House owned by the Bank of New South Wales for A$1.3 million. The Glensborough Hotel was renamed Islanders Place and designated for use by Nauruan students in Melbourne.

TABLE 6.1 Nauru Phosphate Royalties Trust Investments

	30 June 1981	30 June 1982
Book Value		
LTIF	A$166,320,005	A$189,449,043
NLRTF	101,651,812	122,469,887
NHF	3,162,234	3,083,251
NRF	61,325,773	75,403,884
	332,459,773	390,406,065
Equities	86,474,226	116,761,036
Fixed Interest	123,553,593	118,992,466
Property	39,673,601	41,853,769
Cash/Dep	82,758,302	112,798,794
	332,459,773	390,406,065
Market Value		
Equities	138,619,541	129,851,872
Fixed Interest	119,558,071	105,554,665
Property	74,172,500	91,783,000
Cash/Dep.	82,758, 302	112,798,794
	415,108,418	439,985,331
Royalties		
LTIF	2,963,548	2,991,369
NLRTF	8,043,916	8,119,431
NHF	846,728	854,677
NRF	5,503,732	5,555,401
	17,357,924	17,520,878
Collateral Securities (Market Value)		
NLRTF	19,519,722	18,737,003
NHF	2,302,325	1,166,163
NRF	45,554,240	14,846,896
	63,376,287	34,750,062

Source: Nauru Phosphate Royalties Trust, *Annual Reports* for the years 1980-81 and 1981-82.

The trust also purchased properties elsewhere besides Australia. It purchased hotels in Western Samoa, New Zealand, and the Marshall Islands; apartments in Guam; Saipan House on Saipan; a large site for development in Honolulu, near the Ala Moana Shopping Center; and additional property in New Zealand, the Philippines, and Hong Kong. In June 1985, the trust signed an agreement to begin construction of the nineteen-story, 450-room Pacific Star Hotel in Guam. Construction and management of the hotel was placed in the hands of Japanese interests. Among Nauru's more recent purchases are the Grand Pacific Hotel in Suva, from interests closely associated with Prime Minister Mara of Fiji; 601 acres in Portland for U.S.$16 million in cooperation with an American developer in April 1988; another 668 acres in Houston; and the construction of Pacific House for U.S.$5 million in Washington, DC, which opened in March 1988. In regard to the latter, the plan is to entice other Pacific island countries to house their diplomatic offices in the building. Construction began in late 1989 on a large multipurpose complex on its holdings near the Ala Moana Shopping Center in Honolulu. The Nauruans ran afoul of local regulation and neighboring landowners with several of these investments and, overall, their reputation among the locals was not a particularly favorable one. Nauru also invested A$40 million in phosphate mining in India, where it assumed a forty per cent interest in Paradip Phosphate Ltd., a joint venture with the Indian government. The partnership was a difficult one and the were Nauruans not always keen to accept Indian laws and regulations.

During the 1970s and early 1980s, Hammer de Roburt developed increasingly close ties with the Marcos regime in the Philippines. Nauru began recruiting Filipino workers in 1977, and Air Nauru began service to Manila and opened an office there primarily to service the laborers. The trust also invested A$38 million in the Philippine Phosphate Fertilizer company in 1981, giving Nauru a forty-five per cent share and Filipino interests associated with the Marcos crony business group Zobel assuming the remaining fifty-five per cent share. The Leyte-based company is the largest producer of phosphate fertilizer in Asia and Nauru's interest in the company was intended, in part, to secure an Asian market for Nauru's phosphate. The two governments also discussed the possibility of resettling the people of Nauru on an island in the southern Philippines but no concrete plan resulted—fortunately for the Nauruans.

TABLE 6.2 Properties of the Nauru Phosphate Royalties Trust, 1990

Country	Property
Guam	Pacific Star Hotel
Fiji	Grand Pacific Hotel (Suva)
Philippines	Pacific Star Building (Manila)
New Zealand	Sheraton (Auckland)
	Sheraton (Rotorua)
Australia	Nauru House (Melbourne)
	Prime House (Melbourne)
	Islanders Place (Melbourne)
	Savoy Plaza Hotel (Melbourne)
England	Office Building (London)
United States	Nauru Tower Project (Honolulu)
	Pacific House (Washington, DC)
	Singer Building (Houston)
	668 acres of land (Houston)
	601 acres of land (Portland)

These investments contributed to a reduction of government reliance on phosphate revenue. The government depended on phosphate for eighty-five per cent of its revenue in 1970-71. By 1981-82, this had been reduced to sixty-five per cent (A$60.5 million out of a total of A$91.3 million). Such diversification also helped to underwrite the overall growth of the government's budget, which grew dramatically during the 1970s and early 1980s (to A$87 million for the year 1981-82). Nauru's mineral wealth had allowed its government to establish several ventures (such as Air Nauru, Nauru Pacific Line, and Nauru Fishing Corporation). From the beginning, these operations had to be subsidized. Initially, the amounts involved were not large and were well within the bounds of what could be afforded. But, it was not long before the situation had gotten out of hand.

Development and expansion of these ventures took place in the face of increasing fuel costs and lax fiscal control and losses began to grow. By 1980-81, Air Nauru was reporting earnings of A$29.4 million against expenditures of A$59 million—representing a loss of A$29.6 million, or around one-third of the government's budget. The problem worsened, until, by 1983-84, Air Nauru was losing around A$45 million a year. The situation with Nauru Pacific Line was much the same, with annual losses reaching A$12-A$15 million. Nauru Fishing Corporation's losses of only a few million dollars a year seemed modest in comparison.

Losses of over A$60 million a year on these ventures threatened the future security of the nation. And the situation became even worse as phosphate revenue began to decline. The drop in phosphate earnings would not have been so serious if it were not for the huge losses being run up elsewhere, since phosphate earnings were still considerable for such a small population. Thus, although representing a decline of about twenty-five per cent from a couple of years earlier, total phosphate earnings for 1985-86 were still around A$90 million.

The government made a token effort to come to terms with these financial problems in 1984. The year began with a supplementary appropriation to the budget of A$3.8 million—A$2.6 million of which was for Air Nauru—but the 1984-85 budget, announced a short time later, was a conservative A$88 million. The government was almost able to live within this amount (a supplementary appropriation of A$341,000 was made in February 1985), but it was becoming increasingly clear that soon it would no longer be able to sustain expenditure even at this level. By the mid-1980s, Nauru was not only being hurt by lower phosphate earnings, but also by the downturn in the Australian economy, to which most of its overseas investments were tied.[16] Not the least of its problems was the devaluation of the Australian dollar in 1985.

In the May 1985 session of Parliament, De Roburt announced that "owning to the economic climate and financial constraints which the country presently is experiencing Government has decided to scale down the activities of Air Nauru."[17] A decision was made to reduce Air Nauru's fleet of 737s and to suspend some routes. On the same day, a budget of A$76.8 million was announced, with an anticipated surplus of A$516,000. But, by June, such restraint was already being undermined with the announcement of a supplementary appropriation of A$3.3 million. It was also not long before Air Nauru recommenced some of its suspended routes. And, in November, a supplementary allocation was requested for A$26.4 million (including A$16.7 million for the public debt and A$6 million for Air Nauru).

Hammer de Roburt and his associates have not gone unopposed in their handling of Nauru's economy and criticism increased as the economic situation worsened. Even before the crisis of the early 1980s, there had been opposition. Reference has already been made to the debate over the distribution of phosphate earnings around the time of independence. This issue, along with others (including criticism of what some perceived to be "His Excellency's" authoritarian manner), continued to simmer after the granting of independence.

De Roburt's opponents in Parliament managed to defeat a bill dealing with phosphate royalties in December 1976 and forced him to resign. Bernard Dowiyogo, a twenty-nine year old former teacher who had only been elected to parliament in 1973, became the new president. Dowiyogo was defeated in the national election a short time later, and was replaced as president by Lagumot Harris. One week after assuming office, however, Harris was defeated, when the parliament rejected an appropriations bill, and De Roburt returned to the presidency after only twenty-two weeks out of office. During most of the boom period De Roburt was able to overcome threats to his power by using the country's wealth in a patronizing and sometimes authoritarian manner. So long as the money was good few seemed overly bothered about the lack of democracy and the veil of secrecy that covered most government activities.

As the economic picture worsened in 1985-86, political opposition grew. Although it was passed, the 1985-86 budget did not go through without a few critical remarks. Thus, one member of parliament noted that no provision had been made for the construction of additional homes for Nauruans.[18] An even more important debate was taking place over the funds held in trust. In December 1985, a proposal was placed before Parliament as a result of a petition from a group of landowners seeking to amend the Nauru Phosphate Royalty Trust Ordinance of 1968. The landowners, suspicious of De Roburt's handling of trust funds, sought to move the date of payment of interest accrued from the Nauruan Landowners Royalty Trust Fund forward to November 1986.[19] The total value of the fund at this time amounted to A$202 million.

Debate over the proposed amendment continued during parliamentary meetings in February and March 1986. The amendment was passed by the Parliament, despite strong opposition from De Roburt, who then had the matter referred to the Supreme Court. On 25 June, the Chief Justice gave his opinion against the petition.[20] When Parliament met the following day, a motion of no confidence was moved against the government. The motion ended in a tie (eight to eight) and, thus, was lost. A short time later, however, Hammer de Roburt was not so lucky and was defeated in Parliament by a group led by Kennan Adeang, who became the new president in September 1986.

Adeang's first item of business was presenting the 1986-87 budget. In his opening remarks, Adeang stated that his government was committed to "the principle of minimization of government expenditure...maximize popular participation in government [and] increased accent on public accountability." Beyond this, and perhaps more to the point, he followed these generalities with five specific matters that he intended to take up. Of these, he listed as his first concern: "we intend to promote the interests of the Nauruan landowners in all possible ways."[21] This meant pushing immediately for withdrawal of the money in the landowners' trust.

The appropriation bill introduced by the new government, which differed little from that presented by the previous government, called for expenditure of A$71.1 million. Since anticipated revenue was only A$59.5 million, this resulted in a deficit of A$11.6 million. The meeting adjourned without the budget being passed. Adeang and his supporters were unable to pass the budget at the next meeting of Parliament, and Adeang sought to assume emergency powers. De Roburt responded with a motion of no confidence, which was passed, and Adeang was out as president.[22]

De Roburt's quick return to power meant that the landowners group was stopped from getting its hands on the trust fund for the time being, but pressure from landowners and others on the government did not end. The struggle within Parliament, essentially, was between Hammer de Roburt and members of his clique, who favored an authoritarian-paternalistic approach, and the more individualistic landowners. Beyond Parliament, however, there were other sources of discontent—including those Nauruans who must work for a living.

TABLE 6.3 Employment on Nauru, 1981

Ethnic or National Origin	Number Employed			
	Admin.	NPC	LGC[a]	Total
Nauruans	1,474	102	182	1,758
Europeans	106	181	10	297
I-Kiribati	40	1,224	8	1,272
Tuvaluans	14	797	0	811
Fijians	14	0	6	20
Other Pacific	16	16	0	32
Filipinos	10	89	73	172
Chinese	42	333	7	382
Japanese	2	0	1	3
Indians	12	10	0	22
	1,730	2,752	287	4,769

a) Local Government Council.
Source: Department of Island Development and Industry, 1981.

The employment situation in Nauru has changed in a number of ways in recent years, although many of the fundamental problems remain much the same. The employment breakdown in 1971 was: 117 Nauruans, 140 Europeans, 750 Pacific Islanders (mostly Gilbertese), and 480 Chinese. Minimum wages in the mining industry were A$1.52 per day for unskilled labourers and A$2.40 per day for tradesmen (with maintenance provided as well). The Nauru government began to recruit skilled workers from Fiji and the Solomon Islands in the mid-1970s. The practice was frowned upon by the Solomon Islands government, which in 1981, complained that it could not afford to have skilled workers lured away since they were in short supply at home. As was noted above, Filipino workers began to be recruited in 1977. Many of these were relatively skilled workers. In the early 1980s, Nauru began to recruit Indians and Sri Lankans to replace more expensive and more demanding Europeans. Table 6.3 outlines the employment picture in 1981.

A look at labor relations on Nauru tells us a great deal about politics, economic, and ethnic relations in the republic. Nauru has witnessed numerous labor disputes over wages and working conditions. Shortly before independence, In April and May 1967, 600 Chinese, Gilbertese (I-Kiribati), and Ellice Islanders (Tuvaluans) went on strike for three weeks over wages and conditions. The Australian authorities raised the spectre of communist influence and one hundred of the Chinese workers had their contracts cancelled and were flown back to Hong Kong.[23] There were numerous minor disputes in the early 1970s, mostly involving Gilbertese and Ellice Islanders. A major strike, in February 1978, threatened an end to recruitment from the Gilbert and Ellice Islands.[24] It was around this time that Nauru began to recruit Filipinos, who were considered to be less strike-prone. Nauru's shipping line also had labor troubles in the 1970s. The line's management strongly resisted attempts to unionize the largely Gilbertese crews and the maritime workers union in the Gilbert Islands was highly critical of conditions on board Nauruan ships. The line also ran afoul of New Zealand unions. In mid-1973, the Nauruan ship *Enna G* was strike-bound in New Zealand for a couple of months.[25] Relations with New Zealand unions became very strained again in late 1976, when Nauru threatened to sue the New Zealand maritime union.[26]

There are no unions for non-Nauruan workers on Nauru. The government tolerates ethnically-based associations in the mining industry, but has made it clear that these are not to become overly involved in matters pertaining to labor relations. Labor legislation is limited and no new legislation has been drafted since the mid-1950s.[27] Wages for unskilled workers in the mining industry rose to A$3.20 a day by 1977 and to A$4.00 a day by 1981. In 1977, the average monthly income for European employees was A$575, for Chinese A$125 (this often being augmented by a second job or some other form of earning supplemental income), and A$75 for other Pacific islanders.

Whereas the wages of unskilled and semi-skilled workers mentioned above are only marginally better than those found in many other Third World countries, salaries for professionals have been closer to those paid in developed countries. Taking just one example, a position of Curriculum Officer in the Department of Health and Education in 1985, intended for a Nauruan, had a salary range of A$8,958 to A$10,086 (on which no income tax is paid). Positions which have to be held by skilled expatriates, because of a lack of qualified Nauruans, tend to be even better paid. Professionals from poorer Asian countries find the salaries particulary attractive. The main detraction is the lack of security. As one reporter has commented:

> If the foreigners complain about anything (and especially if they criticize the rather autocratic ways of the president), they are usually expelled within 24 hours: a letter is slipped under the door, and they are on the next flight out. But the pay is good and the life is easy, so there are always plenty of applicants to take their place.[28]

Among Nauruan workers, there have been occasional rumblings of disquiet. It must be remembered that not all Nauruans can live off of their royalty earnings and some must or wish to work to rise above the basic wage. An association was formed among Nauruan public servants before independence and public servants complained about their conditions in 1974.[29] The economic boom did much to reduce dissatisfaction and the association became little more than a hazy memory. But the economic crisis of the 1980s brought on renewed grumbling. The fifth point made by President Adeang in his September 1986 speech dealt with public servants:

> We have decided to have a closer look at the Nauruan Basic Wage regimen. The existing regimen has been set up in the early 1970's. It requires to be reviewed urgently, as many of the old premises of the old regimen and commodities whose prices constitute the basis for the half yearly revision of basic wage are no longer valid or in existence today.[30]

While this issue may not be of much importance to those with large royalty incomes, it is for many of the over one thousand Nauruans who were in paid employment in 1986.

Wages and conditions of employment cannot be divorced from the overriding concern with maximizing income from phosphate. It is a fixation that has led independent Nauru to have a record of labor relations that is little better and is perhaps even worse than that of the BPC. The government and NPC have viewed anything spent on workers as something subtracted from profitability and, indirectly, therefore as a detriment to national well-being. This has been easiest to rationalize in the case of foreign workers, but the issues are more difficult with Nauruan workers, and it is here that the contradictions concerning division of the spoils from mining among Nauruan surfaces again.

Back in office, in a February 1987 speech, De Roburt emphasized the need for Nauruans to tighten their belts, work harder, and not depend so much on the welfare state if the republic was to survive. He also sought to defuse opposition from landowners. To refute allegations that there was little money left in the Nauruan Landowners Royalty Trust Fund, De Roburt sent financial statements to twelve of the leading landowners. The statements provide a glimpse into the degree of inequality existing on the island and indicate how much worse it would get once the landowners begin drawing on the interest in the fund with the termination of mining around 1995. The twelve statements averaged A$1 million each, with the largest amounting to A$9 million.[31]

The most important new initiative launched by De Roburt was setting up of the Nauru Rehabilitation Inquiry in February 1987.[32] The inquiry was concerned with the prospects for rehabilitation of the four-fifths of the island that would have been mined when the phosphate ore ran out during the latter half of the 1990s, and, more specifically, to assess the liability of the countries that had comprised the BPC in paying for rehabilitation. Hearings took place in Nauru as well as in Melbourne and Wellington. At the outset, Australia, New Zealand, and Britain ignored the inquiry, and, when Foreign Minister Garth Evans of Australia visited Nauru in September 1988, he stated that no more money would be forthcoming beyond what had been agreed to at the time of independence.

The inquiry's ten volume report was tabled in the Nauruan Parliament in December 1988. The report concluded that rehabilitation was possible and estimated that the total cost would be around A$216 million. Not surprisingly, the inquiry found the BPC countries liable and made a claim against them for A$72 million.

In presenting the report, De Roburt proclaimed: "It charts the course of progress for this island extending over the next twenty years or even more."[33] On 19 May 1989, the Nauru government filed a claim against the three BPC countries with the International Court. In doing so, Nauru, confident of victory, had managed to get Australia to agree to accept the court's findings.

In the midst of the excitement over the pending inquiry report, Hammer de Roburt's labor policies led to a crisis with the country's airline. Many of Air Nauru's pilots had long been concerned about the operating safety of the airline and on several occasions its planes had been grounded at overseas airports for safety problems. In an effort to confront the government on this issue and to gain wage parity with other pilots in the region, a majority of the pilots formed the Nauru Airline Pilots' Association in early 1988. Hammer de Roburt, who was also chairman of Air Nauru, responded by firing the secretary of the association. In May, the pilots (most of whom were Australian) went on strike. The following month, New Zealand authorities withdrew their safety certification of the airline and Australia did the same a short time later.

Efforts by the government to recruit new pilots in Asia were unsuccessful. Relations between Nauru and New Zealand airline authorities deteriorated further when the De Roburt government decided to allow an agreement by which New Zealand officials advised Air Nauru on operations and airworthiness to lapse. De Roburt was able to get the airline operating on a limited commercial basis in September, but by December it was clear that it would not be resuming regular service any time soon. Given the amount of money normally lost by the airline, the strike might be seen as a blessing, but even a grounded airline has expenses and, between December 1988 and January 1989 alone, losses were estimated to have amounted to NZ$3 million.[34]

Air Nauru was not the only problem confronting De Roburt. Declining profits and rising debts of the Philippine Phosphate Fertilizer company (Philphos) after the fall of Marcos resulted in the company ceasing to purchase Nauru phosphate. After the fall of Marcos, the state-owned National Development Company, had assumed control of the 50.1 per cent share held by Marcos's associates. In 1988, the National Development Company announced a restructuring plan for Philphos that would substantially reduce Nauru's share of the company.[35] Members of Parliament decided that Nauru should consider getting out of the company altogether and, in early 1989, set up a select committee to investigate the situation. De Roburt, who had been instrumental in promoting

Nauru's involvement with the company to begin with, was anxious to rush the committee's report, but several members of Parliament felt that it should be given an extension on its 31 July deadline. Disagreement over the issue led to a vote of no confidence being placed before Parliament on 17 August by Kennan Adeang. The vote went ten to five and, once again, De Roburt was ousted.[36] In the balloting for president, Adeang withdrew in favor of Kenas Aroi, a former finance minister and chairman of the board of the NPC, who won by a vote of nine to six. Among those named to the new cabinet were Adeang (minister of finance) and former president Bernard Dowiyogo (minister of health and education).

Aroi announced that general elections would be held on 9 December 1989. In the meantime, he pledged his new administration to a policy of greater fiscal restraint, including a balanced budget. The government closed several overseas offices which had been a drain on the treasury (such as those in London, Tokyo, and Hong Kong) and took steps to reorganize Air Nauru. The latter included selling two of its planes, eliminating many of its international routes, and renewing the New Zealand advisory agreement.[37] The plan was for the airline to start small again and to build it up as finances justified— an important symbolic gesture to differentiate the new administration from the old.

Aroi and his allies won the general election, but Aroi himself suffered from a stoke and did not contest the presidency. When Parliament met to vote for the president on 12 December, Bernard Dowiyogo won by a vote of ten to six.[38] While this time it looks as if Hammer de Roburt might be finished, past experience cautions not to count him out yet. But whether the younger generation of Nauruans, represented by Dowiyogo, remains in power or De Roburt and his cronies return, Nauru faces a very difficult future. The Australian Development Assistance Bureau has characterized Nauru as an "Expiring Resource Boom State" and the date of expiration is only a few years away (twenty at the most). How well is Nauru prepared for the cessation of mining?

De Roburt's strategy was to concentrate his government's efforts in maximizing its foreign holdings, largely in stocks and real estate, and to limit decision-making about these holdings to a small group of individuals. Little serious attempt has been made to improve the productive capabilities of individual Nauruans through participatory democracy, training and education, and other means. It is a population accustomed to living off of rent rather than producing its own wealth and used to leaving decisions about this wealth largely in the hands of others. Even among younger Nauruans, there are relatively few who have the education to run the administrative and financial affairs of the country.

By the late 1980s, Nauru's public overseas investments were worth somewhere in the neighborhood of A$500 million. Optimistically, their worth might rise to as much as A$700 million by the mid-1990s.[39] On a per capita basis this equals about A$20,000; it would generate far less if figured simply in terms of earnings derived from the principle. The money, of course, will not be divided in this way. A proportion would remain tied to the government for the continuance of even much reduced services. And, for a government accustomed to spending A$60-A$70 million a year, even a "bare-bones" budget is likely to amount to a lot. Then there is that amount held in the name of the landowners (over A$200 million in the late 1980s), on which they alone are entitled to draw interest.

Should the people of Nauru choose a collective future, based on continued residence on the island, it seems unlikely that they will be able to maintain a life style equivalent to that which they have grown accustomed. Even with a great deal of luck, it is improbable that their earnings will be able to compensate for the loss of mining revenue. Moreover, it seems quite likely that their assets will be reduced through efforts to rehabilitate the island and maintain a reasonable administrative infrastructure. In the case of rehabilitation, even a court victory over the former BPC countries will leave Nauru having to spend a great deal, especially in the likely eventuality that there are substantial cost overruns.

Such financial difficulties will effect Nauruans differently, thereby placing greater strains on the prospects for a collective future. The wealthier landowners should be able to weather the transition without too much difficulty, but access to and control of their trust fund will undoubtedly be an ever hotter political issue. Given that the locus of their wealth will be entirely away from Nauru, their interest in the country also could diminish. The poorest and least educated Nauruans face the prospect of survival within the context of a much reduced welfare state. Island rehabilitation will do them little good in their present, state since they have few abilities to exploit their homeland through fishing, agriculture or other means. Improving their livelihood would require concerted educational efforts on the part of the government and, given the record in this regard, it is hard to be optimistic. The middle sector of Nauruan society is in an equally difficult position. For many of them, it is the very state structure that has provided the income to lift them above the level that they would otherwise occupy and it would be hard for them to find comparable employment outside of Nauru. It is understandable that members of this group have been prominent among those opposed to the De Roburt regime, but even with De Roburt out of the way their future is going to be a difficult one.

Nauru became independent with more promise than many other Third World countries, and in many ways Nauru has made much more out of its mineral wealth than have other countries. Like most Third World counties, however, newly independent Nauru suffered from a poorly developed infrastructure and this infrastructural poverty has contributed to its inability to maximize the potential benefits of phosphate mining. But the situation could have been far worse and the authoritarian De Roburt regime has left the country with a sizeable bankroll. However, given the continued poor state of the country's infrastructure capabilities and its numerous social and political problems, it is going to prove very difficult for Nauru to make adequate use of its investments as it enters a new era once mining ceases—difficult, but not impossible, and it remains to be seen whether Nauru's younger and more educated political leaders can do any better than those who came before them.

As a final note on the closing days of mining on Nauru, the country's financial problems are also of some relevance to neighboring Pacific Island states. For example, the reduction of air routes by Air Nauru has led to even greater isolation for some of the smaller countries in the region such as Niue and Kiribati, which depended, to a large extent, on the airline for air service. There are also the hundreds of mineworkers who will soon be sent back to their homes. Thus, when mining ceases around 1995, about 700 Tuvaluan mineworkers and their families will be forced to return to their overcrowded atoll country of 8,500 people, where their earnings have provided an important source of foreign exchange and where jobs are already at a premium. The Tuvaluan government in its 1988-91 *Development Plan* has proposed employing the returning miners on land reclamation projects, to be paid for with overseas aid funds, but such schemes can only ease the burden of such dislocation to a limited extent.[40]

Banaba and Rabi

Pacific Islands Company employee Albert Ellis discovered phosphate in 1900 not only on Nauru but on Banaba (also known as Ocean Island) as well.[41] Ellis persuaded a local chief named Temati, whom he viewed as "king and chief" of the island, to sign an agreement giving the company the right to mine phosphate on the island for 999 years at a rate of £50 per year—blatant theft, even by the standards of the day. Temati was chief of Tabwewa district, and his rights included control of commercial relations with Europeans. What he did not have the right to do was to alienate land, which, as on Nauru, was individually owned. In fact, the other islanders clearly repudiated the right of Temati, or any other chief, to sign such an agreement and the other chiefs refused to sign it. Despite the obvious problems with the agreement, with Arthur Gordon serving as a lobbyist, it was accepted by the Colonial Office. Also, at Gordon's urging, in September 1901, the Colonial Office decided to annex Banaba and to make it part of the Gilbert and Ellice Islands Colony.

The Pacific Islands Company had become extremely prosperous by 1904 and, over the next few years, was able to pay large dividends to its shareholders. Between 1904 and 1913 (with the contribution of Nauru after 1907), the company recorded profits of over £1,750,000. The Banabans, for their part, were paid around £10,000 during this period as their share from the proceeds from mining.

As phosphate exports increased (exports for 1908, for example, were 200,000 tons) so did government revenue, although certainly not in equal proportions. Government revenue rose from £4,300 in 1906 to £42,792 for the 1913-14 financial year. Added revenue and the ascendancy of Banaba as the economic center of the colony led to important changes in the administration. In particular, British authorities decided to move the administrative headquarters of the colony to Banaba. It was a move that was to isolate the administration from the rest of the colony and to promote unequal development, with the rest of the colony serving as little more than a labor reserve for the mine.

As in the case of Nauru, local labor was not used for mining on Banaba. By 1905, around 1,000 Gilbert Islanders had been recruited for mine work, a small number of Ellice Islanders had been recruited as boatmen, and mechanics were being brought from Japan. Later, about three hundred Japanese were recruited to work in the mine as well. Workers were poorly treated and, in 1911, the industry had its first strike, which was staged by Gilbertese over altered working hours.

The majority of Banabans remained opposed to mining or at least to the conditions under which it was being conducted. John Dickson was appointed chief administrator of the colony in 1907, and proved to be more sympathetic to the islanders than his predecessors. In part because of his favorable attitude towards the Banabans and Gilbertese copra producers, he was transferred in 1912. By this time, however, the Colonial Office itself was becoming more critical of the company's treatment of its non-European employees, its apparently excessive profits, and its destruction of Banaban food sources. As a result, the new agreement with the Banabans in 1912 that increased the original mining lease area of 105 acres by an additional 145 acres (the total area of the island is around 1,500 acres) included provisions more favorable for the Banabnans. The land was to be leased for £40-£60 per acre, there was to be compensation for food trees destroyed, and the company agreed to pay a royalty of six pence per ton into an interest bearing trust fund for the Banabans (equal to about £5,000 per year)—a rate comparable to that paid to the colonial administration. The following year, the company also agreed that food trees would be replanted once mining was finished in an area.

Phosphate exports declined during the First World War, but the Pacific Phosphate Company continued to record substantial profits. There were problems with both the Banabans and the mineworkers during the war. There was a renewal of hostility with the Banabans community in 1914, when, in an extremely petty move in light of the profits it was making, the company declared that it would pay compensation for coconut trees and not pandanus or wild almonds. Next, Gilbertese workers went on strike in 1916, after the company announced plans to reduce the wages of newly recruited workers. The action by the Gilbertese forced the company to drop the plan. Later, there was an additional labor dispute over the company trade store practice of charging Japanese and Europeans one-half of what it charged Pacific islanders. Protests were sufficient for the company to agree to uniform prices. It then, however, gave European workers a salary rise as compensation. Nothing was done to compensate the Japanese workers, who went on strike in 1919 and won a twenty per cent wage increase.

After the British Phosphate Commissioners took over from the Pacific Phosphate Company in 1920, the BPC sought to expand the lease area on Banaba by another one hundred acres. The Banabans refused and the BPC went directly to the Colonial Office in 1923 and asked for 150 acres. The Banabans continued to resist since the land in question included important food sources. The colony's newly appointed high commissioner for the western Pacific,[42] Cecil Rodwell, recommended that the entire island, except for "native reserves," be placed at the disposal of the BPC—an idea inspired no doubt by his eighteen years previous experience in South Africa—and stated that he felt further negotiations were pointless. Rodwell's recommendation was rejected by the Colonial Office and talks with the Banabans continued.

The Banabans asked for £5,000 per acre in 1925, instead of the existing £60. In effect, they were refusing to sell. Their position was viewed with some sympathy by the new high commissioner, Eyre Hutson, who noted that the BPC's revenue from mining amounted to between £37,500 and £48,000 per acre. The Banabans went even further and demanded £5 per car load of phosphatic rock (one car equalling about one ton), which would amount to around £1 million a year. Arthur Grimble, who had become resident commissioner after thirteen years' experience in the Gilbert and Ellice Islands, took on the difficult task of negotiations in 1926. After six weeks of intense discussions, the Banabans, led by Rotan Tito, still refused to give in. The Colonial Office was growing impatient: "The need of the Empire for the supplies of phosphate necessitates the taking of steps to make more land available for mining."[43]

The Banabans rejected the final offer in 1927. The response of the administration was to enact the mining ordinance of 1928, which allowed for land to be placed at the disposal of the BPC without the acquiescence of the Banabans, provided that the resident commissioner felt that the agreement was fair. This was followed in 1931 with an edict by High Commissioner Murchison Fletcher, stating that the initial agreements with the Banabans concerned surface rights only and not mineral rights, over which colonial subjects had no say.

Rotan Tito petitioned the secretary of state for colonies in 1932, thinking that the British government was unaware of what was going on. Significantly, throughout the entire ordeal, although the Banabans had become bitter against the BPC, such feelings did not carry over to the British administration and they never became critical of their colonial status. By the early 1930s, however, the Banabans had become fatalistic about their eventual loss. Even Rotan Tito went to work for the BPC.

One point that Rotan Tito, in particular, had felt strongly about was that royalty payments should be distributed to individuals and not given to the community. He argued in favor of this on the basis of the Banaban tradition of individual ownership of land. Some of the British administrators took a cynical view of this position since Rotan Tito and his family were the largest landowners on the island and stood to gain the most by a policy favoring individuals. Most Banabans did not see things in this light, however, and continued to support Rotan Tito as their spokesman.

The agreement that was put into effect set the level of royalty payments at 10s 1/2d per ton. The Banaban Provident Fund, intended for purchase of a future home for the Banabans, took two pence of this, with the balance going to the Banaban Royalties Trust Fund on behalf of the whole community. The agreement was to be reopen to negotiation in 1931. With Rotan Tito continuing to fight in favor of individual rights, the 1931-37 agreement allowed for the payment of annuities. All Banaban adults were to receive £8 per year and an additional £4 was paid for children. Individual landowners also were to receive payments, but with a weighting against the largest landholders, such as Rotan Tito.

With the end of the First World War, the colony's exports rose sharply: to £342,599 in 1920-21. The value of imports increased as well: £212,406 for 1920-21. There was a brief drop in the trade figures for 1921-22, as a result of the world economic slump, but they remained relatively high for the remainder of the 1920s. Government finance also recovered after the war (reaching £54,079 in 1920-21), but soon there were difficulties with the colonial budget. The BPC adopted a policy that royalties and taxes paid to the administration should not exceed those paid to Nauru (about £10,000 a year) and that they should only go to cover administrative expenses on Banaba. The policy was an attempt to play Banaba off against Nauru and to disassociate the BPC's operations on Banaba from activities elsewhere in the colony. The administration saw things differently, holding the view that Banaba had to be treated as part of a larger colony and that the BPC should be taxed for the benefit of the colony as a whole, and not necessarily in accordance with practices on Nauru.

In 1921, Acting High Commissioner T.E. Fell advocated increasing the tax on phosphate to improve the financial position of the colony. Lobbying efforts by the BPC in England succeeded not only in stopping the increase, but helped to convince the Colonial Office to cut administrative expenses in the Gilbert and Ellice Islands Colony. High Commissioner Cecil Rodwell agreed. The image which was being built up in government circles outside the colony was that it was a scattered and isolated group of islands which, except for Banaba, had no economic potential. Therefore, money spent on trying to improve things was a waste.

Government revenue levelled off in 1923-24 and, thereafter, declined, allowing the BPC to reduce its costs even further. The British considered the idea of establishing an advisory council for the Gilbert and Ellice Islands, but decided that it was unnecessary and impractical, given the difficulties of transportation between the islands and the small size of the European community, if one excluded those employed by the BPC. Budgetary cuts led the government to sell its only ship, the *Tokelau*, making the transportation situation in the colony even worse. One result of the loss of the ship was that colonial officers could visit islands only once or twice a year on private trading vessels.

After the First World War, Japanese labor no longer was available to Banaba, being diverted to Japan's new possessions in Micronesia. As it did with Nauru, the BPC turned to recruiting Chinese laborers in Hong Kong. Initially, about five hundred workers were recruited from Hong Kong for Banaba. In addition, Gilbertese continued to be recruited, as were Ellice Islanders in smaller numbers. The supply of workers from the rest of the colony, however, was unstable, depending in part on the price of copra and the occurrence of droughts. The total number of mineworkers in any given year during the 1920s varied from 1,200 to 1,500.

In general, the BPC's record of labor relations and its treatment of workers on Banaba was abysmal, and its policies served to heighten communal tensions. Relations between Chinese and Gilbertese workers were especially poor. One of the problems was a lack of outlets for recreation. But there were many other problems as well and tension between these two groups built up until a full-scale riot erupted in 1920. Chinese workers became upset in 1925, when the BPC failed to provide them with clothing and food that had been promised as part of their conditions of service, and a short time later there was an attack by Chinese workers on the Gilbertese. These events led to a further clampdown on workers by the management rather than to any attempt to alleviate the situation.

Phosphate exports from Banaba reached 230,000 tons a year by 1930. About three-fifths of this went to Australia and about one-fifth to New Zealand. The onset of the world depression in 1929 led to a lowering of overseas demand for phosphate as well as for copra. As a result, the value of the colony's exports declined to £231,328 in 1929-30. The BPC used the situation to argue for an even lower tax rate. The administration was opposed to the idea, arguing that the BPC could easily afford the £27,000 a year it was paying. To this the BPC responded by pointing out that it was paying much lower royalty rates on Nauru and that it could meet most of the existing demand for phosphate from that source if pressured to do so.

A five-year agreement was reached in 1932, according to which the BPC would meet the shortfall between approved administrative expenses and revenue. The six pence a ton royalty was to continue, but the BPC was exempted from most other taxes, fees, and duties. For the colonial administration, the agreement was a disaster.

Phosphate exports began to rise again in 1931, reaching 400,000 tons by 1937, with a value of around £450,000. At the same time, colonial revenue declined to around £25,000 a year.

The agreement also had an impact on labor recruitment. With the removal of the capitation tax, Gilbertese workers began to be replaced by cheaper Chinese laborers. The overall size of the workforce remained around 1,000, with the number of Chinese rising to about 700. For the Gilbertese, already suffering from low copra prices, this meant a significant reduction in incomes. As for the Chinese, they went on strike in 1931, when the BPC tried to repatriate 250 of them early.

Arthur Richards, who served briefly as high commissioner in 1936-37, was critical of the extent to which the Gilbert and Ellice Islands Colony administration had capitulated to the BPC. His replacement, Henry Luke, sought to establish greater administrative power in relation to the BPC and even advocated returning the colonial headquarters to Tarawa. During the course of negotiations with the BPC, Luke was able to exact an additional £10,000 a year in revenue for the administration and to remove the BPC's veto power over government expenditure. Further reforms were interrupted by the Second World War.

The Japanese bombed Banaba a short time after their December 1941 attack on Pearl Harbor. Most of the island's European residents were evacuated. Remaining behind were the Banabans, around eight hundred Gilbert and Ellice Islanders, and a few European government officials and missionaries. The Japanese landed on Banaba in August 1942. The Europeans on the island were killed and most of the Banabans and a number of Gilbertese were sent to Kosrae, where over two hundred died, many of starvation. Most of the other Gilbertese were shipped to Nauru or Tarawa. About two hundred Gilbertese were kept on Banaba to work as fishermen. Those remaining on the island were treated harshly and all but one was killed by the Japanese in August 1945, shortly before the Allies landed. As with Nauru, Banaba was increasingly isolated as the war progressed, until it was virtually cut off from outside contact. It too was bypassed as the Allies moved north and was not reoccupied until the end of the war.

When the Allies landed on Banaba in mid-1945, they found a great deal of the mining infrastructure destroyed. Reconstruction began quickly, but exports did not resume until 1947. A relatively large labor force was required for both reconstruction and mining. In addition to skilled workers from Australia, the recruited included: 100 Chinese from Hong Kong (mostly as mechanics), 200 Ellice

Islanders (mostly as boatmen), and around 1,000 Gilbertese (largely as unskilled workers). Labor relations were far from cordial. There was unrest among the Australian tradesmen and, in January 1947, they formed a Workers' Committee—the first thing even to resemble a union among BPC employees on the island. The BPC management accused the committee organizers of "possessing what is generally known as communistic tendencies."[44] Nevertheless, anxious to avoid an interruption of the reconstruction work, the BPC did agree to improved work conditions and pay.

Industrial peace did not last long and the Gilbert and Ellice Islands workers went on strike in May 1947, after their demand for a pay increase was rejected.[45] At the time, they were paid £2 15s, plus an eight shilling bonus per month and accommodation and rations. They had asked for £10 per month. Motivation for the demand came, in part, from the islanders' experience of being able to earn higher wages from the occupying Allied forces near the end of the war and, in part, from the example of the Australian workers. The management did not agree and brought in Resident Commissioner H.E. Maude to try to convince the Gilbert and Ellice Islanders to return to work through traditional paternalistic appeals. This strategy received a poor response from the workers, but after two weeks the Ellice Islanders, who were accustomed to better treatment than the Gilbertese by the colonial authorities and BPC management, decided to resume work. They were attacked by the Gilbertese and the strike continued. The management then decided to break the strike by sending seven hundred of the Gilbertese back to their homes, replacing them, for the time being, with Chinese from Hong Kong.

Towards the end of 1942, the island of Rabi, off the east coast of Vanua Levu in Fiji, was purchased by the British to serve as an eventual home for the Banabans, once the phosphate deposits were depleted, with money from the Banaban trust fund. In September 1945, the remaining 702 Banabans and 300 Gilbertese who had been sent to Kosrae from Banaba by the Japanese were brought to Tarawa by the British. In light of poor conditions on Banaba as a result of wartime destruction, the Banabans were asked if they would be willing to be resettled on Rabi immediately rather than returning to Banaba. The BPC's reasons for supporting such a move are not difficult to assess, for it is clear that the commissioners would have liked nothing better than to get the troublesome islanders out of the way. Understanding why the Banabans agreed is a little more complicated. One important reason would seem to be the belief of Rotan Tito that the move would facilitate lobbying the high commissioner in nearby Suva.[46] The move also, apparently, was seen by some Banabans as a means of helping to retain a sense of community, since Rabi was far more isolated from outside influences than was Banaba.

Life on Rabi proved difficult at first. This was, in part, simply a matter of having to adjust to a different environment. Eventually, the Banabans did adapt, but the focus of the community leaders and many others remained on getting a bigger share of the profits from phosphate mining on Banaba rather than on economic development on Rabi.

The royalty rate established in 1947 was one shilling three pence per ton, which was similar to that prevailing on Nauru. This rate remained in effect until 1958, when it was increased by five pence (again close to Nauru's rate). The Banabans seemed relatively happy with the advice given to them by British colonial officials during this period, feeling that their advisors sided with them against the BPC. Among other things, what the British advised was patience and moderation. One point of disagreement, however, was that the British continued to favor payment on a communal basis, while the leading Banaban landowners argued for greater payments to individuals. The amount of money involved had become more significant as production increased. Phosphate exports from Banaba were around 200,000 tons a year by 1950, and they soon exceeded 300,000 tons. Taking 1958 as an example, 323,550 tons of phosphate were exported, yielding £28,311 in royalties for the Banabans. While certainly a significant sum for fewer than one thousand Banabans, it was not a great deal in relation to the total amount involved.

Increased phosphate production also was of importance for the colonial administration. Starting in 1946, the BPC paid the administration £50,000 a year on an estimated production of 200,000 tons of phosphate. In 1950, the administration suggested raising the amount to £100,000. The outcome of the negotiations between the two parties marked a turning point in the involvement of the colonial authorities in the mining industry and tied government income more closely to the value of phosphate production. Now, as production increased, government revenue rose substantially. Thus, government revenue in 1959 amounted to A£663,916. Phosphate royalties accounted for A£215,455 of this and duties, most of which were directly or indirectly related to phosphate mining, accounted for another A£275,363. Copra production, the colony's only other export, remained of minor importance—in 1958 amounting to only 7,590 tons.

More money meant that the administration could offer more services, but there was still a strong sense that the colony's future economic prospects were extremely limited. With this in mind, in 1956 the administration set up the Revenue Equalization Reserve Fund with money from savings and the sale of assets related to the Japanese occupation. The fund was intended primarily to provide a reserve to compensate for fluctuations in copra earnings. With phosphate becoming the main source of additional revenue for the fund, its balance grew from an initial A£555,580 to A£1.2 million in 1962.

In 1959, the BPC again found itself under pressure from both the colonial administration and the Banabans to provide them with more money. The British went so far as to mention the "world price" of phosphate in discussions with the BPC—something which the BPC had fought for a long time against as a pricing standard. The BPC resisted the notion, but it did agree to provide the administration with more money. In the same year the Banabans noted that the BPC was paying the Nauruans a much higher royalty rate as well as spending more on housing for them. In response, when the commissioners visited Rabi in 1960 they agreed to spend A£230,000 for projects on the island. The following year, 1961, the BPC was confronted with trouble from another front. Early in the year rumors began to spread among workers on Banaba that the government was planning to tighten customs laws relating to many items that Gilbert and Ellice Islanders were able to purchase and take home with them from Banaba duty-free. This sense of unease combined with perceived mistreatment by Gilbertese and Australian overseers, led to a strike a few months later.[47]

The strike, led by Tito Teburor (who was later to become an important political figure in Kiribati), lasted a month, during which time the HMNZS *Pukaki* stood offshore in case the situation deteriorated further. The strike finally was settled, with the BPC agreeing to substantial wage increases and other benefits. Among the steps taken, in the hope of avoiding further strikes, was a A£5 million program to upgrade the workers' quarters. In addition, a number of Gilbert and Ellice Islanders were appointed to senior level positions. The BPC still sought to avoid the formation of unions, but it did allow for the creation of workers' committees along ethnic lines and established a pattern of fairly regular meetings between management and representatives of the committees.

The Nauruans' success in their negotiations in the mid-1960s had ramifications for mining on Banaba, as both the Banabans and the colonial administration sought a larger share of the profits, which continued to increase along with production (which reached 350,000 tons in 1965). A new agreement was reached in 1964, in which the colony as a whole was to receive eighty-five per cent and the Banabans fifteen per cent of a new rate, which worked out to £1 3s and 2s 8d per ton respectively. The example of Nauru had other implications as well. For one thing, it helped to promote greater self-confidence among the Banabans. This manifest itself in the Banabans deciding to break with the practice of hiring a British colonial officer as their adviser. A group of them, armed with sticks and other implements, confronted their adviser and demanded his immediate departure. About this decision, Dagmar comments that it "put an end to direct government interference with the spending of Banaban funds and in local political matters on Rabi."[48]

The pace of change quickened in the 1970s, as the Gilbert and Ellice Islands Colony moved towards and then became independent, as the Banabans launched an even more sustained effort to increase their earnings from phosphate, as the price of phosphate soared, and, then, as the deposits on Banaba were depleted and the mine closed in 1979. Phosphate production climbed from 509,000 tons in 1970 to 742,300 tons in 1973, after which it declined to 530,000 tons a year for the next two years. The value of phosphate exports went from A$6.0 million in 1972 to a high of A$26.7 million in 1975 (when the price of phosphate peaked). The financial implications for the colony were considerable. The per capita gross domestic product went from A$278 in 1972 to A$704 in 1975 (thereafter declining to A$687 in 1978, before it rose to A$737 in 1979). The Revenue Equalization Reserve Fund balance grew from U.S.$7 million in 1972 to U.S.$70 million in 1979. Most realized, however, that the boom would be short-lived since the mine was nearing exhaustion.

In February 1975, Rotan Tito filed suit against the British Phosphate Commissioners (actually against Her Majesty's attorney general) on behalf of the Rabi Council of Leaders in the British High Court. The Rabi council claimed some £7 million in back mining royalties and for damage to the island. The court case received considerable international attention and lasted until June 1976, making it the longest High Court case in British history. For the most part, the judgement went against the Banabans, although some fault was found with the British government and the BPC. A short while later, however, the British, Australian, and New Zealand governments decided to make an *ex gratia* payment of U.S.$10 million to the Banabans, which was put into a trust.

The phosphate boom took place amidst movement towards granting independence to the Gilbert and Ellice Islands. The colony was not provided with a nominated Executive Council and Advisory Council until 1963—a year after Western Samoa received its independence. In 1967. As Nauru was preparing for its independence, the Advisory Council was replaced by a House of Representatives, which still had no actual power. The pace of political reform picked up in the early 1970s, starting with the creation of an elected Legislative Council in 1971. Three years later, in 1974, this was replaced by a House of Assembly with a chief minister—the year that the phosphate boom had reached its peak, and at a time when it was apparent that phosphate mining on Banaba had only a few more years to run.

During this period of gradual political reform, sentiment had been building in the Ellice Islands in favor of an independent future separate form the Gilbert Islands. This reflected not only cultural differences between the two island groups, but also a legacy of distinct treatment by employers on Banaba and, in general, by colonial authorities. Having received special and generally better treatment, the Ellice Islanders tended to consider themselves superior to the Gilbertese. There was also the fear of being dominated by the Gilbertese once independence was achieved. A referendum was held in the Ellice Islands on the issue of separate independence in 1974 and the population voted overwhelmingly in favor of independence as a separate state (3,799 to 293). This was in spite of their being told not to expect a share of the phosphate royalties should they choose this course of action. Accordingly, in October 1975, the Ellice Islands was separated from the Gilbert Islands under the new name of Tuvalu. Full independence was granted to this nation of seven thousand people in October 1978.

The Ellice Islanders were not alone in desiring separate independence. With Nauru as an example, a small group of Banabans from Rabi landed on Banaba in 1975 to push for separate independence for the island. The move did little for already strained relations between Banabans and Gilbertese. Initial talks aimed at arriving at a solution agreeable to both parties came to nothing. An agreement finally was reached toward the end of 1977, known as the Rakiraki Resolution, several months after the Gilbert Islands had been granted internal self-government. The agreement called for a referendum concerning the future political status of Banaba in relation to the Gilbert Islands and on the fate of mining royalties and the mining industry. It was little more than an awkward compromise, in which both parties remained committed to different goals. By this time, however, some of the debate over economic issues had become academic since mining was about to cease and the price of phosphate had declined. For the Gilbertese, there was little question of giving up the remaining phosphate wealth altogether, since doing so would have made a fairly desperate situation even worse. Survival was not at stake for the Banabans, but they were driven by a sense of injustice and envious comparison with Nauru.

During the 1978 constitutional conference on the Gilbert Islands, the Banabans again pressed for secession. The Banaban leadership was well aware that mining would soon cease, but hoped that some economic use could still be made of the island. Neither Britain or Kiribati agreed to secession, but provision was made for a Banaban seat in the Kiribati House of Assembly and the Banabans were given back land that had been acquired from them on Banaba and were given the right to live on Banaba. The Independent Commission of Inquiry Relating to the Banabans was convened in 1985, as part of the agreement to review the status of Banaba and the Banabans. While there were still a few Banaban leaders who hoped for independence, by 1985 most Banabans no longer saw this as a possibility. Accordingly, the Rabi Council of Leaders accepted the recommendations of the commission, which more or less confirmed the status of Banaba and the Banabans as contained in the Kiribati constitution.

The income that the Banabans received as a result of phosphate mining, as well as the special status that they received in Fiji under the Banaban Settlement Act, allowed them to maintain a relatively autonomous existence on Rabi. They themselves, and not the government of Fiji, provided most of the island infrastructure, and administration of the island was largely in the hands of the Council of Leaders, which is comprised of eight elected members (two from each of the island's four villages) Their income also allowed the Banabans to maintain a substantially higher standard of living than nearby Fijian villagers on Vanua Levu (who were sometimes hired to work for the Banabans). Hans Dagmar comments on the impact of their dependence on royalties in terms of the development of Rabi by the Banabans:

The transformation of the Banaban economy from one dominated by subsistence fishing into one based on royalty payments has deeply affected the Banaban mentality. The peculiar nature of this monetary income has not given the Banabans as a group, much experience with working for money. The rising expectations of a steadily growing number of Banabans have mainly been satisfied by their leaders' fighting for a larger share of phosphate income and distributing this to the community. Development in the Banabans' eyes was associated with improving the cash flow to the Rabi Council of Leaders. Through this, the option of building up the community step by step, by means of small-scale local projects, has not been given the attention it needed.[49]

As income from phosphate royalties increased in the early 1970s, the council established Rabi Holdings Ltd. to invest their phosphate wealth for the purpose of improving living conditions on Rabi and to generate additional income as a basis for sustaining their relative prosperity after the cessation of mining. The company proved a disaster and near the time that mining was coming to an end on Banaba it was forced into receivership, with losses in excess of F$5 million.[50] This left the council solely dependent on income generated from the trust fund. The fund's U.S.$10 million was invested in overseas banks, largely in Western Europe, under the direction of Kenneth Walker (who also served as Hammer de Roburt's financial adviser). On average, these investments have generated an income in excess of F$1 million per year. The council's only other source of income has been from rent on a building that it owns in Suva. The building houses the council's offices as well as spaces that are rented to private businesses and is the sole property remaining from its once much more extensive real estate holdings.

Some two-thirds of the council's yearly income is used to pay for administrative expenses. The largest expense within this category is the maintenance of a small community on Banaba, in part, to maintain their claim to the island. This community on Banaba leads a precarious and dependent existence on the now quite isolated island, as evidenced by a food shortage in mid-1989 which required the sending of emergency assistance by the Kiribati government.[51] There are also salaries of council employees (whose number had to be cut back drastically with the cessation of mining) and the expenses of the council members to be met. The council maintains offices in Suva and on Rabi and many of the councillors spend a good deal of their time in Suva. The remaining one-third is paid directly to the Banaban community. A portion of this amount is paid on an equal basis to all members of the community in the form of annuity payments. The rest consists of bonus payments, which are made on the basis of the size of a person's landholdings on Banaba.

During most of the council's existence, it has received widespread support in its financial and political activities from the Banaban community. During the 1980s, however, following the fall of Rabi Holdings, the council's actions were subjected to increasing controversy. Council elections in recent years have been hotly contested, primarily because the salaries and benefits accruing to the office are considerable in local terms. The office of councillor provides substantial patronage possibilities and lax fiscal accountability has created opportunities for personal enrichment. Such practices have proven to be the primary attractions of office as well as serving as important points of debate in jockeying for electoral support. Thus, those trying to get elected accuse those in office of mishandling funds, but, if successful in getting elected, they often soon resort to similar practices themselves. The result has been a general deterioration of respect for the council among the islanders.

In a survey conducted in 1985, Dagmar found "that while most Banabans did not question the institution of the council, many expressed concern or outright disapproval of the execution of office by the councilors and were upset by the lack of financial accountability of the council."[52] Popular disapproval of the behavior of the council forced it to hold a referendum in 1985 on whether to continue the pattern of distributing two-thirds of the funds to the council and one-third directly to the community. The outcome was a decided majority favoring a reversal of the percentages, reducing the council's share to one-third. Matters did not end with the reversal of payment shares, and the outcome led to increased debate over individual versus communal distribution of payments similar to that encountered on Nauru—a debate that continues at present.

Debate over such economic issues has taken place in the context of declining standards of living on Banaba and of considerable economic inequality. Whereas, during the 1970s and early 1980s, Banabans were seen by neighboring Fijians as wealthy and free-spending, by the latter part of the 1980s, the situation had changed dramatically. Island infrastructure had deteriorated markedly and the average per capita income of Banabans now was only twenty per cent of that for all Fijians—they had become poor even in comparison with many Fijians living in relatively isolated villages. The money that had been so freely spent on taxi rides to the nearest large town of Savusavu, for shopping and partying had left the taxi drivers and merchants of Savusavu with large houses and new or expanded businesses, but had proven to be of no lasting benefit to the Banabans.

With no more money coming from mining and the income from the trust fund severely dissipated, those who had no formal employment on Rabi, a group comprising seventy per cent of the households on the island, found themselves among the poorest people in Fiji. The mean income of these non-wage earning households was a mere F$113 in 1985.[53] Most of the income for non-salaried households is derived from copra cutting. Largely through the sale of fish, the better-off households within this category (about twenty per cent of all households) have been able to raise their mean income to F$342. For those households with a wage-earning member, the mean income in the same year was F$712, making them somewhat poorer than most Fijians, but substantially better off than most Rabi islanders. About half of the jobs on the island are provided by the Rabi council and most of the other half by the government of Fiji.

Given the fact that employment and incomes from all of these sources have limited potential for growth, Rabi's population faces even more serious problems in the near future. The seriousness of the situation is even more apparent when one considers that some three-quarters of the island's four thousand people is under thirty years of age. It remains largely to the council that Rabi Islanders turn for solutions to their economic problems. The council, for its part, has continued to emphasize external schemes for enhancing its pool of wealth upon which to draw, rather than developing the island itself, but in recent years a little more attention has been paid to promoting economic development on the island.

Among the externally-oriented schemes, the most important ones have focused on trying to derive some new source of wealth from Banaba. Those discussed have included prawn or fish farming, offshore fishing royalties, and even leasing the island to the Soviets. The only one to graduate to formal consideration has been a plan to explore the prospects for remining the island. Negotiations in 1988, involving the Rabi council and Kiribati government, led to an agreement for an Australian company, Roche Brothers, to undertake a feasibility study, but the plan was suspended in early 1989. There was also an attempt in the mid-1980s to lobby the Japanese government for war reparations. In this instance, after spending a good deal of money and embroiling itself in a financial scandal, nothing was accomplished by the council.

The island of Rabi has considerable economic potential in terms of its timber and sea resources and agricultural possibilities. The island had an established coconut plantation when the Banabans arrived. A replanting scheme ended in failure and most of the trees are now extremely old and production is very poor. Plans for various other commercial crops have not been implemented. An aid-funded artisanal fishing project, begun in the late 1980s, may still succeed, but for the moment it has been held up by island politics.[54] Feasibility studies for exploiting the island's timber resources span a number of years, but nothing came of them until the mid-1980s, when negotiations began with foreign interests looking for sources of tropical hardwoods in Fiji. In the cases of both fishing and forestry development, council members have shown a clear preference for schemes involving foreign financial interests and the prospects of quick and easy cash over grass-roots development projects that would be of more direct benefit to the island's poor.

Returning to the Gilbert Islands, it became independent as the Republic of Kiribati in July 1979. When mining ceased on Banaba a few months later, the new finance minister was led to comment: "I doubt if there have been many other ministers of finance who have had the doubtful honour of declaring the country's main economic asset officially dead."[55] With copra, fish, and overseas remittances as its only other possible sources of income, the country faced a severe economic crisis which the Revenue Equalization Reserve Fund assumed an important role in alleviating.

The end of mining caused export earnings to drop by ninety per cent in 1980, from A$22.1 million in 1979 to A$2.8 million in 1980. Copra accounted for A$2.2 million of the latter amount. The gross domestic product fell by forty-six per cent, with per capita gross domestic product declining from A$737 in 1979 to A$398 in 1980. Government revenue fell by forty-seven per cent and the budget went from a surplus of A$0.7 million in 1979 to a deficit of A$5.5 million in 1980 (equal to twenty-six per cent of gross domestic product). By 1982, despite savings measures, the deficit had grown to A$9.5 million (thirty-seven per cent of gross domestic product). These deficits were covered by interest earnings from the Revenue Equalization Reserve Fund and budgetary aid from Britain. The deficit the following year was U.S.$8.7 million, with U.S.$5.7 million of this being in the form of debts incurred by the country's fledgling airline, Air Tunguru. Revenue Equalization Reserve Fund interest and British aid continued to help cover the debt, but it was also necessary to borrow U.S.$2.7 million from the Westpac bank of Australia and U.S.$1.0 million from Nauru at a fixed interest of twelve per cent. The country's debt service in 1983 was only U.S.$0.8 million, but this represented a debt service ratio of six per cent.[56]

The mineworkers on Banaba succeeded in establishing a union in 1977, the BPC General Workers' Union. The union staged a strike in 1978 over wages, but its main concern was negotiating termination pay and other arrangements relating to the end of mining. The following year, Kiribati was faced with a severe unemployment problem, as hundreds of mineworkers returned to their home islands or took up residence on already overcrowded Tarawa. Remaining

TABLE 6.4 Kiribati, Government Revenue and Phosphate Exports

	Total Govt Revenue (A$m)	Govt Revenue from Phosphate (A$m)	Phosphate Exports ('000 tons)	Phosphate Value (A$m)
1975	26.3	22.8	530	26.7
1976	14.6	9.6	427	17.2
1977	14.7	8.3	425	15.7
1978	14.4	8.0	502	18.9
1979	17.3	8.4	446	18.0

From the Revenue Equalization Reserve Fund

1980	8.8	4.3	0	0
1981	8.7	4.3	0	0
1982	12.9	4.3	0	0
1983	12.9	5.0	0	0
1984	13.0	5.0	0	0

Sources: Asian Development Bank, *Economic Survey on Kiribati*, August 1983; and Government of Kiribati, *1984 Estimates of Revenue and Expenditure.*

sources of overseas employment included work on Nauru and as seamen (mostly on West German ships). The numbers involved in mid-1983 were 375 working on Nauru and about 1,200 serving as seamen.

In addition to foreign aid and revenue from fishing licences,[57] the most important source of money available to the government is the Revenue Equalization Reserve Fund. The balance in the fund as of December 1981 was A$66 million. By the end of 1984, it was A$104.6 million. The fund is managed by a London stockbrokerage firm and its annual yield in the early 1980s averaged a little over eight per cent. Most of the money is invested in bonds, primarily in government bonds from Western Europe, North America, Japan, and Australia. The largest single investment is in the European Investment Bank (investments in the bank in 1984 amounted to U.S.$5.6 million, DM6.3 million, and ¥110.6 million). Some of the fund is invested in cash deposits. Stirling deposits were diversified in 1984 to include U.S. dollars, Japanese yen, and German marks. In contrast with Nauru's funds, a relatively small amount of the Kiribati money is invested in stocks. The nominal value of the stock investments in 1984 was U.S.$12 million: distributed between Atlantic Richfield, Beatrice Food, General Electric, R.J.Reynolds, Gulf Oil, and Campbell

Soup.[58] The breakdown of Kiribati investments in dollar terms in 1983, by country, is: thirty-three per cent in the United States, twenty-four per cent in Japan, twenty per cent in Britain, fourteen per cent in West Germany, and eight per cent in Australia.

Each year since 1982 approximately A$5 million has been taken from the fund and placed in an income account to help pay for the running of the government. In the 1982-83 financial year, A$1 million was used for the purchase of Fanning and Washington Islands, which subsequently became the focus of government resettlement plans to ease crowding elsewhere in the country (more recently, Christmas Island has been used for the same purpose). Since the non-Banaban people of Kiribati were not landowners on Banaba, there is no landowners' lobby pressing for a slice of the fund's earnings. There is also no thought of dividing it among the people of Kiribati on an individual or regional basis. At its estimated level in the mid-1980s, such a move would result in a payment of only around A$2,000 per person. The money is seen to be for use exclusively for purposes of national development.

Kiribati's economy remains in a very precarious state. Its 1988 trade deficit amounted to U.S.$16 million, based on exports of only U.S.$6 million and imports of U.S.$22 million. Revenue from fishing fees (from South Korea, Japan, and the United States) have hovered around the U.S.$1.5 million mark, with remittances from overseas workers adding another couple of million dollars a year to the national coffers. The country therefore remains highly dependent on foreign aid and earnings from the Revenue Equalization Reserve Fund (the balance of which stood at U.S.$160 million at the end of 1986). Aware of this dependency and the economic balancing act that is necessary for the survival of the country, the government of Kiribati has invested much more conservatively than Nauru. It has also sought investment advice through more established channels than have either Nauru or the Banabans and handled its money in a much less erratic manner. The pattern is in keeping with the overall financial behavior of Kiribati and it can be argued that it has been much more successful in handling its mining-derived wealth in the interest of the population as a whole than has the Hammer de Roburt government of Nauru or the Rabi Council of Leaders.[59]

Makatea

Phosphate was discovered on the small island of Makatea in the Tuamotu archipelago around the turn-of-the-century.[60] At the time, the island had about two hundred and fifty inhabitants. John Arundel of the Pacific Phosphate Company came to Pape'ete in 1906, and the following year a joint venture was formed between the Pacific Phosphate Company (which held a fifty-one per cent interest) and the French Société Français des Iles du Pacifique to mine the phosphate. Arundel visited Makatea and drew up contracts with the islanders which allowed for a royalty of one franc per ton (less than one pence). The joint venture became the Compagnie Français des Phosphate de l'Océanie in 1908, with initial capital, mostly of British origin, of £240,000. When rival German interests associated with phosphate mining on Angaur sought to intrude on Makatea, a compromise was reached incorporating them into the Compagnie Français des Phosphate de l'Océanie.

The French colonial administration took steps to legalize the phosphate operation in 1910 and decided that it too should be paid a royalty of one franc per ton. Although a formal concession was not granted until 1917, mining began in 1911. Initial infrastructural costs were relatively high. in part, because, like Nauru and Banaba, the waters around the island were extremely deep and required the construction of special moorings. The company had trouble recruiting sufficient labor. What labor it did recruit came from other islands in the Tuamotus (especially Tubuai) and from Tahiti. The Makateans, for their part, were content to live off their royalties and rents. Between 1911 and 1913, a total of 200,000 francs (around £800) was paid to individual families for rents and 150,000 francs (around £600) was paid to the district council. Because of the labor problems and large outlays for infrastructure, initial profits were low.

German interests in the Compagnie Français des Phosphate de l'Océanie were confiscated during the First World War. The war also led to a change in the nature of British interests in the company. After Pacific Phosphate Company holdings on Nauru and Banaba were taken over by the British Phosphate Commissioners, individuals with interests in Pacific Phosphate Company formed the Anglo-French Phosphate Company in 1921 to assume control of Pacific Phosphate Company operations on Makatea.

Although Makatean phosphate prices were higher than those charged for BPC phosphate, by world standards the Anglo-French Phosphate Company's prices were still quite low, and the company had no trouble finding markets for its phosphate. France at this time relied mainly on phosphate from Morocco and most Makatean phosphate was shipped to Japan, with a small amount going to Australia and Europe (especially Scandinavia). Phosphate production on Makatea increased during the interwar years. In 1925, before the depression, it reached 100,000 tons. Following the depression, it rose to 123,545 tons in 1936 and reached 159,678 tons by 1939. At the same time, however, the price of phosphate declined.

The Compagnie Français des Phosphate de l'Océanie successfully petitioned French authorities to be allowed to recruit indentured laborers from Japan in 1919. The next year, twenty-one Japanese laborers arrived, followed by another 260 in 1921. The Anglo-French Phosphate Company was able to convince the administration to allow it to recruit additional workers from China and Vietnam. A group of 287 Vietnamese workers arrived in 1925, along with 272 Chinese recruited in Hong Kong. The depression, rising labor costs, and other factors, led to a reduction in the number of indentured workers on the island in the early 1930s, and to a shift towards recruiting a greater percentage of workers from neighboring islands in French Polynesia. As production picked up, the number of workers rose once again in the late 1930s. The Makateans themselves continued to avoid mine work.

Exports of phosphate from Makatea to Japan ceased with the outbreak of the Second World War. The BPC assumed control of the industry during the war and exports were redirected to Australia and New Zealand. The loss of Nauru and Banaba as sources of phosphate placed considerable importance on Makatea for these two countries and production on the island was increased substantially.

Greater demand for phosphate meant that more labor was needed. Wartime conditions in French Polynesia, however, made labor recruitment difficult. The presence of large numbers of American soldiers on Bora Bora and a rise in the price of copra led to an economic boom for the islanders. As a result, the islanders were not inclined to work on Makatea, where wages remained relatively low and the work was more arduous. The mine's management complained that economic conditions had given the islanders "so much money that they were not working well." To solve this problem, the BPC approached the French administration to allow it to import workers from poorer islands under New Zealand's control. Permission being granted, the BPC arrived at an agreement with New Zealand authorities in 1943 to recruit workers from the Cook Islands. By early 1945, there were 485 Cook Islanders, including wives and children, on Makatea (the total population of the Cook Islands at the time being 14,088). They were paid £4 per month plus food and accommodation.

In April 1945, a group of mineworkers returning to the Cook Islands complained of poor food and accommodation on Makatea and accused company employees of encouraging immorality among workers and their families. The complaint was taken up by the Cook Islands Progressive Association, church leaders, and the Auckland Trades Union Council. These groups called on New Zealand authorities to investigate conditions on the island. In response, a short time later, a New Zealand Labour Commissioner was sent to Makatea. The BPC agreed to improve food and accommodation and to raise the wage rate to £7 a month. In response to the complaint of its employees encouraging immorality, the BPC decided in the future not to have the workers bring their wives and children.

The 1951 census of Makatea recorded 1,343 islanders from Makatea and elsewhere in French Polynesia, 289 Cook Islanders, 62 Chinese, 30 French, and 34 others, for a total of 1,758 inhabitants. The workers lived in a separate village in the interior of the island, the Europeans

TABLE 6.5 Phosphate Exports, Makatea, 1939-1966

	Quantity ('000 tons)	Value of Phosphate Exports (million francs)[a]	Total Value of Exports, Fr.Poly. (million francs)	Phosphate Exports as a % of Total
1939	159.7	9.5	63.5	15
1940	173.2	17.2	47.8	36
1941	192.3	46.6	124.5	37
1943	197.9	48.5	142.6	34
1944	203.3	56.7	178.4	32
1945	231.7	83.4	185.4	45
1946	231.8	83.5	282.2	30
1947	208.3	120.9	431.6	28
1948	183.1	99.5	443.2	27
1949	239.5	127.6	472.6	27
1950	254.8	146.9	479.4	31
1951	227.9	152.6	643.8	24
1952	213.6	136.0	500.9	27
1953	245.0	157.7	513.2	31
1954	228.9	186.0	663.2	28
1956	264.9	219.9	658.5	33
1957	314.1	264.7	739.6	36
1959	310.6	337.1	1,103.2	30
1961	368.8	437.0	1,035.0	42
1962	354.0	na	na	na
1964	318.6	369.5	996.7	37
1965	200.0	245.6	1,537.0	16
1966	200.1	na	na	na

a) CFP100 = US$1.00 (1968).

maintained an enclave complete with sports and other facilities, while the Makateans remained in their own villages. The recruitment of Cook Islanders came to an end in 1955. They were replaced by workers from elsewhere in French Polynesia: unskilled workers coming mainly from Tubuai and semi-skilled tradesmen from Tahiti. The 1956 census recorded 1,995 islanders from Makatea and elsewhere in French Polynesia, 191 Chinese, 85 French, and 59 Others, for a total of 2,330 inhabitants. The total number of workers on the island in 1961 was around 700, and the island's population in 1962 was 2,273.

Production dropped briefly after the war, but then recovered and was maintained at relatively high levels through the 1950s. After the war, most of the phosphate once again was exported to Japan. The BPC withdrew and the Compagnie Français des Phosphate de l'Océanie resumed management of the mine. Phosphate exports assumed an important place in the colony's economy and, by the 1950s, concern was being expressed about the size of the reserves remaining on Makatea. In the late 1950s and early 1960s, production increased sharply. It was then realized that only a few years of mining remained. The reserves were considered exhausted by the latter half of 1966, and the mine was closed in September 1966. The mining had turned the island into a virtual desert and it was no longer able to support its pre-mining population of about 250. The workforce was sent home and by the following year only fifty-five inhabitants remained on Makatea. This small indigenous community had grown to seventy-eight by 1971, but then declined to less than thirty people during the 1970s. As for French Polynesia as a whole, the crisis caused by the closure of the mine was quickly superseded by the rise in importance of another island at the other end of the Tuamotu Archipelago—Mururoa.

French Polynesia became the site of a new phosphate venture in the late 1980s, on Mataiva Atoll.[61] Mataiva measures ten kilometers by six kilometers and is located in the north-western corner of the Tuamotu Archipelago. The population of the atoll in 1983 was two hundred and fifteen people, mostly living in a single village. The phosphate deposit is located in the atoll's lagoon under three meters of water and seven meters of mud and sand near the village. Initial studies of the site indicated that the phosphate was of comparable quality to that on Nauru and estimated reserves to be twenty million tons. Development of the site will entail considerable environmental disruption and have a major impact on the inhabitants. The mining venture is being carried out by Australmin Holdings Ltd (with a 49.5 per cent share in the venture), Cominco Ltd., and Bureau de

Recherches Geologiques. Final clearance for the mine concession went ahead in early 1990, with French government approval for the project expected by March 1990. Australmin is particularly interested in the project because of the closure of one of Australia's main sources of phosphate on Christmas Island, in the Indian Ocean, and the pending end of mining on Nauru.

Angaur

The last remaining phosphate island to be discussed is Angaur, in the Palau Group.62 The account offered here is extremely brief and intended, in part, to draw attention to the need for further study. The Germans began mining on Angaur in 1909, and then Japan assumed control of the island as a result of the First World War. Mismanagement of the open-pit phosphate mines by speculators led the Japanese navy to take the mines over during the war. The Japanese government-owned Nan'yo Takushoku Kaisha ran the mines until 1936, when it was replaced by the Nan'yo Takushoku (South Seas Colonization Corporation), a government agency with close ties to business, which was given overall responsibility for development of the region.

All phosphate was exported to Japan, where it was used for fertilizer and, later, in the manufacture of explosives. By the mid-1930s, phosphate deposits were estimated to be around 2.4 million tons. About 60,000 tons a year were exported during the early 1930s, rising to 65,000 tons in 1937, and to an estimated 70,000 tons around the time when the war began. Available figures for the period 1922 to 1931 give annual values of phosphate exports to Japan ranging from ¥0.9 million to ¥1.5 million. Phosphate exports were roughly comparable to copra exports and slightly less than dried bonito. Until 1929, sugar exports to Japan amounted to only a few million yen, but after then sugar production increased sharply, with the value of sugar exports reaching almost ¥20 million in 1937. The rise of the sugar industry meant that phosphate assumed less economic significance, although it retained considerable strategic importance.

Labor for the mine was recruited primarily from among Chamorros in the Marianas and from Truk, Palau, and Yap in the Carolines. The workers were recruited by village chiefs and headmen, who were paid a small bonus, and there is evidence that many were recruited against their will.

The region became increasingly closed to foreigners during the interwar years, especially after Japan left the League of Nations in

1935, and as preparations for war were stepped up. Angaur was the site of a major battle near the end of the Second World War and much of the mining infrastructure was damaged. The Americans assumed control of the island after the war and a short time later mining was resumed. Mining continued until 1954, when the deposits were depleted.

Notes

1. For additional historical material on these islands and the phosphate industry in the Pacific, see Nancy Viviani, *Nauru: Phosphate and Political Progress* (Canberra: Australian National University Press, 1970); and Maslyn Williams and Barrie Macdonald, *The Phosphateers: A History of the British Phosphate Commission and the Christmas Island Phosphate Commission* (Melbourne: Melbourne University Press, 1985).

2. See Arthur Ellis, *Ocean Island and Nauru* (Sydney: Angus & Robertson, 1935). Also see Arthur Grimble, *A Pattern of Islands* (London: John Murray, 1952), pp. 27-29, on Ellis's discovery.

3. Australian writers, including Nancy Viviani, for years have claimed that Japan also sought to take possession of Nauru, using as proof the arrival of a Japanese naval vessel off Nauru a short time after the arrival of the Australians. Recent research by Hiroshi Nakajima, using Japanese naval records, however, indicates that the Japanese did not intend to take Nauru, limiting their postwar claims to former German territories north of the equator, and that the visit of the visit of the Japanese ship was a friendly one intended only to take on coal and water (cited in "The Japanese and Nauru," in *Pacific Islands Monthly*, September 1987, p. 58).

4. Viviani, *Nauru*, p. 47.

5. Viviani, *Nauru*, p. 86.

6. Viviani, *Nauru*, p. 131.

7. Statistics are derived from a variety of sources, including various editions of the *Pacific Islands Yearbook* (Sydney: Pacific Publications), and government publications from the Republic of Nauru.

8. Fiji Airways had initiated regular air service to Nauru in April 1968.

9. John Connell, *Migration, Employment and Development in the South Pacific: Country Report No. 9, Nauru* (Noumea: South Pacific Commission, 1983), p. 4.

10. Gwyne Dyer, "Nauru: Where Life is Short, Sweet and Pointless," in *Times-Colonist* (Victoria, BC), October 1985.

11. Michael Field, "Nauruans Dying of Wealth," in *Pacific Islands Monthly*, October 1988, p. 29.

12. Connell, *Nauru*, p.4.

13. Nauru Phosphate Royalties Trust, *Annual Report 1980-1981, 30 June 1981* (Republic of Nauru, 1981); Nauru Phosphate Royalties Trust, *Annual Report, 1981-1982, 30 June 1982* (Republic of Nauru, 1982).

14. For more information on Nauru's stock portfolio see Michael C. Howard, *The Impact of the International Mining Industry on Native Peoples* (Sydney: Transnational Corporations Research Project, University of Sydney, 1988), pp. 144-45.

15. *Pacific Islands Monthly*, August 1989, p. 38.

16. Phosphate exports were further undermined by a decision of the New Zealand government, as part of its overall economic reform policy in agriculture, to cut subsidies for phosphate fertilizers; see Hamish McDonald, "Wanting their Cake Now: Nauruans call for Distribution of Phosphate Earnings," in *Far Eastern Economic Review*, 12 June 1986, p. 127.

17. "Ministerial Statement," in *The Bulletin* (Nauru), No. 20/85, 15 May 1985, p. 1.

18. "Motion of Amendments at Second Reading of the Appropriation Bill," in *The Bulletin* (Nauru), No. 20/85, 15 May 1985, p. 1.

19. "Reports Laid Before Parliament," in *The Bulletin* (Nauru), No. 52/85, 18 December 1985, pp. 1-2.

20. "Supreme Court Decision on Constitutional Reference," in *The Bulletin* (Nauru), No. 26/85, 2 July 1986, pp. 1-17.

21. Quotations from "Policy Statement by H.E. the President," in *The Bulletin* (Nauru), No. 39/86, 30 September 1986, pp. 1-3.

22. "Declaration of Emergency" and "Motion of No Confidence," in *The Bulletin* (Nauru), No. 40/86, 8 October 1986, p. 1.

23. "Red Links Seen in Nauru Strike," in *Pacific Islands Monthly*, June 1978, p. 25.

24. "Strike Jeopardises Future of Gilbertese Employment in Nauru," in *Atoll Pioneer* (Kiribati), No. 284, 9 February 1978, p. 2; "Strike Ends in Nauru," in *Atoll Pioneer* (Kiribati), No. 285, 16 February 1978, p. 1.

25. "Enna G is Still Strike Bound," in *Pacific Islands Monthly*, August 1973, p. 87; "Determined Islanders Prepare to Fight for Enna G Principle," in *Pacific Islands Monthly*, September 1973, pp. 79, 81-82; "The Enna G Sails Again," in *Pacific Islands Monthly*, October 1973, p. 13.

26. "Nauru to see NZ Maritime Unions," in *Pacific Islands Monthly*, October 1976, p. 79. It is also worth pointing out that Nauru's airline, Air Nauru, is not a member of IATA and that its employees also have few rights beyond those associated with kinship and personal whim.

27. The Workman's Compensation Ordinance (1956) being the most recent labor law. The other laws are as follows: Chinese and Native Labour Ordinance (1922), Overseas Workers Ordinance (1928), and Chinese and Native Labour Ordinance (Amendment) (1953). On a visit to Nauru in 1984, when I asked about recent or pending labor legislation, those responsible for drafting Nauru's laws appeared not even to have considered the topic, despite a considerable amount of work being carried out in other legal areas.

28. Dyer, "Nauru."

29. "Nauruan Workers' Plight," in *Pacific Islands Monthly*, May 1974, p. 29; "Nauruan Workers," in *Pacific Islands Monthly*, August 1974, pg. 25;

"Nauruan Public Servants Unhappy," in *Pacific Islands Monthly*, November 1974, pg. 93; "Nauruan Workers," in *Pacific Islands Monthly*, December 1974, pg. 23. As can be seen from table 6.3, relatively few Nauruans work for the Nauru Phosphate Commission. This reflects their preference for the better conditions and salaries available to those employed by the government, which is, in part, because few Nauruans have the skills to qualify for higher paid jobs in the mining industry.

30. *The Bulletin* (Nauru), No. 39/86, 30 September 1986, p. 2.

31. *Pacific Islands Monthly*, July 1987, p. 9.

32. The inquiry was chaired by Christopher Weeramantry, formerly a judge on the Sri Lankan Supreme Court and at the time a professor of law at Monash University in Melbourne. He was assisted by an Australian engineer, Robert Challen; another Australian law professor, Barry Connell; and the Nauruan director of the Nauru Language Bureau, Gideon Degidoa. See John Dunn, "Fighting for a Future," in *Pacific Islands Monthly*, November 1987, p. 20. Relevant writing on Nauru's environment includes: H.I. Manner, R.R.Thaman, and D.C. Hassall, "Plant Succession After Phosphate Mining on Nauru," in *Australian Geographer*, Vol. 17, 1985, pp. 185-195; and J.F. Dupon, *Pacific Phosphate Island Environments Versus the Mining Industry: An Unequal Struggle* (Noumea: South Pacific Environment Programme, 1989).

33. Richard Dinner, "Australia, NZ Silent on Nauru Compensation Claim," in *Pacific Islands Monthly*, February 1989, pp. 36-37. After interruptions, Nauru decided to proceed with its case in mid-1990 (see "Nauru's Million-dollar War," in *Pacific Islands Monthly*, June 1990, p. 25; and "Nauru Seeks Phosphate Earnings Boost," in *Financial Times*, 17 October 1990, p. 37). The latter article also discusses efforts by the Nauruan government in 1990 to boost its phosphate earnings, including consideration of the feasibility of setting up its own super-phosphate works.

34. See Phil Twyford, "Air Nauru's Woes Spread across the Region," in *Islands Business*, February 1989, pp. 48-49; Robin Bromby, "Nauru Still Flightless," in *Pacific Islands Monthly*, October 1988, p. 15; and "NZ-Nauru Deal Ends," in *Pacific Islands Monthly*, March 1989, p. 36.

35. In June 1990, the National Development Company of the Philippines announced that it wanted to sell half of its equity in Philphos to Nauru or another party in an effort to find a buyer willing to assume guarantees on some U.S.$400 in foreign debts owned by the company (*Fiji Times*, 20 June 1990, p.23).

36. See *Islands Business*, September 1989, p. 28; and "The Fall of De Roburt," in *Pacific Islands Monthly*, October 1989, p. 20.

37. "Air Nauru Back, with Clipped Wings," in *Islands Business*, December 1989, pp. 43-44 (the article includes a brief interview with Aroi).

38. "Dowiyogo's Back Again," in *Pacific Islands Monthly*, January 1990, p. 21. See also "Nauru: We Shall Overcome," in *Pacific Islands Monthly*, April 1990, pp. 22-24.

39. One important issue concerning the future of Nauru's overseas wealth is the future of the Australian economy. Despite some

decentralization of investments, the bulk of Nauru's wealth remains in Australia. A serious downturn in the Australia stockmarket, in particular, would have serious repercussions for Nauru.

40. "Tuvalu Plans to Fill in the Holes," in *Islands Business,* February 1989, pp. 35-36.

41. Historical material on Banaba is taken largely from: Barrie Macdonald, *Cinderellas of the Empire* (Canberra: Australian National University Press, 1982); Michael Howard and Simione Durutalo, *The Political Economy of the South Pacific to 1945* (Townsville: Centre for Southeast Asian Studies, James Cook University, 1987), pp. 168-178; Maslyn Williams and Barrie Macdonald, *The Phosphateers;* Pearl Binder, *Treasure Islands* (London: Blond & Briggs, 1977); and Martin Silverman, *Disconcerting Issue* (Chicago: University of Chicago Press, 1971).

42. The office of High Commissioner for the Western Pacific was created in 1877. During the first half of the twentieth century the high commissioner was responsible primarily for the administration of the Solomon Islands, Tonga, the Gilbert and Ellice Islands, Pitcairn Island, and the New Hebrides (which was jointly administered with France). The high commission was based in Suva, where the commissioner also served as governor of Fiji. Serving under the high commissioner in the Gilbert and Ellice Islands was a resident commissioner, below which were administrative officers for each of the colony's five districts and native magistrates on most of the individual islands.

43. Quoted in Macdonald, *Cinderellas of the Empire,* p. 107.

44. Williams and Macdonald, *The Phosphateers,* p. 374.

45. See Williams and Macdonald, *The Phosphateers,* pp. 372-78, on the 1948 strike.

46. See Silverman, *Disconcerting Issue,* p. 146. Hans Dagmar ["Banabans in Fiji: Ethnicity, Change and Development," in Michael C. Howard, ed., *Ethnicity and Nation-Building in the Pacific* (Tokyo: United Nations University, 1989), p. 217] cites a statement concerning a discussion between Rotan Tito and lawyer Richard Brown in 1972 about the role of Major Kennedy, the Banabans first adviser on Rabi, concerning the decision to move to Rabi: "at one time he approached Major Kennedy to try to find a way of getting a lawyer to take up the Banaban case. The advice Rotan was given was that they should buy an island in Fiji where they would be closer to the Governor General and Major Kennedy would approach the Governor General to help Rotan find a better way of presenting their case."

47. On the 1961 strike, see Williams and Macdonald, *The Phosphateers,* pp. 453-455; "Phosphate Workers' Strike: Explosion Averted on Ocean Island," in *Pacific Islands Monthly,* October 1961, pp. 18, 142; and "Ocean Island and Nauru Settle Down," in *Pacific Islands Monthly,* December 1961, p. 125.

48. Dagmar, "Banabans in Fiji," p. 201.

49. Dagmar, "Banabans in Fiji," pp. 207-08.

50. It is not possible here to discuss in detail the reasons or possible reasons for the fall of Rabi Holdings. Questions remain about the extent to

which its problems were a result of mismanagement and the extent to which actual malfeasance was to blame, but the affair resulted in increased political tensions on the island and served to deprive the people of Rabi of the benefit of much of the wealth accumulated from mining royalties.

51. Islands *Business*, September 1989, p. 28.

52. Hans Dagmar, "Cooperative Artisanal Fishing on Rabi Island, Fiji," *Practicing Anthropology*, Vol. 12, No. 1, 1990, pp. 6-7, and 18.

53. All figures in this paragraph are from Hans Dagmar's two publications: "Banabans in Fiji" and "Cooperative Artisanal Fishing."

54. Dagmar, "Cooperative Artisanal Fishing." These schemes also became entangled in the web of sometimes questionable business interests surrounding Fiji strongman Kamasese Mara and his close associates.

55. Quoted in Michael Howard, et al, *The Political Economy of the Pacific: An Introduction* (Townsville: Centre for Southeast Asian Studies, James Cook University, 1983), p. 231. Also of relevance to the impact of the cessation of mining is an interview with Kiribati president Iremaia Tabai (in *Islands Business*, July 1989, p. 13).

56. Source of figures: Asian Development Bank, *Economic Survey on Kiribati*, August 1983.

57. Foreign aid to Kiribati in 1984 amounted to A$14.4 million (the largest donor being the European Community, followed by Britain, Japan, and Australia). Fishing Access agreements with Japan between 1979 and 1984 generated about A$4 million in income. Agreements with South Korea between 1979 and 1981 were worth A$0.4 million. More recently, Kiribati has signed agreements with the Soviet Union (for one year) and the United States.

58. Information on the Revenue Equalization Reserve Fund is provided in, Government of Kiribati, *1984 Estimates of Revenue and Expenditure*, pp. 77-84; and Asian Development Bank, *Economic Survey*, pp. 12, 17, and 45.

59. One other fund has been established in the Pacific which is indirectly related to phosphate mining. This is the fund that Tuvalu established in the late 1980s in the hope of providing a more secure economic future for the country. Britain, Australia, and New Zealand provided about A$9 million at the outset, and Japan and South Korea added small amounts later.

60. Material on Makatea is drawn largely from: Virginia Thompson and Richard Adloff, *The French Pacific Islands* (Berkeley: University of California Press, 1971); Colin Newbury, *Tahiti Nui* (Honolulu: University Press of Hawaii, 1980); Richard Golson, *The Cook Islands 1820-1950* (Wellington: Victoria University Press, 1980), on Cook Island workers; Recherche Géologique et Minérale in Polynésie Français (Paris: Inspection Générale des Mines et de la Géologie, 1959); and various volumes of the *Pacific Islands Year Book* (Sydney: Pacific Publications).

61. See J.F. Dupon, *Pacific Phosphate Island Environments*, p. 8; and *Pacific Islands Monthly*, March 1990, p. 25.

7

Conclusions

About the safest conclusion that can be reached with respect to the influence of natural resource endowments on development, viewed historically, is that although a superior resource endowment is a facilitating condition for faster overall development, it is neither a necessary nor a sufficient condition for it. Clearly, possession of a particularly rich mineral deposit can have an extremely strong influence on the development of the immediate area where it is located, but the impact on the national economy need not even be noticeable.

James H. Cobbe,
Government and Mining Companies in Developing Countries, p. 6.

Mining in the South Pacific initially developed under European colonial rule according to the common enclave pattern, geared to demand from abroad and with a limited range of linkages to the surrounding society and even the colonial state. The primary role of the colonial state in relation to mining was to provide a legal framework for gaining access to land and labor, in return for which mining enterprises paid duties and taxes. For the most part, the mining companies provided their own infrastructural requirements and made their own arrangements for labor recruitment, more or less within the guidelines established by the state. By and large, the colonial state was of importance to the mining companies only indirectly, while the state, for its part, ever short of funds, often relied heavily on what monies it could pry from the mining sector and tended to do what it could to encourage mining by way of incentives and favorable treatment. In almost every case, mining interests clearly had the upper hand in their dealings with the colonial state.

223

From the perspective of the foreign interests that dominated the mining sector, the results of their efforts from the late nineteenth through the middle of the twentieth centuries were mixed. For some, the 1930s, in particular, produced considerable profits, but for many mining wealth remained elusive. For the colonial administrations, mining did not prove to be the hoped for easy route to salvation from their fiscal concerns. Even in the case of the Morobe goldfields, the nickel mines of New Caledonia, and the phosphate riches of Banaba and Nauru, colonial governments had to struggle constantly to derive any direct benefits and, as often as not, they found themselves under pressure to provide subsidies to mining interests.

The impact of mining on the indigenous populations of the various countries under colonial rule in the region varied a great deal. In the case of Fiji, mining provided one of the few employment outlets available to native Fijians, and, thus, one of the limited means for native Fijian commoners potentially to escape chiefly control. Recognizing the danger, the chiefs frequently intervened in the labor process to assert their authority. Moreover, wages from work in Fiji's mines often served to maintain the quasi-traditional social order established under colonial rule by providing finance for religious and other ceremonial activities.

Mining in Papua New Guinea was of relevance to the indigenous population in a number of ways, all of which contributed to the creation of a colonial society that was partly capitalist and partly a variant of traditional society. The most obvious contribution to this social formation was through the provision of wage labor and the recruitment act itself. Mining also provided limited market opportunities for local agricultural products. In addition, the presence of larger mining enterprises, as in Morobe province, played a role in promoting the establishment of colonial law and order. In all instances, however, the impact of mining activities in Papua New Guinea was localized and far from overwhelming even for those living adjacent to mining areas.

The relevance of mining for the Melanesian population of New Caledonia prior to and immediately after the Second World War was largely indirect. The dislocation of the Melanesian population during the late nineteenth and early twentieth centuries was only in small part related to mining. However, the progressive dominance by mining of the colonial economy served to promote even further marginalization of the Melanesian population. The mining industry's use of migrant labor also provided a basis for the demographic changes that were to result in the Melanesians losing their majority status.

The most immediate effects of mining on indigenous peoples were to be found on the small phosphate islands, where mining came to dominate the entire landscape. By and large, the indigenous islanders did not engage in wage labor in the mines. Rather, their relationship with the mining sector was as recipients of rent for the use of the land in combination with paternalistic colonial control. As other means of providing for their livelihood receded into insignificance, the islanders became almost entirely dependent on wealth derived from mining and their political behavior focused on increasing this wealth and debate over its distribution. The small size of the indigenous populations made them even more vulnerable than elsewhere to being overwhelmed by migrant laborers. Steps were taken by European authorities to ensure that most of these migrants did not remain, but, in the case of both Banaba and Nauru, the situation helped to promote an pronounced defensiveness on the part of the islanders that colored virtually all of their relations with other communities.

The transition to independence for Fiji, Nauru, and Papua New Guinea provided opportunities to ensure that mining was of more direct benefit to the people within whose country the mining was taking place. In Fiji, that such a change was possible was clearly demonstrated by the sugar industry, but no such change occurred in mining. The alliance between mining interests and the chiefly oligarchy which retained power after independence ensured that mining in Fiji maintained its enclave characteristic. Nauru represents a situation that is almost the opposite of that in Fiji, an instance where the local population succeeded in gaining complete control of what previously had been an alien mining industry. The impact of their success on the Nauruans was, in many ways, devastating. It can be argued that too much wealth was heaped upon the Nauruans too fast—not simply because of their takeover of the mining industry, but also because of the rapid rise in the price of phosphate. Gradually, the Nauruan government has become more adept at managing its investments, although many problems in this regard remain, and Nauruan society continues to suffer a variety of ills associated with mining. Their mineral wealth has not so much gone to provide for a productive infrastructure for Nauruan society as it has been invested in such a way as to allow them to live off of the productive work of others.

The situation in independent Papua New Guinea is far more complicated because of the size and complexity of the country and of its mining industry. The amount of wealth generated from mining in Papua New Guinea over the past couple of decades has been considerable and the government has been able to retain a sizeable proportion of this wealth. What has proven more elusive than taxing mineral wealth is moving beyond dependency on mining revenue merely to cover operating costs to using this wealth to create a more diversified developing economy. Moreover, while, to some extent, mining-derived wealth no doubt has helped Papua New Guinea, such wealth also has contributed to problems of national fragmentation, corruption, and inequality. The mining industry cannot solely be blamed for these conditions, but the lumpiness of the wealth it has generated can be isolated as a major contributing factor to them.

Turning to one of the South Pacific's few remaining colonies, New Caledonia, mining can be seen as one of the most important forces behind the colony's misdevelopment. Mining (along with French government expenditure) has helped to give the colony one of the highest standards of living in the South Pacific, but the wealth is unevenly divided. In particular, little of this wealth has found its way to the colony's large indigenous population. In recent decades the presence of mining has encouraged the continuance of colonial rule and contributed to the colony's communal problems and its inability to develop a more diversified economy. Many of these problems would no doubt exist even without mining, but the industry has served to exacerbate the situation and it has yet to provide, in a demonstrable way, for the sustainable development of New Caledonia.

The scars left by mining throughout New Caledonia also raise another important issue in relation to the environmental impact of mining and its regulation by government authorities. The environmental degradation caused by mining has not been much of an issue in the region until quite recently. Local landowners often demanded compensation for a mine's destruction of trees or agricultural land, but that was about as far as it went. On the phosphate islands, those conducting the mining, the colonial authorities, and many of the islanders themselves more or less took it for granted that mining would one day make the islands uninhabitable and that the best solution was to resettle those living on the islands. The situation today is quite different. The people of the South Pacific are much more aware of environmental problems and politicians and mining companies are under considerable pressure to limit the damage.

In the case of Nauru, the result of this change of consciousness has been for the government to search for ways to rehabilitate the island, while abandoning the search for an alternative homeland. The cost of such an undertaking will be substantial, but it has become a political necessity for any government in power to support the goal of rehabilitation. Nauru has sought to have the countries responsible for mining when it was a colony share some of the expense, making it the first country in the region to seek compensation for environmental damage sustained under colonial rule. A crucial question for the future is how the Nauruan government and population will react to efforts to rehabilitate the island should the undertaking threaten the future of their overseas investment portfolio.

Emperor Gold Mining's close alliance with the Mara government in Fiji served to shield it from close scrutiny by environmental critics. The environmental impact of the mine became a political issue during the 1987 election, but since the military coups of that year there has been little opportunity for critical analysis or discussion of the issue. Again, the situation in Papua New Guinea has been much more complicated. Popular support for greater environmental protection has been much in evidence and, on the whole, the various governments have taken steps to improve regulation of mines. Experience has shown, however, that only limited environmental protection has been forthcoming in practice, especially when safeguards threaten the economic viability of a project. Disagreements over appropriate environmental safeguards between ministries are common and, in general, the environmental impact of mining has become a highly sensitive political issue at all levels of government.

Mining and Development

Mining in the South Pacific therefore has a problematic record where the question of economic development is concerned. It has produced some benefits but, more often than not, these are offset by an array of problems. Worldwide, this is not an unusual situation. While in the immediate term mining has always generated hope and promise, historical analysis has shown that for much of the world mining has failed to live up to its developmental promise. Harking back to a warning issued by an official in Papua New Guinea, in relation to Latin America, William Culvert and Thomas Greaves note: "The map of the Americas is dotted with the names of once well-known mining communities now but a shadow of their former eminence... When the mines of these regions opened they promised to lift individuals and even whole nations into the bosom of material progress, but in time the mines spawned communities of marginality, if not poverty."[1] The situation in the South Pacific may not be quite so bleak, but neither is it all that much better.

Debate about how best for developing countries to derive benefits from mining, and, conversely, why countries have not done better in the past, is divided into a number of distinct tendencies on either side of a left-right divide. On the right, there are those who argue that the best way for a country to develop its mining industry is to try to keep costs down, maximize production, and maintain close and cordial relations with the metal consumers.[2] This, essentially, was the approach of the Pinocet government in Chile. Others, such as Rex Bosson and Bension Varon of the World Bank express a more moderate view, arguing that it is important to try to maximize production and exports, but at the same time developing countries should try to negotiate arrangements that are of more benefit to themselves.[3] A similar view is held by Cobbe, who perceives the crucial factor for promoting development to be improved understanding by governments and transnational corporations.[4]

The left critique in the mining literature generally has fallen within the dependency perspective in development studies which focuses on unequal exchange or the appropriation of surplus from underdeveloped countries by the developed. The leading exponent of this point of view in the 1960s and 1970s was Norman Girvan, who argues that exports now going at relatively cheap prices to developed countries will deprive developing countries of resources that they will need for themselves in the future.[5] This is what Michael Tanzer refers to as the "leave it in the ground school" which argues that since minerals are a non-renewable resource "every ton produced today is a ton not available for future production."[6] This view leads Tanzer to suggest that ideally developing countries might be better off without mining—to delay utilizing mineral resources until they are in a better position to take advantage of them.

While holding off on mineral development might be a good idea, in practice it is usually extremely difficult to do so. After reviewing the poor record of mining in Latin America, where "mining has severely distorted the national economies, with wealth transfers and jobs being traded against heavy concessions of national autonomy (whether or not the mines are nationalized), bitterly contentious labour relations and chronic political stress," nevertheless, comment Culvert and Greaves, "the mineral economies of the hemisphere are so desperate for income and development options that national leaders must regard mining as a strategic resource" since mining "produces critical foreign exchange..., employs and concentrates sectors with immense political potency, and holds the promise of critical revenues in these tax-poor countries."[7] Recognizing such difficulties, Tanzer concedes that "what is required is not an 'all or nothing' approach, but a pragmatic yet principled strategy that will maximize independence and the capacity for self-development."[8]

Distinctions among these various perspectives can be seen in debate over the role of transnational corporations in mining. Thus, Bosson and Varon argue that since transnational mining companies control needed technology, capital and markets, developing countries need to work with them. Cobbe recognizes that there is a price to be paid for working with foreign companies, but that there are important benefits in terms of efficiency of marketing and production. He also points to the high cost of exploration as something discouraging governments to go it alone. In contrast, Girvan calls for "disengagement," or keeping transnational corporations out at all costs. Tanzer is also wary of transnational mining companies and the extent to which they deprive a developing country of "a crucial opportunity to assimilate its own capital from the potential profits" derived from mining.[9] But he feels that the best strategy will depend on the specifics of a situation such that where, for example, production of a particular mineral requires substantial capital inputs or the use of certain technology it may be necessary or even most beneficial to work with a foreign corporation. Under even these circumstances, however, Tanzer argues that developing countries should rely on transnationals as little as possible and continually seek to reduce their reliance.

The appropriate role of foreign corporate interests in the mining industry in the South Pacific has elicited considerable debate. While Nauru's mining industry may not have lived up to all of the expectations prevalent at the time of independence, the government-run industry has done relatively well financially and it has demonstrated the extent to which even a group of poorly educated Pacific islanders can manage a mining operation largely for their own benefit—purchasing technology and expertise where needed. The Fiji Labour Party pursued a similar goal in relation to Emperor Gold Mine in its 1986-87 electoral campaign. Drawing upon very successful local examples of industries whose benefits to Fiji had been greatly enhanced once foreign control had been removed, in contrast to the limited benefits for Fiji derived from Emperor Gold Mine over the years, the Fiji Labour Party felt confident that the situation could be improved through nationalization, government participation as a joint venture, or, minimally, through much more careful government regulation. The Fiji Labour Party was not opposed to future mining developments being carried out by foreign interests, but it felt that safeguards were necessary to ensure that any new mines maintained better relations with workers and landowners that they were monitored more carefully for their economic and social impact than it felt had been the practice in the past. In contrast, the current chiefly-military regime favors continuance of the practices which prevailed under the former Alliance government.

Participation by foreign corporate interests in mining in Papua New Guinea also has been the subject of considerable political controversy. The large scale and technological difficulties which have characterized the country's mining projects has made it virtually impossible for the government to consider undertaking them on its own. And, given the potential wealth to be derived from the mines and the income needs of the government, it is unlikely that any of Papua New Guinea's governments would have considered leaving development of the sites until some time in the distant future when the country was in a better position to use the resources. Instead, the government's policy has been one of limited participation (usually in the ten to twenty per cent range) so as not to tie up too much of its capital, with additional income being derived from taxation, promotion of localization where feasible, and steps to regulate the social and environmental impact of the mines. On the fiscal side, the government has done relatively well for itself and in the Papua New Guinea context localization has been fairly successful. Environmental regulation has been more of a problem, but the government has met with some success. Foreign capital has not been saintly in its behavior, but, overall, it has not behaved that badly either (especially when compared with, say, Fiji).

Where problems have occurred in Papua New Guinea, and there certainly have been many, transnational corporations generally have not been solely responsible. Rather, often the problems are more the result of internal political and economic difficulties related to mining in general than to any specific acts of foreign capitalists. Likewise, in Fiji, the problems associated with Emperor Gold Mining cannot all be laid at the feet of its foreign owners (or at least its expatriate manager), for the actions of members of the chiefly oligarchy and the Alliance Party government also have been important factors. Turning attention to local considerations, Tanzer makes "a distinction between those progressive and honest governments that can effectively use mineral revenues for the benefit of the mass of people, and those conservative and corrupt governments where the revenues benefit only a privileged few."[10] Fiji, through most of its independent history would certainly fall into the latter category and, despite attempts to ensure that Papua New Guinea's mineral wealth is used for the national good by many politicians and public servants, it has been the wealthy and influential few who have benefitted most from the industry and government corruption in the mining sector has been widespread.

Attention to local problems leads us to a more recent current on the left within the literature on mining and development. This is the articulation of modes of production approach, which seeks to understand barriers to development through attention to relations of production and the class structure within a country. Elizabeth Dore is one of the more prominent authors to use this perspective specifically in relation to mining. Dore notes that those seeking to explain barriers to growth in the Peruvian mining industry generally have adopted a dependency perspective, feeling that it is particularly appropriate when dealing with an extractive industry.[11] Those following the dependency approach point to extraction of surplus as a major cause of Peru's underdevelopment. Dore argues that this idea cannot be sustained. Specifically, she states that it is hard to prove that foreign companies have extracted a net surplus from Peru and, more importantly, that "It is even more difficult to show that had a higher portion of profits remained in Peru this money could or would have been productively invested."[12]

For Dore the central problem is the "inflexibility of precapitalist social relations."[13] Thus, she argues that "The uneven development of the productive forces among countries is primarily caused by fundamental differences in the nature of social relations of production."[14] Following Bill Warren, Dore views capitalism as progressive in nature since it transforms all social relations to economic ones, thereby allowing economic growth to assume center stage.[15] Development then is closely associated with the replacement of precapitalist social relations with capitalist relations of production and the question of the export of capital becomes less important than the extent to which capitalist institutions transform social relations.

Modern variants of precapitalist social relations are much in evidence in all of the Pacific island states discussed and are of considerable relevance to the mining industry and, more generally, to national political and economic issues. The importance of these relations has been seen in regard to questions of land ownership, the distribution of mining royalties, as well as political leadership and decision-making. While each case differs to some extent, in all of the countries studied, the relevance of mode of production analysis for understanding the question of mining and development is apparent.

For the phosphate islanders from Nauru and Banaba, their developmental problems in recent years have not so much been a matter of acquiring more money, but of productive utilization of the funds available. They have had to confront the modern capitalist world while still heavily influenced by precapitalist features in their society. For the Banabans of Rabi Island, the contradictions proved almost overwhelming and only gradually are they recovering from the disaster of Rabi Holdings. Nauru not only has had to face the difficulty of managing a modern mining industry and international investment portfolio with a society ill prepared for either task, but its traditionalism also has wedded the Nauruans to a desire to rehabilitate their island rather than move, despite the cost. The decision to rehabilitate Nauru is not necessarily wrong in a cultural sense, but it is likely to have important negative implications for the economic development of Nauru for reasons that have more to do with the present state of Nauruan society than past exploitation by the British Phosphate Commissioners. Recent political turmoil on Nauru can also be examined in light of a struggle between social forces representing quite different strategies for articulating with Nauru's modern capitalist environment—Hammer de Roburt being associated with a traditionalist enclave approach that sought to shield Nauruan society from the world, while his opponents seem to desire greater participation in the world from which Nauru derives its wealth.

Fiji has witnessed a similar political struggle, as exemplified in the conflicting views of the Alliance Party and Fiji Labour Party. Prime Minister Mara gave Fiji a debilitating stability that allowed some economic growth while, at the same time, creating tensions which ultimately undermined stability as his political machine was no longer able successfully to control the communalism it had promoted nor adequately to service the demands of its own patronage system. Put another way, the Mara government advocated a primitive form of capitalism that was reliant on a quasi-feudal political structure and economically inefficient patronage practices. The Fiji Labour Party developed out of the frustrations with this situation among those desiring the creation of a more progressive mixed economy. Reflecting upon this aim, in his speeches Timoci Bavadra often spoke of "releasing the productive potential of the Fijian people" that had been frustrated by Alliance Party rule.

In promoting capitalist development, the Mara government constantly was confronted with contradictions of its own making. For example, although it advocated native Fijians going into business, in practice, the funds supposedly set aside by the Alliance Party government to help entrepreneurs were given out as spoils to prominent party supporters. Among those who joined the extremist

Fijian Nationalist Party were would-be native Fijian entrepreneurs who were unable to secure even small loans from government sources. In the case of the Emperor Gold Mining, rather than serving productive purposes contributing to national development, under Alliance Party rule, the mine was able to retain an enclave status. Such a position ensured that most of its profits were, in fact, taken out of the country, while within Fiji the mining company pursued a rather primitive pattern of industrial relations and helped to support a structure of rule linked to quasi-feudal social relations. In Fiji, then, the alliance of mining interests and chiefly rule has served more to hinder development than to promote it.

Mining in New Caledonia has helped to sustain a relatively high standard of living for many of the residents in the colony, but, to the extent that it has contributed to communalism and the perpetuation of colonial rule, mining also has served as a force against development. Colonial class and communal relations have been crucial factors blocking further development from mining. Despite the economic wealth produced by mining, New Caledonia's economy beyond the mining sector remains either underdeveloped or dependent on government assistance and mining.

Likewise, in Papua New Guinea, mining has produced substantial wealth, but the context within which the wealth has been produced has proven poorly fit to take full advantage of the wealth. Precapitalist social relations remain a potent force in Papua New Guinea, touching upon almost all aspects of the mining industry. Where mining wealth has gone directly to local populations, as at Mt. Kare, the result has been an orgy of consumerism with little lasting developmental benefit. More generally, the lumpiness of the wealth produced from mining enclaves has served to exacerbate many tensions and to encourage corruption and patronage politics. The government of Papua New Guinea has proven itself increasingly adept at dealing with foreign mining interests, but relating to its own citizens has been more difficult.

In reviewing mining in the South Pacific, the developmental record of the industry has not been very good. The mining sector has not proven to be particularly effective at encouraging the development of other productive sectors. In fact, mining has tended to undermine them, especially where people are turned into mere renters. At best, mining has provided some cash to prop up a state's bureaucracy, but even here there is a distorting tendency that is at odds with long-term development. The practices of foreign companies sometimes have been at odds with national interests, but, as we have seen, the shortcomings of the mining sector must also be placed within the context of the local societies themselves. To benefit more from mining, the governments of the states discussed face the difficult task of overcoming many of the contradictions facing their own societies. Failing in this task, the mining wealth that does not go to foreign interests will continue to be dissipated and contribute little to national development.

Notes

1. William C. Culvert and Thomas C. Greaves, "Miners and Mining in the Americas: An Introduction," in William C. Culvert and Thomas C. Greaves, eds., *Miners and Mining in the Americas* (Manchester: Manchester University Press, 1985), p. 5.

2. See Theodore H. Moran, *Multinational Corporations and the Politics of Dependence: Copper in Chile* (Princeton: Princeton University Press, 1974).

3. Rex Bosson and Bension Varon, *The Mining Industry and the Developing Countries* (New York: Oxford University Press, 1977).

4. James H. Cobbe, *Government and Mining Companies in Developing Countries* (Boulder: Westview Press, 1979).

5. Relevant works by Norman Girvan include: *Corporate Imperialism: Conflict and Expropriation* (New York: Monthly Review Press, 1976); "Multinational Corporations and Dependent Underdevelopment in Mineral-Export Economies," in *Social and Economic Studies*, December 1970; and *The Caribbean Bauxite Industry* (Mona, Jamaica: Institute of Social and Economic Research, University of the West Indies, 1967).

6. Michael Tanzer, *The Race for Resources* (London: Heinemann Educational Books, 1980), p. 230. James H. Cobbe (*Government and Mining Companies*, p. 5) makes a similar point concerning the nonrenewability of mineral resources, although the implications that he draws from this are different, when he writes, "to the extent that the proceeds of resource extraction...are used for consumption rather than investment, the country is living off capital."

7. Culvert and Greaves, "Miners and Mining," p. 5.

8. Tanzer, *Race for Resources*, p. 237.

9. Tanzer, *Race for Resources*, p. 235.

10. Tanzer, *Race for Resources*, p. 232.

11. Elizabeth Dore, *The Peruvian Mining Industry: Growth, Stagnation, and Crisis* (Boulder: Westview Press, 1988), p. 25.

12. Dore, *Peruvian Mining*, p. 26.

13. Dore, *Peruvian Mining*, p. 27.

14. Dore, *Peruvian Mining*, p. 13.

15. See Bill Warren, *Imperialism: Pioneer of Capitalism* (London: New Left Books, 1980). See also John Weeks, *Limits to Capitalist Development: The Industrialization of Peru, 1950-1980* (Boulder: Westview Press, 1985).

Appendix: Seabed Mining

The 1970s and early 1980s witnessed a major innovation in the mining industry of considerable importance to the South Pacific with the advent of efforts to develop seabed mining. Interest focused on deposits of lead, zinc, copper, iron, phosphorites, silver, gold, cobalt, nickel, mercury, cadmium, and oil found on the bottom of the sea. The deposits were produced largely by minerals seeping onto the sea floor through cracks known as hydrothermal spread centers. Seabed mining came to feature prominently in negotiations for the Law of the Sea, with industrial countries such as Britain, West Germany, and, especially, the United States opposed to efforts to create international regulations for seabed mining. Despite such opposition, the signing of the United Nations Law of the Sea Convention and establishment of a two hundred nautical mile Exclusive Economic Zone for countries with coastlines in 1982 served as a catalyst for further development of seabed mining.

By the early 1980s, corporate interests in seabed mining were represented by several consortia. These included: Ocean Mining Associates (Deepsea Ventures Group), equally shared between U.S. Steel, Sun Oil, and Union Minière of Belgium; Kennecott Exploration Corporation, in which Kennecott held a fifty per cent share, and RTZ, Consolidated Gold Fields, Noranda Mines, Mitsubishi, and British Petroleum each held a ten per cent interest; Ocean Management Inc., which was divided equally (twenty-five per cent each) between Inco, a group of three West German companies, a consortium of Japanese companies, and SEDCO of the United States; Ocean Minerals Company, seventy-five per cent of which was held by Ocean Minerals Inc., which in turn was owned by Shell, Lockheed, and BKW of the Netherlands, with the remaining twenty-five per cent being owned by Standard Oil of Indiana; AFERNOD, a French group comprised of CNEXO, CEA, BRGM, SLN, and Chantiers de France; and, finally, Deep Ocean Minerals Association, a consortium of thirty-five Japanese companies. Bechtel International of the United States was also active in developing seabed

235

mining technology and was particularly interested in the area between Hawaii and California and Hawaii and Micronesia.

In the South Pacific, seabed mining primarily was the concern of AFERNOD within French territories and UNDP-sponsored CCOP/SOPAC in the non-French areas. CCOP/SOPAC was founded in 1972 to conduct seismic surveys and related activities. It was headquartered in Fiji with an initial budget of only A$750,000. Activities relating to seabed mining remained minimal until 1981-82. In mid-1981, the UNDP appealed to the United Nations for a member country to undertake a survey of offshore oil, gas, and mineral prospects in the southwest Pacific. When the Soviet Union offered to undertake the survey, Australia, New Zealand, and the United States were quick to make a counter offer, which was accepted. Their joint project involved two ships and more than fifty scientists working for two months testing petroleum prospects off Tonga, Vanuatu, and the Solomon Islands, and mineral deposits off Fiji and the Solomon Islands. The surveys were completed in June 1982, and preliminary findings indicated the possibility of commercially significant finds, but a further eighteen months was required to collate the data.

Next came a spate of research, starting in 1985, involving sophisticated research vessels from West Germany, France, Britain, and the United States working with CCOP/SOPAC, to carry out further exploration. In February 1990, an English survey company, working under contract, completed a survey of 300,000 square kilometers of seabed around Fiji, Western Samoa, Vanuatu, and Tonga using the Marconi Long Range Inclined Asdic (GLORIA) sonar scanning device. Data from the ships started to be processed in 1989 by a French-supplied computer, which will produce three-dimensional maps. The next phase of exploration involves the careful examination of sites selected as the most likely to produce significant results. A third phase is to commence shortly with arrival of the drilling ship *Joides Resolution*, operated by the Ocean Drilling Programme (an international consortium). At a cost of A$35 million, the ship will spend two years drilling at depths of six thousand meters near Vanuatu and Tonga.

The Japanese also became involved, through the Metal Mining Agency of Japan (MMAJ). In April 1989, the MMAJ expressed interest in assessing the feasibility of mining manganese nodules on the sea floor, primarily to see if the nodules contain yttrium (used for super-conductivity technology). In agreement with SOPAC, the MMAJ conducted preliminary surveys of the seabed off Kiribati, Tuvalu, and the Cook Islands. In March 1990, the MMAJ renewed its research deal with SOPAC, agreeing to spend A$20 million on a five-year program of exploration off of the Cook Islands, Kiribati, Papua New Guinea, the Solomon Islands, Vanuatu, and Western Samoa. Plans have also been announced for exploration in the waters of northern Fiji.

Among the discoveries to attract the most attention so far are an "interesting" hydrocarbon find in Tonga and deposits of manganese nodules and cobalt in the Cook Islands. The main site of manganese nodules in the Cook Islands is an area covering several thousand square kilometers lying at depths of 4,500 to 5,000 meters on the Manihiki Plateau in the South Penryhn Basin. These deposits appear to be the most valuable discovered in the South Pacific to date.

In January 1988, a French consortium obtained exclusive rights for the exploration and exploitation of mineral bearing rocks in French Polynesia from the International Seabed Authority. This allowed France to mine mainly manganese-bearing rock in a 75,000 square kilometer area. French interest in the project, however, has waned because of a glut of minerals from nodule sources, relatively low mineral prices, and the high cost of recovery.

The factors influencing the decline of French private sector interest in seabed mining have influenced private sector mining interests elsewhere as well. This includes private Japanese interests and the situation is reflected in remarks by MMAJ executive director Yoichi Yamaguchi on the prospects for seabed mining: "All we can say is that it [seabed mining] won't be in this century, but the resource is potentially huge for mankind" (*Fiji Times,* 16 March 1990, p. 10). Such market conditions mean that, for time being, exploration will have to depend primarily on public sector support.

Meanwhile, CCOP/SOPAC has expanded its activities. Following its annual meeting in September 1989, the member states (Australia, Cook Islands, Fiji, Guam, New Zealand, Papua New Guinea, Solomon Islands, Tonga, Vanuatu, Western Samoa, Tuvalu, and Kiribati) decided that SOPAC, now to be called the South Pacific Applied Geo-science Commission, was to become a fully-fledged regional organization under the South Pacific Forum. With a 1990 budget of A$5 million, priority was to be given to continuing coastal mapping activities and exploring possibilities for nearshore and coastal development. The coastal mapping primarily involves looking for offshore oil in Fiji, Tonga, Solomon Islands, and Vanuatu and offshore mineral research into manganese nodules in the Cook Islands, Kiribati, and Tuvalu. In addition to Japan and the European Community, funding for the projects comes from Australia, New Zealand, Canada (which has agreed to provide A$1 million for a nearshore mineral research program commencing in 1990) the UNDP, the CFTC, the United States, and the Netherlands.

Bibliography

Bain, 'Atu. 1985. Vatukoula—Rock of Gold: Labour in the Gold Mining Industry of Fiji, 1930-1970. Ph.D Thesis, Australian National University.

_____. 1986. "Labour Protest and Control in the Gold Mining Industry of Fiji, 1930-1970." *South Pacific Forum* 3 (1): 37-59.

Bedford, Richard, and Alexander Mamak. 1977. *Compensation for Development: The Bougainville Case.* Christchurch: Department of Geography, University of Canterbury.

Binder, Pearl. 1977. *Treasure Islands.* London: Blond & Briggs.

Bird, Eric C.F., Jean-Paul Dubois, and Jacques A. Iltis. 1984. *The Impact of Opencast Mining on the Rivers and Coasts of New Caledonia.* Tokyo: United Nations University.

Brou, Bernard. [no date] *Richesses Miniéres en Nouvelle-Calédonie.* Dossier 3. Paris: Nouvelles Editions Latines.

Brown, M.J.F. 1974. "A Development Consequence: Disposal of Mining Waste on Bougainville, Papua New Guinea." *Geoforum* 18: 19-27.

Brunton, Brian. 1978. Prices, Mining and Taxation in Papua New Guinea. LL.M. Thesis, Monash University.

Burchett, Wilfred G. 1941. *Pacific Treasure Islands: Voyage through New Caledonia, its Land and Wealth, the Story of its People and Past.* Melbourne: Cheshire.

Carol, Jean. 1900. *La Nouvelle Calédonie Minière et Agricole.* Paris: Ollendorf.

Connell, John. 1983. *Migration, Employment and Development in the South Pacific: Country Report No. 9, Nauru.* Noumea: South Pacific Commission.

_____. 1989. *Sovereignty and Survival.* Sydney: Department of Geography, University of Sydney.

Conyers, Diana. 1976. *The Provincial Government Debate.* Boroko: Institute of Applied Social and Economic Research.

Curtain, Richard. 1984. "The Migrant Labour System and Class Formation in Papua New Guinea." *South Pacific Forum* 1 (2): 117-141.

Dagmar, Hans. 1989. "Banabans in Fiji: Ethnicity, Change and Development," in Michael C. Howard, ed., *Ethnicity and Nation-Building in the Pacific.* Pp. 198-217. Tokyo: United Nations University.

———. 1990. "Cooperative Artisanal Fishing on Rabi Island, Fiji." *Practicing Anthropology* 12 (1): 6-7, 18.

Daniel, Philip, and Rod Simms. 1986. *Foreign Investment in Papua New Guinea: Policies and Practices.* Pp. 47-70. Canberra: National Centre for Development Studies, Australian National University.

Demaitre, Edmond. 1936. *New Guinea Gold: Cannibals & Gold Seekers in New Guinea.* London: Geoffrey Bles.

Dornoy, Myriam. 1984. *Politics in New Caledonia.* Sydney: University of Sydney Press.

Doumenge, François. 1966. *L'Homme dans le Pacifique Sud: Étude Géographique.* Publications de la Société des Océanistes 19. Pp. 443-494, 512-529. Paris: Musée de l'Homme.

Dove, J., T. Miriung, and M. Togolo. 1974. "Mining Bitterness," in P.G. Sack, ed., *Problems of Choice: Land in Papua New Guinea's Future.* Pp. 182. Canberra: Australian National University Press.

Dupon, J.F. 1989. *Pacific Phosphate Island Environments Versus the Mining Industry: An Unequal Struggle.* South Pacific Study 4. Noumea: South Pacific Environment Programme.

Ellis, Arthur. 1935. *Ocean Island and Nauru.* Sydney: Angus & Robertson.

Emerson, Criag. 1982. "Mining Enclaves and Taxation." *Development* 10 (7): 561-571.

Espie, F. F. 1972. "Bougainville Copper: Difficult Development Decisions," in R.J. May, ed., *Priorities in Melanesian Development.* Pp. 335-342. Canberra: Australian National University.

Fages, J. 1975. *Les Tahitiens de Nouvelle Caledonie.* Papeete: ORSTOM.

Fraser, Helen. 1989. *New Caledonia: Anti-Colonialism in a Pacific Territory.* Canberra: Peace Research Centre, Australian National University.

Garnault, R., and A. Clunies Ross. 1975. "Uncertainty, Risk Aversion and the Taxing on Natural Resource Projects." *Economic Journal* 85 (338): 272-287.

Glasser, E. 1904. *Les Richesses Minérales de la Nouvelle-Calédonie.* Paris: Dunod.

Grimble, Arthur. 1952. *A Pattern of Islands.* London: John Murray.

———. 1957. *Return to the Islands.* London: John Murray.

Grover, John C. 1955. "A Concise History of the Search for Gold in the Solomons." *Transactions of the British Solomon Islands Society* 2: 1-11.

———. 1955. "The History of Exploratory and Mining Ventures in the Solomons." *Geological Survey of the British Solomon Islands Memoir* 1: 10-15.

Hannett, Leo. 1975. "The Case for Bougainville Secession." *Meanjin Quarterly* 34 (3): 286-293.

Healy, Allan M. 1967. *A History of the Development of the Bulolo Region, New Guinea.* New Guinea Research Bulletin No. 15. Canberra: Australian National University.

Howard, Michael C. 1988. *The Impact of the International Mining Industry on*

Native Peoples. Pp. 83-172, 239-249. Sydney: Transnational Corporations Research Project, University of Sydney.

Hughes, Philip and Marjorie Sullivan. 1989. "Environmental Impact Assessment in Papua New Guinea: Lessons for the Wider Pacific Region." *Pacific Viewpoint* 30 (1): 34-55.

Idriess, Ion. 1933. *Gold Dust and Ashes: the Romantic Story of the New Guinea Goldfields.* Sydney: Angus.

Jackson, Richard. 1980. "Mineral Resources and Mining in Papua New Guinea: Digging in for a Difficult Decade." *Yagl-Ambu* 7 (2):, 1-8.

_____. 1982. *Ok Tedi: The Pot of Gold.* Boroko: University of Papua New Guinea.

_____. 1989. "New Policies in Sharing Mining Benefits in Papua New Guinea: A Note." *Pacific Viewpoint* 30 (1):, 86-93.

_____, and T.S. Ilave. 1983. *The Ok Tedi Monitoring Project.* Report No. 1. Boroko: Institute of Applied Social and Economic Research.

Jorgenson, Dan. 1981. Taro and Arrows. Ph.D. Thesis, University of British Columbia.

_____. 1981. "Life on the Fringe: History and Society in Telefolmin," in *The Plight of Peripheral People in Papua New Guinea: Volume I: The Inland Situation.* Pp. 59-79. Cambridge, MA: Cultural Survival.

Kobayashi, M. 1980. "Les Japonais en Nouvelle-Caledonie." *Bulletin de la Societe d'Etudes Historiques de la Nouvelle-Caledonie* 43: 57-72.

Kotabalavu, J. and D.J. Tiffin. 1989. "Ocean Minerals: Prospects for South Pacific Islands." *Pacific Viewpoint* 30 (1): 22-33.

Macdonald, Barrie. 1982. *Cinderellas of the Empire.* Canberra: Australian National University Press.

Mamak, Alexander, and Richard Bedford. 1974. *Bougainville Nationalism: Aspects of Unity and Discord.* Christchurch: Department of Geography, University of Canterbury.

_____, and Richard Bedford. 1977. "Inequality in the Bougainville Copper Mining Industry: Some Implications," in F.S. Stevens and E.P. Wolfers, eds., *Racism: The Australian Experience: Volume 3: Colonialism and After.* Pp. 427-455. Sydney: Australian and New Zealand Book Company.

_____, and Richard Bedford. 1979. "Bougainville Copper Mineworkers' Strike, 1975," in A. Mamak and A. Ali, eds., *Race, Class and Rebellion in the South Pacific.* Pp. 76-85. Sydney: George Allen & Unwin.

McCarthy, John K. 1963. *Patrol Into Yesterday.* Melbourne: F.W. Cheshire.

Mikesell, Raymond F. 1975. *Foreign Investment in Copper Mining: Case Studies of Mines in Peru and Papua New Guinea.* Baltimore: Johns Hopkins University Press.

Momis, John, and Eugene Ogan. 1972. "Bougainville '71: Not Discovered by CRA." *New Zealand and Australia, the Pacific and Southeast Asia* 6 (2): 32-40.

Monberg, Torben. 1976. *Mobile in the Trade Wind: The Reaction of the People on Bellona Island towards a Mining Project.* Working Paper No. 1. Copenhagen: National Museum of Denmark.

Moulik, T.K. 1977. *Bougainville in Transition.* Canberra: Development Studies Centre, Australian National University.

Nelson, Hyland N. 1975. Black, White and Gold: Goldmining in Papua New Guinea, 1878-1930. Ph.D. Thesis, University of Papua New Guinea.

_____. 1976. *Black, White and Gold: Gold Mining in Papua New Guinea, 1878-1930.* Canberra: Australian National University Press.

Newbury, Colin D. 1975. "Colour Bar and Labour Conflict on the New Guinea Goldfields 1935-1941." *Australian Journal of Politics and History* 21 (3): 25-38.

_____. 1975. "Labour Migration in the Imperial Phase: An Essay in Interpretation." *Journal of Imperial and Commonwealth History* 3 (2): 234-256.

O'Faircheallaigh, C. 1982. *Mining and the Papua New Guinea Economy 1880-1980.* Occasional Paper in Economic History No. 1. Port Moresby: University of Papua New Guinea.

_____. 1984. "Review of Papua New Guinea's Mineral Policy 1964-82: Some Preliminary Findings," in D. Gupta and S. Polume, eds., *Economic Policy Issues and Options in Papua New Guinea.* Canberra: Development Studies Centre, Australian National University.

Oliver, Douglas. 1973. *Bougainville: A Personal History.* Honolulu: University Press of Hawaii.

Pintz, William S. 1984. *Ok Tedi: Evolution of a Third World Mining Project.* London: Mining Journal Books.

_____. 1987. "Environment Negotiations for the Ok Tedi Mine in Papua New Guinea," in C.S. Pearson, ed., *Multinational Corporations: Environment and the Third World.* Durham, NC: Duke University Press.

_____. 1989. "Mining and Social Conflict: Planning Strategy in Melanesia." *Pacific Viewpoint* 30 (1): 75-85.

_____, and A. Clark. 1984. "Resource Assessment in National Planning: Papua New Guinea Case Studies." *Materials and Society* 8 (4): 681-698.

Premdas, Ralph. 1977. "Secessionist Politics in Papua New Guinea." *Pacific Affairs* 50: 64-85.

_____. 1977. "Ethnonationalism, Copper and Secession on Bougainville." *Canadian Review of Studies in Nationalism* 4 (2): 247-265.

Reed, S.W. 1943. *The Making of Modern New Guinea, with Special Reference to Culture Contact in the Mandated Territory.* Philadelphia: American Philosophical Library.

Rizer, James P., et al. 1982. *The Potential Impacts of a Namosi Copper Mine: A Case Study of Assimilation Planning.* Suva: Centre for Applied Studies in Development, University of the South Pacific.

Ruthven, David. 1979. "Rennell Bauxite," in Peter Larmour, ed., *Land in Solomon Islands.* Pp. 94-104. Suva: Institute of Pacific Studies, University of the South Pacific.

Sharp, N. 1975. "The Republic of the North Solomons." *Arena* 40: 119-127.

Silverman, Martin. 1971. *Disconcerting Issue*. Chicago: University of Chicago Press.

Sinclair, James. 1978. *Wings of Gold: How the Aeroplane Developed New Guinea*. Sydney: Pacific Publications.

Stephensen, H.E., ed. [no date] *Bougainville: The Establishment of a Copper Mine*. St.Kilda: Construction, Mining, Engineering Publications.

Thompson, Herb. 1989. "The 'Barbarous Relic' and the 'Rim of Fire': Gold in Papua New Guinea." *Raw Materials Report* 6 (4): 20-31.

Thompson, Virginia, and Richard Adloff. 1971. *The French Pacific Islands*. Berkeley: University of California Press.

Tilton, John, John Millett, and Richard Ward. 1986. *Mineral and Mining Policy in Papua New Guinea*. Discussion Paper No. 24. Port Moresby: Institute of National Affairs.

Treadgold, M.L. 1971. "Bougainville Copper and the Economic Development of Papua New Guinea." *Economic Record* 47 (118).

_____. 1978. *The Regional Economy of Bougainville: Growth and Structural Change*. Canberra: Development Studies Centre, Australian National University.

Umeng, Ephaim. 1976. The Impact of Bougainville Copper Limited Operations on Local Business on Bougainville: A Study of Underdevelopment. B.Ec.(Hons) Thesis, University of Papua New Guinea.

Vernon, D.C. 1983. *The World Economy—and Prospects for Development of Papua New Guinea's Mineral Resources*. Speech Series No. 18. Port Moreby: Institute of National Affairs.

Viall, L.G. 1938. "Some Statistical Aspects of Population in the Marobe District, New Guinea." *Oceania* 8 (4): 383-397.

Viviani, Nancy. 1970. *Nauru: Phosphate and Political Progress*. Canberra: Australian National University Press.

Wesley-Smith, Terence A. 1988. Melanesians and Modes of Production: Underdevelopment in Papua New Guinea with Particular Reference to the Role of Mining Capital. Ph. D. Thesis, University of Hawaii.

West, Richard. 1972. *River of Tears: The Rise of the Rio Tinto Zinc Mining Corporation*. London: Earth Island. [Contains material on mining in Papua New Guinea.]

Williams, Maslyn, and Barrie Macdonald. 1985. *The Phosphateers: A History of the British Phosphate Commissioners and the Christmas Island Phosphate Commission*. Melbourne: Melbourne University Press.

Winslow, Donna. 1986. "Labour Relations in New Caledonia to 1945." *South Pacific Forum* 3 (1): 97-112.

_____. 1988. Changement Social et Identité Ethnique en Nouvelle-Calédonie. Ph.D. Thesis, University of Montreal.

Zorn, S. 1977. "Bougainville: Managing the Copper Industry." *New Guinea and Australia, the Pacific and Southeast Asia* 7 (4): 23-40.

Index